Looking and Seeing

Looking and Seeing: The Role of Visual Communication in Social Interaction

D R Rutter

Social Psychology Research Unit,
University of Kent at Canterbury.

JOHN WILEY & SONS

Chichester · New York · Brisbane · Toronto · Singapore

Library of Congress Cataloging in Publication Data
Rutter, Derek.
  Looking and seeing.

  Includes bibliographical references and index.
    1. Nonverbal and communication (Psychology) 2. Gaze –
Psychological aspects. I. Title.
BF637.C45R9 1984   153.6   83-25894
ISBN 0 471 90415 5

British Library Cataloguing in Publication Data
Rutter, D.
  Looking and seeing.
    1. Social exchange   2. Communication
  I. Title
    302.1   HM258
ISBN 0 471 90415 5

Typeset by Oxford Verbatim Limited.
Printed by St Edmundsbury Press, Suffolk

CONTENTS

For my parents

PREFACE

Research on visual communication began in the 1960s. In the 1970s it accelerated, and in the 1980s it consolidated, and the purpose of what follows is to chart the major developments and to integrate the literature theoretically and empirically. The book began in 1981, when I was Visiting Scholar in the Department of Psychology at the University of Pennsylvania, but I had been working in the area for more than a decade, and my own research will provide the focus for much of the discussion. I am most grateful to my sponsors for their continued support – the Social Science Research Council, the Medical Research Council, and the Mental Health Foundation; and I am delighted to thank my friends and colleagues – especially Rupert Brown, Noel Clark, Michael Dewey, Kevin Durkin, Delice Gambrill, Patricia Grounds, Ann Harding, Nigel Kemp, Ian Morley, Donald Pennington, Geoffrey Stephenson, Janet Thomas, Hilarie Tucker, and Julius Wishner. Without them, the book would not have been written.

INTRODUCTION

The purpose of this book is to review the literature on visual communication and to integrate the findings theoretically and empirically. Experimental research on visual signalling began in the 1960s. Nonverbal communication was just emerging as a significant and identifiable area of investigation, and there were many issues to tackle. How should communication be defined and should nonverbal behaviour be included (Wiener *et al.*, 1972)? What were the most useful theoretical (Cranach & Vine, 1973) and methodological (Scherer & Ekman, 1982) approaches to take? What were the functions of nonverbal signals (Patterson, 1982; Edinger & Patterson, 1983)? How were the signals combined together (Mehrabian, 1971) – and with language (Moscovici, 1967) – and did it make sense to examine them one by one (Weitz, 1979)? How might the findings be applied in everyday life? Gaze was central, many were to argue, and the growth of research was rapid.

The first concern of the literature was to describe the 'normal pattern' of looking (Chapter 1). From time to time during most encounters we glance at one another in the region of the eyes, and sometimes our eyes meet. Gaze at the eyes is *looking*, and mutual looking is *eye-contact*, and a number of regularities were soon discovered. People looked more when they listened than when they spoke; looks were more frequent at certain points in utterances than others; and eye-contact was generally very brief. What is more, while a particular individual might behave consistently from encounter to encounter, there were noticeable differences between individuals, and sex, personality and psychopathology were important sources of variance.

By the late 1960s, structure had given way to function, and the evidence began to suggest that the purpose of gaze was threefold: to express our emotions and attitudes, to regulate the flow of conversation, and to monitor the other's behaviour for feedback. Expression attracted the most attention (Chapter 2), and the central concept was emotion and the leading model was intimacy (Argyle & Dean, 1965). Theory, however, concerned very few, and what mattered to most was data – but seldom were the findings consistent and still less did they make sense theoretically. But then, in the late 1970s, came a new development, in the work of Ellsworth and Patterson. Gaze, it was argued, was a salient and arousing stimulus, which the receiver could not ignore – but it had no meaning of its own, and a meaning had to be attributed. A positive attribution would lead the sender to look more, and the receiver to react more favourably, and a negative attribution would do the opposite. Not intimacy but attribution was the key to expression, and a significant advance had been achieved.

The remaining functions of looking were regulation and monitoring (Chapter 3) and this time emotion played no part. Regulation was concerned with how we open and close encounters and synchronize transitions from speaker to speaker, while monitoring was concerned with feedback, and, for both, the central concept was information. Emotion had dominated the literature for many years, but by now a change was under way.

Two main developments took place, and the first concerned the status of eye-contact. By tradition, eye-contact and looking were regarded as independent, and the former was seen as the more important – so much so that it had provided the explicit foundation for the intimacy model, and looking had been all but ignored. But then, in the mid-1970s, the illusion was shattered: eye-contact was exposed as a chance event. From time to time, when two people look, their eyes will meet by chance, and what the evidence showed was that the duration of eye-contact in a whole range of encounters was almost precisely what chance would predict. All that eye-contact could communicate was a piece of information: I am looking at you, you are looking at me, and we have each other's attention. Emotion was irrelevant.

The second development concerned the concept of information itself, for what emerged from regulation and monitoring was that looking, in fact, played little part in either. Certainly, people communicated information, but it was information about facial expression and gestures and posture – none of which was available through looking, since looking was defined as gaze at the eyes. What people needed most was visual access to the whole person – not just the eyes – and for that we introduced the term *seeing*.

By, the mid-1970's, then, a turning point had been reached. For more than a decade the literature had been preoccupied with looking, but first eye-contact had been attacked, and with it the significance of emotion, and now looking itself was under threat. Seeing was the focus of attention now, and its importance was quickly established for without it, we found, people were depersonalized and task-oriented in what they said, they were stilted and unspontaneous in their style, and they were immoderate and uncompromising in the outcomes they reached. The pattern, it seemed, was consistent and clear, and the findings were strong and reliable (Chapter 4).

There arose, however, a number of problems, and now was to come the most important development of all (Chapter 5). There were two issues in particular which attracted attention, and the first concerned methodology. To examine the role of seeing, the most common approach had been to compare face-to-face with audio-only encounters but in the process visual presence had often been confounded with physical presence. Disentangle them, we found, and the result was striking, for what mattered above all was the interaction. The xii

significant change from face-to-face to audio was the *aggregate* of social cues, not just *visual* cues, and the concept we proposed was *cuelessness*. The more cueless the encounter, the greater the feeling that one is psychologically distant from one's partner – and so the more depersonalized and task-oriented the content of the discussion, the less spontaneous the style, and the less likely an eventual compromise. Visual cues were certainly important, but so too were the others, and it is through cuelessness, I hope to demonstrate, that the literature can at last be integrated.

The other problem was how cuelessness operated. Content, style, and outcome, we had known for some time, were all affected by social cues, but what we discovered only later was that the measures were closely related. Content predicted style, and it also predicted outcome, but style and outcome were independent. Thus content, we believe, is influenced directly, and style and outcome are secondary. The more cueless the encounter, the more depersonalized and task-oriented the content – and, *by mediation*, the less spontaneous the style and the less likely an outcome of compromise.

And so, our analysis was almost complete. From looking we had moved to seeing, and from seeing we had moved to cuelessness, and in cuelessness we had found our theoretical framework. Now we were ready to test the model outside the laboratory and to explore its practical applications (Chapter 6) – and it is there that the book will end.

CHAPTER 1.

THE PATTERN OF LOOKING

The normal pattern

In 1967 there appeared a paper which was to become a classic in the literature on visual communication. It was published by Kendon. From time to time, during many forms of social encounter, people look at one another in the region of the eyes, and sometimes their eyes meet to make eye-contact. What interested Kendon was whether any regularity or pattern may be detectable – and, if so, what significance it might have for social interaction – and to try to find out, he set up an 'exploratory' study. Seven pairs of unacquainted students were recruited and, as they 'got to know one another' in the laboratory, they were filmed and tape-recorded. The subjects sat across a table, and a mirror was placed beside them so that both could be monitored in full-face close-up, one directly and one by reflection. The conversations lasted 30 minutes, and small segments were later selected from each film and subjected to a careful frame-by-frame analysis. From six of the conversations a 5 minute section was taken from near the end and, from the seventh, 7 minutes were taken from the beginning and 9 minutes from the end – a total of just 46 minutes.

The main findings were as follows. On average, subjects looked at their partners about 50% of the time, but there was a wide range, from 28% to 70%. In general, they looked more as they listened than as they spoke, and the length of individual looks was greater during listening than speaking. Thus, typically, Kendon suggested, people looked at the speaker in long gazes as they listened, broken by very short glances away; but when they spoke they alternated between looks and looks away of more equal length, and the looks away were generally longer than during listening.

As well as measuring individual looking, Kendon also examined mutual looking, or eye-contact as it is generally known. The analysis this time was based on samples from only five of the pairs and, here too, there was a considerable range of scores. The proportion of time spent in eye-contact ranged from under 10% to almost 40%, with a mean of 23%, and the bursts were very short, lasting only a second on average, with a range of 0·7 seconds to 1·4 seconds. Almost as soon as eye-contact was made one or other member of the pair broke it.

1

Shortly, we shall turn to Kendon's more detailed description of the precise timing of looks in relation to speech patterning, but for the time being, these were his main findings. Interestingly enough, they were very similar to those of the Scandinavian writer, Nielsen, who had, independently of Kendon, completed a similar study some 5 years earlier but whose work is, for some reason, not so well known (Nielsen, 1962). Like Kendon, Nielsen had reported a wide range of scores – 8% to 73% of the time spent looking – and the question therefore arose whether stable individual differences might be responsible. That is, might some individuals look a lot, consistently across encounters, while others looked less? In fact, Kendon's own data had included preliminary evidence which, at first sight, appeared to contradict such a notion. When the behaviour of the individuals within each pair was examined, it emerged that both the length and frequency of looks for the first subject were strongly associated with the corresponding values for the second: the more frequently one subject looked, and the longer his looks, the longer and more frequent were the looks of the other. As Kendon commented:

> it seems as if each dyad comes to a kind of 'agreement' whereby each looks at the other for particular [sic] length of time, on the average, though for how long at a time each looks at the other depends upon the dyad. . . . There remains the possibility, however, that though people may all adjust their looking behaviour in accord with situation specific factors, each will do this to an extent and in a way that is characteristic of him. (Kendon, 1967, p. 30).

The 'possibility' to which Kendon drew attention has been examined in only one major study, and that was conducted by Kendon & Cook (1969). Fifteen people took part in the experiment, and they were divided into two groups, so that each of eleven subjects (five male, six female) met each of four others (two male, two female), giving a total of forty-four two-person encounters. None of the eleven was acquainted with any of the four and, at the start of each session, the subject and partner were simply introduced and asked 'to make each other's acquaintance' for 30 minutes. A variety of measures were taken of looking and speech, and it was found that subject and partner were both major sources of variance for the subject's behaviour. In other words, although individuals behaved consistently across encounters and could each be identified irrespective of partner, they did nevertheless modify their behaviour to some extent. In general, though, consistency was the stronger effect.

Speech patterning and the timing of looks

As well as analysing the gross frequency and duration of looks, Kendon conducted a very detailed description of precisely when they occurred in the flow of conversation, and it was principally for this that the paper became so well known. There were two main analyses, and both were based on so-called 'long' utterances, those which lasted 5 seconds or more. The first examined what happened during the utterance, and the second was concerned with what happened when the utterance ended and the new speaker took over. The following discussion will, I hope, demonstrate that Kendon was able to make some fascinating and important suggestions – but, unfortunately, we do have to bear in mind that both analyses were based on very small samples of the data, often taken from fewer than the seven conversations Kendon recorded, and sometimes from only one.

What happened within long utterances was this. During continuous passages, where there were no significant pauses at phrase boundaries, people looked more when they were speaking quickly than when they were speaking slowly, and they tended to avert the gaze if they hesitated or stumbled. The likely explanation, Kendon suggested, was that we try to avoid distraction when we are planning what to say but, once we begin to 'run off' well-planned or well-practised phrases, we are free to look again since distraction is now less of a threat. At phrase-boundary pauses, in contrast to hesitations, speakers often looked up at the listener, as if seeking feedback or reassurance that they were being understood. Frequently a response came, in the form of an accompaniment signal such as a nod or 'mhmm', and the speaker would then look away and begin his new phrase.

Already the data began to suggest two things: by looking away the speaker shuts out potentially distracting information, and by looking he sends the listener a signal. The implications became even clearer in the second analysis, an examination of the beginnings and endings of long utterances. This time Kendon used all 46 minutes of data, and the number of long utterances totalled almost 100. In ½-second units each utterance was inspected from 2 or 3 seconds before it began to 2 or 3 seconds after it ended, and a clear pattern was revealed. As the speaker came to the end of his utterance he generally looked up at the listener; and the new speaker generally looked away as he began to speak and continued to do so until he was well under way. Over 70% of the utterances began with the speaker looking away from the listener, and over 70% ended with the speaker looking up at the listener. What is more, if the speaker ended without looking up, there was likely to be a delay before the new speaker took over, if indeed he took over at all. In Kendon's words:

> In withdrawing his gaze, [the speaker] is able to concentrate on the organisation of the utterance, and at the same time, by looking away he signals his intention to continue to hold the floor, and thereby forestall any attempt at action from his interlocutor. In looking up, which we have seen that he does briefly at phrase endings, and for a longer time at the ends of his utterances, he can at once check on how his interlocutor is responding to what he is saying, and signal to him that he is looking for some response from him. As for his interlocutor, these intermittent glances serve as signals to him, as to when [the speaker] wants a response from him. (Kendon, 1967, p. 42).

The analysis was impressive. Kendon had apparently demonstrated that looking is closely synchronized with the patterning of speech, and he had suggested that it might serve to regulate the flow of conversation. Perhaps, therefore, it is not surprising that both his data and his interpretation went unchallenged for more than 10 years. But then, in 1978, two independent pieces of research were published side by side in the *British Journal of Social and Clinical Psychology* and both raised a number of doubts.

The first paper was by Beattie, and his principal concern was whether a look by the speaker at the end of an utterance really did serve to invite the partner to take over the floor Beattie (1978). He was sceptical because Kendon's analysis of what happened when there was no look was based on only two conversations. Nevertheless, if Kendon was correct, then the presence of a look should, as he suggested, lead to shorter speaker-switch pauses and/or an increase in the proportion of switches which occurred instantaneously. Beattie based his own analysis on tutorials at the University of Cambridge, and neither prediction was supported. Although, like Kendon's, his data were very selective – 15 minutes from the middle of one tutorial between a graduate student and an undergraduate, 10 minutes from the middle of two more tutorials, and 10 minutes from the middle of a long exchange between two faculty members during a seminar – the results were very clear. The presence of a look did not lead to shorter speaker-switch pauses; and the proportion of switches which occurred instantaneously was significantly greater in the absence of a look than when a look had occurred, the reverse of Kendon's finding. Beattie concluded that gaze could not serve to apportion the floor.

Beattie's work drew attention to several weaknesses in Kendon's account – in particular that he had concentrated on long, complete utterances, had said very little about questions, interruptions, and overlaps, and that he had analysed so little data. But there was another problem, and it was this that the second paper, by Rutter *et al.* (1978), took up: although Kendon's interpretation referred to floor changes, his principal data referred only to the beginnings and endings of long utterances. In other words, the data described behaviour within single utterances, and so could not properly be used to comment on the ways in which transitions from speaker to speaker were brought about. If, Rutter *et al.* argued, we wish to find out about turn-taking, then we must examine floor changes specifically: and that is what they did.

The paper reported two experiments, and both were conducted at Nottingham. In the first, thirty-six subjects were recruited, and each was asked to spend 20 minutes with one of the others discussing 'themselves and their interests'. The conversations were recorded on video-tape by means of a close-up split-screen technique introduced by Stephenson, Rutter & Dore (1973), and stereo audio recordings were also made. Verbatim transcripts were prepared – including overlaps, 'mhmms', 'ers' and 'ums', and slips – and the coding and observation were completed by trained assistants.

The analysis was based on only the most relevant data – every utterance which consisted of ten words or more, was deemed to be complete, and ended in a floor change without overlapping speech – and four measures were taken: the proportion of floor changes which began with the speaker looking at the listener; the proportion which began with the listener looking at the speaker;

5

Table 1.1 Rutter *et al.* (1978): proportion (%) floor changes at which looking occurred

	End of old utterance	Beginning of new utterance	d.f.	*t*†
Experiment I				
Eye-contact	51.3	48.4	17	1.1
Looking by speakers	65.6	68.7	17	0.4
Looking by listeners	75.9	66.1	17	1.9
Experiment II				
Eye-contact	64.2	55.3	23	4.1***
Looking by speakers	84.4	59.9	23	4.8***
Looking by listeners	74.7	78.2	23	0.4

† Two-tailed test based on raw frequencies per pair.   ***$P<0.001$.

the proportion which ended with the new speaker looking; and the proportion which ended with the new listener looking. Many types of floor change were excluded, of course – in particular, those which occurred at the end of short utterances, after incomplete utterances, or during periods of simultaneous speech – but the omission was deliberate, and was intended to make our data comparable to Kendon's.

The number of floor changes which met our definition, and so were examined, totalled 195, and the results are given in the first part of Table 1.1 and in Figure 1.1. Overall, 65·6% of floor changes began with the speaker

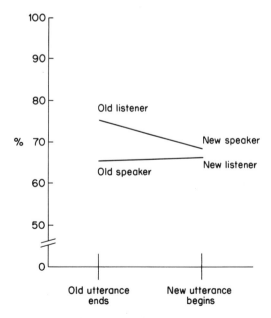

Figure 1.1   Rutter *et al.* (1978) Exp. I: proportion (%) floor changes at which looking occurred

looking, 75·9% with the listener looking, and 51·3% with both looking; and 68·7% ended with the new speaker looking, 66·1% with the new listener looking, and 48·4% with both looking.

The second of our experiments was similar to the first. Twenty-four subjects were recruited, and each was asked to bring a friend of the same sex to the laboratory, so that twelve pairs of friends and twelve pairs of strangers could be formed. Each pair then held a 20-minute discussion about topics from a sociopolitical questionnaire completed shortly before the experimental sessions began. Only items which had revealed a disagreement between the two subjects were used, and half the pairs were assigned to hold a competitive discussion in which the object was to persuade the partner to one's point of view, and half held a co-operative discussion in which the object was to find common ground in preparation for trying later to persuade a third party to the shared view. The conversations were recorded and scored in the same way as in the previous experiment.

Once again, our analysis concentrated on the four principal measures and, because acquaintance and task had little effect, all 257 floor changes were eventually combined. The results are given in the second part of Table 1.1 and in Figure 1.2. Overall, 84·4% of floor changes began with the speaker looking, 74·7% with the listener looking, and 64·2% with both looking; and 59·9% ended with the new speaker looking, 78·2% with the new listener looking, and 55·3% with both looking.

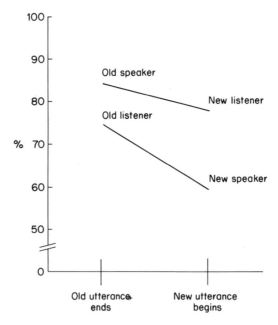

Figure 1.2   Rutter *et al.* (1978) Exp. II: proportion (%) floor changes at which looking occurred

The findings were very similar to those of the first experiment, with one exception: the proportion of floor changes at which the old speaker/new listener looked was greater. Although this may perhaps reflect a difference between the experiments in the patterning of looks at floor changes, the more likely explanation is simply that the differences in subject selection and experimental procedures influenced the overall level of looking, and this was in turn reflected at floor changes.

In both experiments, our approach to Kendon's argument had been rather different from Beattie's. Beattie was concerned with what happens when the speaker fails to deliver a 'terminal look'; we were concerned with how frequently the terminal look was or was not given. Just as Kendon predicted, we found that indeed the majority of long, completed utterances which led to a floor change did end with a look by the speaker – 65·6% in the first experiment and 84·4% in the second – but now comes the crucial issue. Taken alone, this finding is not sufficient to confirm Kendon's interpretation. For that, three further conditions must hold.

The three conditions are these. First, the level of looking by speakers should be higher at the ends of utterances than at the beginnings of new utterances after the floor change, since the new speaker should by now be planning what to say and preventing the old speaker continuing. Although this was confirmed in the second experiment, the first revealed a trend in the opposite direction. Second, there should be a very high level of eye-contact at the ends of utterances. If the speaker's terminal look is to trigger a floor change, the listener must be in a position to receive it – that is, looking, so that eye-contact occurs. In the first experiment eye-contact failed to occur on half the occasions and, in the second, one-third. In other words, for up to half the occasions, either the speaker did not give a look at the end of the utterance or, if he did, the listener missed it because he was looking elsewhere. Third, there should be a lower incidence of eye-contact at the start of the new utterance than at the end of the old utterance, since the new speaker should by now be looking away. Although this was confirmed in the second experiment, where the difference, though small, was consistent across pairs, there was no such evidence in the first. Thus, the first experiment failed in all three respects to confirm Kendon's 'typical pattern', and the second provided only limited support.

Another point concerns the relative importance of speaker and listener. In the event, we found that the incidence of eye-contact at the ends of utterances leading up to floor changes was considerably less than Kendon predicted. Suppose, however, that eye-contact had occurred on every occasion. Might not the listener's look rather than the speaker's be the signal which triggered the floor change? As Kendon himself acknowledged, it might be that the speaker looks up as a means of receiving, not sending, a signal. Either interpretation would be possible, and there is no obvious reason for concentrating one's account on the speaker.

Like Beattie, we were led to conclude that there is no good evidence that looking serves to apportion the floor. Kendon, however, was not convinced. In a comment on both papers, published alongside them, he conceded that Beattie's findings went against him (Kendon, 1978), though he suggested they may well have been in part the result of status effects. Our own experiments, however – or, at least, the second – he received with enthusiasm, for here the methodology was closer to his own, he argued, and so, correspondingly, was the outcome:

> The kind of conversation that was in progress . . . was . . . a conversation in which a serious topic of conversation had been established. . . . It did not include the more ritualised exchanges which occur early in 'getting acquainted' conversations, before a topic of mutual interest has been found. Rutter *et al.*'s Expt. I would almost certainly have included conversation of this sort (Kendon, 1978, p. 23).

In fact, neither of Kendon's arguments is persuasive. The topic which came closest to his own was the one we used in Experiment I, not Experiment II – 'yourselves and your interests' against divisive items from a sociopolitical questionnaire – but it was Experiment I which produced the greatest discrepancy with his findings. Furthermore, effects of status have been reported only for gross measures of the frequency and duration of looking, and there is no published evidence to suggest that it influences the timing of looks.

Nevertheless, Kendon's reply did include two very important and revealing comments.

> whether gaze (or indeed any other specific aspect of behaviour) functions as a floor apportionment or turn-taking signal may be very much dependent upon the kind of interactional situation we are dealing with. I am very much in agreement with Beattie when he comments, at the end of his paper, that 'further research is required into situational differences in the regulation of turn-taking'. I believe that these could well turn out to be overwhelming (Kendon, 1978, p.23).

and

> My own current view is that what can serve to cue the next speaker to his turn is quite variable, depending upon the nature of the turn units being employed and the current conversation structure – for example, what sort of 'conversational sequence' is in progress (cf. Sacks, Schegloff & Jefferson, 1974). I also think that the participants' understanding of each other's current communicational intentions plays a central role. I suspect that the study of single specific variables as turn-taking signals will not be as fruitful as intensive studies in which the internal structure of turn units and their functioning as 'moves' in the conversational organization is taken into account (Kendon, 1978, p. 24).

This was something very different from what Kendon had written 10 years earlier. Perhaps, after all, looking was not so important as a regulator of conversation.

Individual differences

As we have seen, the early descriptive research by Nielsen (1962) and Kendon (1967) revealed a wide range of individual differences in looking, and Kendon

& Cook (1969) were able to show that, to some extent, each individual behaved consistently from situation to situation. Their finding has been confirmed several times since (Harper, Wiens & Matarazzo, 1978): some people simply look a lot and others do not. The question to which experimenters now turned was whether it might be possible to find the main sources of individual variation, and three in particular attracted their attention: sex, personality, and psychopathology.

Sex

Two types of dyadic study have been conducted in the search for sex differences. In the first a confederate is used, and he or she is programmed to stare continuously or to look and look away at specific times according to the experimenter's instructions. In the second the participants are generally two naive subjects who are free to respond as they please, or sometimes a naive subject paired with a partner who, although a confederate, is not under the direct control of the experimenter. Only the second type will be considered here.

Neither Nielsen (1962) nor Kendon (1967) examined sex. Nielsen's descriptions of his sample suggests that all twenty-one participants were male; and Kendon included only three women. Kendon & Cook (1969), however, were able to conduct a systematic analysis, and the results were as follows. For their group of four subjects, the two women looked more than the two men on seven of the nine measures of individual gaze while, for the group of eleven, there was only one effect. For neither group was eye-contact influenced by sex. Thus, another way to present the findings is to say that, of twenty-four possible differences, eight showed women looking more than men, none showed the reverse, and sixteen revealed no difference. It was also found that people looked more at female partners than male partners, and this was true both for men and for women. The same year, interestingly enough, Argyle & Williams (1969) were to report the corresponding finding, that women *feel* more observed than men.

With relatively few exceptions, the subsequent literature has confirmed that women tend to look more than men, and none has reported the opposite, so far as I know. Among the major published studies, for example, Argyle & Ingham (1972), and Levine & Sutton-Smith (1973) both found that women in female–female pairs looked more overall than men in male–male pairs, and so too did Coutts & Schneider (1975), who made their observations on 'unfocussed dyads' in an experimental waiting-room in which subjects were asked to sit in silence. Argyle & Ingham and Coutts & Schneider also examined male–female pairs and found that the average level of looking for the two subjects lay somewhere between the means for male–male and female–female pairs. Other writers who have confirmed the effect include Rubin (1970), Nevill (1974), and Russo (1975). What is more, sex differences also appear to be present even in young children, though here the only study to have used naive subjects and not a programmed confederate is that of Levine & Sutton-Smith (1973). They studied four age groups, 4–6 years, 7–9 years, 10–11 years, and adults, and each subject interacted with a partner who was of the same sex and from the same age group. Although the absolute level of looking varied with age – perhaps because of task differences – and was considerably greater in the adults than the youngest children, females throughout looked more than males, at least while they were speaking, and they engaged in more eye-contact. As Ellsworth & Ludwig felt able to write as early as 1972, 'In research on visual behaviour, sex differences are the rule, rather than the exception' (p. 379). Similar statements are also to be found in the reviews by Argyle & Cook (1976) and Harper, Wiens & Matarazzo (1978).

My own work has produced a variety of findings, some of them consistent with the conclusion that women look more than men, some of them not. None of our studies used a programmed confederate and, in all but four of the twelve in which both sexes were represented, sex was examined systematically. Brief details of all twelve studies are given in Figure 1.3 and, for convenience, the figure is divided into two. The first section presents our experiments with the general population, and the second our series of studies with psychiatric patients. In both sections the order is chronological.

The first of our experiments was conducted by Rutter, Morley & Graham (1972), and was concerned with the personality factor, extraversion. Ten extraverts and ten introverts, half of each group male and half female, held two conversations, one with a male confederate and one with a female confederate. The subjects and confederates were all students, and the conversations, which lasted 4 minutes each, were concerned with university life. Although there were no effects of subject sex for the principal measures of looking and eye-contact, there were several effects for the subsidiary measures. Women engaged in more frequent periods of eye-contact than did men when both people were speaking or both were silent. The duration of their bursts of eye-contact during silence was also longer than for men, and their looks during silence were more frequent, an effect which was especially marked when women interacted with the female confederate. Furthermore, subjects were noticeably affected by whether they were talking to the male confederate or the female confederate. Men and women both spent a greater proportion of their time looking at the female confederate than at the male confederate, and this was reflected in the greater proportions of listening and silence they spent looking at her, the mean length of their looks during speech and listening, and the number of times they looked during silence. Of course, since only one confederate of each sex was used, the effects could not be confidently attributed to sex; but they were, nevertheless, consistent with the common findings that women are generally looked at more than men (Kendon & Cook, 1969; Exline, Gray & Schuette, 1965; Mehrabian & Friar, 1969), and also feel more observed than do men (Argyle & Williams, 1969). There was one unexplained reversal: subjects engaged in more frequent periods of eye-contact when they were

	Focus of investigation	Subjects	Topic
Rutter, Morley & Graham (1972)	Extraversion	10 M; 10 F	University life
Stephenson, Rutter & Dore (1973)	Distance	9 MM pair; 9 FF pair; 9 MF pair	First impressions of Nottingham
Rutter *et al.* (1978) Exp. 1	Timing of looks	6 MM pair; 6 FF pair; 6 MF pair	'Yourselves and your interests'
Rutter *et al.* (1978) Exp. 2	Timing of looks	6 MM pair; 6 FF pair	Sociopolitical debating issues
Rutter & Stephenson (1979b)*	Friendship	6 MM pair; 6 FF pair	Sociopolitical debating issues
Pennington & Rutter (1981)	Distance and friendship	Sex not examined	
Rutter & Stephenson (1972a)	Schizophrenic and depressed patients	20 M patients; 20 F patients; 20 M controls; 20 F controls	
Rutter & Stephenson (1972b)	Patients with neurotic and personality disorders	Sex not examined	
Rutter (1976) Exp. 1	Acute psychiatric patients	18 M patients; 18 F patients; 6 M controls; 6 F controls	CDQ items (Kogan & Wallach, 1964)
Rutter (1976) Exp. 2	Chronic schizophrenic patients	Sex not examined	
Rutter (1977b)	Remitted schizophrenic patients	Sex not examined	
Rutter (1978)	Timing of looks in psychiatric patients	Further data from Rutter (1976, 1977b)	

* The data analysed by Rutter & Stephenson (1979b) were collected by Rutter *et al.* (1978) for Exp. 2.
M = male; F = female.

Figure 1.3   Author's studies of looking

listening to the man than when they were listening to the woman, and this was especially so for the female subjects.

Our other experimental studies of the general population have revealed rather less evidence of sex differences. In their experiment on distance, Stephenson, Rutter & Dore (1973) examined nine male pairs, nine female pairs, and nine mixed pairs, and took five measures of gaze: the duration of looking, the number of looks, the mean length of looks, the duration of eye-contact, and mutual focus, a measure which represents the proportion of a pair's looking which results in eye-contact. There were no main effects of sex, and no interactions between sex and distance. Rutter *et al.* (1978) , in the first of their studies of the precise timing of looks, examined six male pairs, six female pairs, and six mixed pairs, but again found no differences. In the second experiment presented in the paper, sex was included as a factor but the results were not reported, and the same was true for Rutter & Stephenson (1979b). In Pennington & Rutter (1981), sex was not examined.

In one final experiment, which is not included in Figure 1.3 because my colleagues conducted it independently, Swain, Stephenson & Dewey (1982) revealed several further effects. The experiment was concerned principally with seating distance and the relationship between members of the pair, and three types of opposite-sex pair were studied, each of whom held a conversation at 2 feet 6 inches or at 6 feet. The pairs were married couples, platonic friends, or strangers, and there were twelve of each type. The task was to prepare a case either 'for' or 'against' British withdrawal from Northern Ireland, in preparation for the possibility of being asked to return later to present the case at a group meeting. The conversations were terminated after 15 minutes. Although no sex differences were revealed for the principal measures of gaze, there were several effects for the subsidiary measures. The women spent proportionately more time than the men looking while they were listening, but less time than the men looking while they were speaking, and there were two significant interactions between sex and distance. Overall, Swain, Stephenson & Dewey had found that couples who were assigned to sit at 2 feet 6 inches looked less than those who sat at 6 feet, and what the interactions showed was as follows: while the difference between the two distances was greater for men than women in the proportion of time spent looking, the 2 feet 6 inches condition resulted in shorter looks for men than the 6 feet condition, but longer looks for women.

In contrast to our experiments with the general population, my studies of psychiatric patients revealed no evidence of sex differences. The first was conducted by Rutter & Stephenson (1972a), and examined twenty schizophrenic patients and twenty depressed patients, all of whom had been recently admitted to a psychiatric hospital. There were ten men and ten women in each group, and all were matched individually with psychiatrically normal chest patients from a nearby general hospital. One of the criteria for matching was sex. All eighty patients were given a standard, structured, psychiatric interview, and the sessions were video-tape-recorded. Although Rutter &

Stephenson did not analyse the data for sex differences, they did present the means for men and women separately, and it is clear that there were no significant differences for any of the measures they took: duration of looking, mean length of looks, and the proportions of speech, listening, and silence spent looking. In the follow-up study, by Rutter & Stephenson (1972b), the sample was too small for sex to be incorporated as a factor.

In the remaining three experiments, patients took part in free conversations rather than an interview, and their partners were sometimes other patients, and sometimes hospital employees – generally nurses. In the first of the two studies reported by Rutter (1976), four groups of twelve recently admitted patients took part – schizophrenic patients, depressed patients, people suffering from neurotic or personality disorders, and psychiatrically normal chest patients – and each group included six men and six women. No sex differences were found. In the second experiment reported there, a small group of chronic schizophrenic patients were examined, but most were men, and sex differences could not be analysed reliably. Sample size was again small in Rutter (1977b), in which remitted and acute schizophrenic patients were compared, and sex was not examined. In the final paper of the series, Rutter (1978) re-analysed the data from the 1976 and 1977 studies, this time concentrating on the precise patterning of looks, but no evidence of sex differences was revealed there either.

Conclusion.   As to why women might look more than men, there are two main types of interpretation, but both are speculative and lack evidence either for or against. The first, which Argyle & Cook (1976) appear to favour, is based on the assumption that looking is determined largely by motivation, and that men and women have different motives. There are three main approaches of this sort. The most popular takes the view that women have a greater need for affiliation than do men, and that need for affiliation promotes looking. The effect may even be innate, Argyle & Cook suggest, or at least probably develops early in infancy, since baby girls have been reported to give more visual attention to faces than do baby boys (Kagan & Lewis, 1965). The second approach argues that eye-contact is less threatening to women than men for some reason, and the greater reluctance of women to break it means that, on average, they will continue to look longer than men. The third approach, which is really no more than a variant on the other two, favours an interactionist position: motivation interacts with situational factors, and sex differences will therefore be greater in some situations than others. The chief proponent of the interactionist approach is Exline, who was one of the first writers to conduct experimental studies of gaze (Exline, 1971).

The second main type of interpretation, which I do not think has been proposed before, holds that sex differences are best explained by reference not to motivation but to information. There are two parts to the interpretation, and the first is concerned with looking while listening. When we listen to someone else, we have more opportunity to take in information than when we are speaking ourselves, because we do not have to concentrate on planning what to say. The people who look most while they listen are likely to be those who are most dependent on social cues and feedback – and, as Exline himself suggested, women are often characterized in just this way (Exline, 1963). The second part of the interpretation focuses on looking while speaking. One of the main concerns for speakers, in contrast to listeners, is to shut out information rather than seek it, so that they can avoid distraction. Kendon (1967), as we have seen, found that speakers will look away if they hesitate or stumble, and it may therefore be that those who are able to look the most are the most fluent speakers. Thus, if women do look more than men when they speak, we might also expect to find that they are more fluent than men – and there is indeed some evidence to that effect (Harper, Wiens & Matarazzo, 1978).

Personality

The most common approach to personality has been to choose a single trait and then to conduct one of two types of study. In the first, subjects are selected at random from the general population, and their scores on the trait are correlated with measures of their gaze. In the second, extreme or otherwise distinct groups are selected, and their patterns of gaze are compared. A wide variety of traits have been explored, but three have received more attention than most: need for affiliation, dominance, and extraversion.

Need for affiliation.   The first writer to examine need for affiliation was Exline (1963). In a complex study, which has often been poorly reported since, he administered French's Test of Insight (French, 1955) to a large but undefined sample. He then took the ratio of affiliation to achievement responses for each subject, and selected two groups, one with scores above the median and one with scores below. Single-sex groups of three high scorers or three low scorers were formed, and each group held two discussions, one competitive, the other relatively uncompetitive. Measures of individual and mutual looking were taken in both. In the principal analysis, need for affiliation produced no main effects, but it did twice interact with sex, though not with competition. However, in a *post hoc* analysis of eye-contact, in which only the most affiliative and the least affiliative subjects were included, a rather different pattern was revealed. Need for affiliation now interacted significantly with competition, so that subjects with high scores spent proportionately less time in eye-contact in the competitive encounter than the other encounter, while those with low scores tended slightly in the opposite direction. What is more, the means suggested a triple interaction with sex, but the effect was not examined statistically.

In a subsequent study, Exline was able to demonstrate a simple main effect (Exline, Gray & Schuette, 1965) although, as he warned, caution is necessary, because the numbers were small. High and low affiliative subjects were selected on the basis of their scores for inclusion and affection on the FIRO-B test (Schutz, 1958), and high subjects were found to look more than low subjects. The partner was a confederate who was programmed to stare continuously. In the only other 'between-groups' study of which I know, by Libby & Yaklevitch (1973), subjects were asked a series of embarrassing and non-embarrassing questions as part of a structured interview, and one of the dependent measures was whether they maintained eye-contact with the interviewer throughout their answer. Half the subjects had 'high' scores for nurturance on the Edwards Personal Preference Schedule, and half had 'low' scores, and the former maintained eye-contact on more items than the latter. Unfortunately, however, 'high' and 'low' were not defined in the paper.

The remaining studies all used correlational designs, and not one of them was able to corroborate the findings of the 'between-groups' studies. Kendon & Cook (1969), like Exline, Gray & Schuette (1965), used FIRO-B, but they could find no correlations with affiliation, or indeed any of the other scales, beyond the number expected by chance. In contrast, Efran & Broughton (1966) used the Marlowe–Crowne test of social desirability (Crowne & Marlowe, 1960) – which probably taps both affiliation and dependence – and did find a correlation with looking. Subjects were asked to spend a few minutes telling two confederates about themselves, and the higher their score, the more they looked. However, Efran was unable to confirm the finding in his follow-up study (Efran, 1968), and he was therefore compelled to attribute it to Type II error. In both experiments the confederates stared continuously, but one was instructed to behave in a more approving way than the other. As expected, subjects generally looked more at the approving confederate than his partner, irrespective of their Marlowe–Crowne scores.

Dominance. In the first major study of dominance, Strongman & Champness (1968) used neither a correlational nor a 'between-groups' design. Pursuing the notion of agonistic 'cut-off' posture (Chance, 1962), they wondered whether dominance hierarchies might exist for looking in humans just as they do for other types of behaviour in the animal kingdom. They therefore asked ten subjects to interact with one another in all possible paired combinations, and they simply observed which member of each pair was usually the first to break eye-contact. A near-perfect linear hierarchy was revealed, so that the person at the top 'outstared' almost all the others, while the one at the bottom was almost always the first to avert the gaze. Unfortunately, though, as Brand (1969) subsequently pointed out, the data were very difficult to interpret, because no systematic measures of speech were taken. If people look away to prepare to speak, it may be that those who were apparently outstared were the most prolific speakers. If 'outspeaking', as well as 'outstaring', can signal dominance, then a hierarchy based on speech would produce the opposite rankings to one based on looking.

In the remaining literature on dominance, the pattern of findings is very similar to the one which emerged for need for affiliation: correlational studies generally do not produce significant effects, while 'between-groups' studies do. The major correlational studies are those of Kendon & Cook (1969), Argyle &

Williams (1969), and Patterson (1973b). Kendon & Cook (1969), as we have seen already, used FIRO-B and, although 'dominance given' was found to correlate negatively with the frequency of looking, they attributed the result to chance because so few of their many correlations reached statistical significance. Argyle & Williams (1969) administered the FIRO-B 'expressed control' and 'control wanted' scales to a sample of grammar-school pupils and university students, and examined their responses to a series of questions about how they would behave in a variety of hypothetical social encounters. Again, there were few significant effects, and those which did emerge were relatively weak and formed no coherent pattern. Finally, Patterson (1973b), in a study in which subjects were interviewed by a confederate, could find no effects at all, either for looking or for any of the other 'immediacy behaviours' he examined. Dominance was measured by one of the scales from the Personality Research Form of Jackson (1964).

The first of the major 'between-groups' studies was conducted by Exline & Messick (1967). Randomly selected male students were each given FIRO-B, and were classified as either dominant or dependent. Dominant subjects were those whose 'control behaviour' score was greater than or equal to their 'control wanted' score; and dependent subjects were those with the reverse pattern of responses. Each subject was then interviewed by an experimenter, who, although he stared continuously, varied the number of reinforcements (nods, smiles, 'mhmms', and so on) he gave, from only one or two a minute for half the subjects of each type to six or eight for the others. The dependent measure was the proportion of time the subject spent looking at the interviewer as he answered his questions. Main effects of neither personality nor reinforcement were reported in the paper, and the reader is left to infer that they failed to reach significance. There was, however, a clear interaction: while dominant subjects tended to look rather more when they were reinforced strongly than when they were not, the dependent subjects behaved in the opposite way, and markedly so.

In a subsequent study, conducted at Oxford and reported in his review chapter in the *Nebraska Symposium on Motivation*, Exline (1971) again compared dominant and dependent subjects, using the same system of classification as before. This time, however, the interviewer varied his gaze. When he spoke, he looked about 50% of the time, but when he listened, he stared continuously for half the members of each group, and looked away continuously for the other half. Overall, there was a non-significant tendency for the dominant subjects to look more than the dependent group. Furthermore, an interaction occurred, so that dependent subjects looked significantly less when they listened if the confederate stared than if he looked away, while the gaze of dominant subjects was unaffected. To the extent that looking acts as a reinforcer, the findings thus paralleled those of Exline & Messick (1967). In a subsidiary analysis based on rating scales, Exline was able to show that, even though the dominant subjects appeared to be unaffected by the interviewer's gaze, they nevertheless rated him significantly more potent if he averted the gaze than if he looked. 'Powerful people do not monitor less powerful people', Exline concluded. 'Dominant men seem more impressed with the personal force of one who listens without looking and also seem more reluctant to look at those whom they perceive to be forceful' (Exline, 1971, p. 192).

Extraversion. Most studies of extraversion have used either the Maudsley Personality Inventory or the Eysenck Personality Inventory and, again, both correlational and between-groups designs have been employed. In general, the evidence from both types of study suggests that people who look the most are extraverts.

The first of the correlational analyses was reported in the paper by Kendon & Cook (1969) which we have discussed before. All fifteen subjects completed the MPI, and extraversion was found to correlate positively with the frequency of looks when they spoke. Although non-significant, the remaining correlations were all positive. Moreover, in a subsequent questionnaire study on seating position, Cook (1970) found that, when extraverts and introverts chose different seats, extraverts tended to favour positions which allowed the most visual interaction with other people. In a later experiment concerned mostly with distance and looking, Argyle & Ingham (1972) administered the EPI to all their subjects and correlated the scores with four measures of looking. Each subject held one conversation at 3 feet and another at 6 feet, and pairs were either same-sex or opposite-sex. For all thirty-four subjects taken together there were no significant correlations; but when those from the same-sex pairs were examined separately, extraversion was found to correlate positively with the proportion of time the subject spent looking in the 6 foot condition and the proportion of time the pair spent in eye-contact at 3 feet. Of the non-significant correlations, roughly half were positive and half were negative. In the only other correlational study to use the EPI, Rutter & Stephenson (1972a) examined the normal control subjects from their study of looking in psychiatric patients. For the eleven men whose protocols were usable there were no significant effects; but for the sixteen women, both the proportion of time spent looking at the interviewer and the frequency of looks correlated positively with extraversion, though the length of looks did not. Since then, there has been only one more correlational study, as far as I know. Patterson (1973b) administered the social extraversion scale of Bendig (1962) to seventy-two subjects, but could find no association either with looking or with the several other 'immediacy' measures he took.

There have been only two 'between-groups' studies, and the first, conducted by Mobbs (1968), achieved some notoriety. Mobbs selected three groups of subjects on the basis of their scores on a measure of sociability devised by Heron (1956): four extraverts, eight introverts, and seven 'neutrals'. Each subject held a short conversation with a confederate who stared continuously, and extraverts were found to look for longer overall than either of the other groups. As in some of the other studies I have cited, unfortunately speech measures were not reported – which makes interpretation very difficult, of course, since looking and speech are often dependent, and extraverts and introverts may well have different patterns of speech. It should also be added that, again in common with many other writers, Mobbs failed to report whether his method of observation was valid and reliable. The observer was required to peer through the revolving blades of an electric ventilator fan.

The second study was conducted by Rutter, Morley & Graham (1972). They administered the EPI to forty-five undergraduates and selected ten extraverts and ten introverts, five men and five women in each group. The groups were equated for neuroticism so far as possible, and were taken from the ends of the distribution for extraversion so that they did not overlap. Each subject held two conversations, one with a male confederate and one with a female confederate, and three effects of extraversion were found. Extraverts looked more frequently than introverts, spoke more frequently, and engaged in more frequent periods of eye-contact while they were speaking. Mobbs' findings received no support, and the few effects which did occur were small, accounted for very little of the variance, and were perhaps in any case dependent upon speech patterning.

Conclusion. Useful reviews of the literature on personality and gaze can be found in Ellsworth and Ludwig (1972), Argyle & Cook (1976), and Harper, Wiens & Matarazzo (1978). Despite the evidence that personality does have at least some part to play in looking, there have been no systematic attempts to integrate the literature theoretically. As with sex differences, there are two possible types of approach, one based on motivation, the other on information.

The simplest type of motivational account would argue that people with particular personality traits have a strong need for social interaction while those with other traits do not. Extraverts, for example, and people with a high need for affiliation, need social interaction more than others, and they look more to encourage people to interact with them. The first problem with such an interpretation, of course, is that it risks tautology since traits are often defined in terms of social behaviour in the first place. Furthermore, it ignores the influence of both the relationship between the participants and the situation in which the encounter takes place. Since Mischel first provoked the 'person–situation' debate (Mischel, 1968), it has become abundantly clear that personality traits seldom account for more than a small proportion of the variance, whatever behaviour one examines (Bowers, 1973; Bem & Allen, 1974; Magnusson & Endler, 1977; Mischel, 1979). Instead, personality and situation interact, so that the effects of a particular trait in one setting may well be quite different from its effects elsewhere.

The alternative interpretation, based on information, would argue that our personality influences how much we depend on feedback and how much use we make of it. Extraverts, for example, are very dependent upon the requirements of the setting and the responses of other people, and that is why they often look more than others. The salience of information varies from setting to setting, however, and, like the motivational account, the informational interpretation assumes an interactionist perspective.

Psychopathology

Psychopathology has a long history in the literature on gaze, and it has probably been the subject of more research than either sex or personality. Some of the investigators have tried to use their findings to illuminate the normal processes and functions of looking; others have been more interested in developing and testing theories of abnormal social behaviour; and still others have concentrated on the clinical implications for diagnosis and therapy. Research methods have ranged from clinical case studies to controlled experiments, and three main groups of people have been examined: psychotic children; schizophrenic adults; and depressed adults. The early literature on each of the three groups will be reviewed first, and then I shall present my own research.

Psychotic children.   Psychotic children, many of whom are called 'autistic', have received rather more attention than either schizophrenic or depressed adults. Much of the evidence, from clinical and experimental studies alike, suggests that many of them are characterized by marked gaze aversion. Problems of nosology have been considerable (Creak, 1961, 1964; Rutter, 1968), but Norman (1955) observed twenty-five children who were all under 12 years old, and who all had 'reasonably clear pictures of childhood schizophrenia or early infantile autism'. Many showed a marked lack of visual interaction across a variety of settings, and some developed strategies of actively avoiding the gaze of others. Rutter & Lockyer (1967) reported evidence of gaze abnormalities in the case-notes of most of a series of psychotic children admitted to the Maudsley Hospital Children's Department from 1950 to 1958, with almost no such evidence in the case-notes of the control subjects, who were mostly mentally handicapped children. Wolff & Chess (1964) went so far as to suggest that visual behaviour may be important in the diagnostic setting. They argued that the absence of looking in a child was largely responsible for the impression that one was not 'making contact', and that this in turn was crucial to the diagnosis of childhood autism.

There have been no experimental studies of visual behaviour in psychotic children during social interaction as such, but two relevant reports have been published. Hutt & Ounsted (1966) studied eight psychotic boys aged 3–6 years, and a control group of non-psychotic children who were unspecified psychiatric in-patients. Each child was placed individually in a room which contained a number of masks placed at eye level on stands located around the sides of the floor. The child was left there for 10 minutes, and his movements were plotted by observers who sat behind a one-way screen. The psychotic children spent less time than the controls investigating the faces, but more time on the fixtures and fittings in the room – radiators, sink, and so on. Furthermore, the groups differed in the proportion of time they spent on each particular face: the psychotic children spent less time than the controls with the happy and sad human faces, but just as long as the controls with the other faces.

Hutt & Ounsted suggested that their findings were related to gaze avoidance in social interaction, and they went on in the 1966 paper, and a revised version published in 1970, to speculate that gaze aversion in psychotic children has a particular 'biological' significance, and serves to protect them in social interaction. O'Connor & Hermelin (1967), however, argued that it may simply reflect a tendency to avoid all forms of visual stimulation. By means of an ingenious 'inspection box', they presented children with a series of paired simultaneous displays, and measured how long they spent fixating each one in turn, and how long they spent in undirected gaze, looking at neither. A group of psychotic children was compared with a mentally handicapped group and a normal group of equivalent mental age. The psychotic children spent longer then either control group in undirected gazing, and less time looking at the displays. In some of the trials a photograph of a human face was presented, but the psychotic children showed no special tendency to avoid it: indeed, in common with both control groups, they spent longer looking at that display than at any of the others, a variety of shapes and coloured designs.

Schizophrenic patients. Much of the evidence concerning schizophrenic patients comes from the observations and impressions of clinicians. It is important to stress at the outset that, in research on visual interaction, as in other areas, there has been little agreement on what is meant by the term 'schizophrenic patient'. Clinical type, age, length of illness and stay in hospital, degree of social stimulation, the doctor–patient relationship, medication, and a host of other variables may all have important effects upon looking: but clinicians and experimentalists alike have generally selected and described their 'schiozophrenic patients' quite haphazardly.

The first published paper was by the American psychoanalyst, Riemer, who reported his observations on six patients who were characterised by 'gaze aversion' (Riemer, 1949). The definition and extent of 'gaze aversion' were not made clear, but the 'fixedly averted gaze', he concluded, 'is indicative of schizophrenic disorder, usually catatonic' (p. 115). In 1955 he went on to explore other abnormalities of gaze, and to offer a classification which included 'excessive blinking', the 'depressed look', the 'dramatic gaze', the 'guarded gaze', the 'absent gaze', and the 'averted gaze' (Riemer, 1955). Particular abnormalities (some of which, it should be noted, were probably defined by the appearance of the face rather than the activity of the eyes) were held to indicate particular psychopathological conditions. Laing too commented on gaze and, relying like Riemer on clinical experience, described the disturbing significance which the 'Look' (Sartre, 1943) held for some of his patients (Laing, 1960, 1961).

Although some interesting ethological studies have been published (Grant, 1965, 1970, 1972; Hutt & Hutt, 1970), there have been very few controlled experimental studies, and most of them have been no more than exploratory. The first was reported by Lefcourt *et al.* (1967), who attempted to investigate visual behaviour in process and reactive schizophrenics soon after admission to hospital. Unfortunately, the design of the experiment was particularly unsatisfactory. Each subject took part in two encounters: one a very brief initial interview, the other a psychometric testing session in which he or she was given the Wechsler digit-span task. Gaze was recorded on both occasions by an observer who was concealed behind a one-way screen and operated an event-recorder. For each patient, only a sample of behaviour was analysed, and for some it was taken from one or other of the two sessions, while for the remainder it was taken from both. The difference between the two encounters may well have been a source of considerable variance, but this was ignored in the analysis and the results have little, if any, meaning.

Two other studies were reported only briefly. The first was an unpublished piece of work by Argyle & Kendon, cited in Argyle (1967). 'Chronic schizophrenics', it was reported, engaged in less eye-contact than 'normals', looked in very short glances, and tended to gaze at an angle of 90 degrees to the line of regard. Apparently, the patients were observed during interaction with a confederate who stared continuously at their eyes; but in the absence of further details of design and procedure, interpretation is difficult. Moreover, subsequent work by Argyle, again unpublished, indicated that the effects occurred in only some patients, and not all schizophrenics averted the gaze (Argyle, 1970, personal communication).

The second study was by Harris (1968), and it consisted of an examination of the frequency of eye-contact in an experimental 'waiting room'. Each patient was asked to wait with, in turn, his mother, his father, an 'authority figure', and a 'peer'. The schizophrenics were compared with a group of psychiatrically normal subjects, and they were found to engage in less frequent periods of eye-contact, consistently across the four conditions. Unfortunately, however, important details of design and procedure were omitted from the report. In particular it was unclear whether subjects were allowed to speak and, since looking generally occurs less during speech than listening, the findings cannot be interpreted.

More recently, a variety of additional studies have appeared (for example, by Gottheil et al., 1970; Jones & Pansa, 1979; Exline et al., 1979; Fairbanks, McGuire & Harris, 1982), and one of the most interesting was the one by Exline. Schizophrenic patients were asked to recall emotional experiences – happy, sad, and angry – and to relate them to an interviewer. Both 'direct gaze' and 'downward gaze' were measured, and it was found that the most sensitive way to distinguish patients from controls was to take the ratio of the two measures. Absolute values may often be useful – but ratios can sometimes be better still.

Depressed patients. As in other areas of research in abnormal social interaction, relatively little attention has been given to depressed patients and, as with 'schizophrenic patients', there has been scarce agreement on definition and selection. Riemer (1955) included the 'depressed look' in his classification of abnormalities of the gaze, but the appearance owed less to gaze than to the accompanying facial expression. Later, Ekman & Friesen (1969) conducted a series of filmed studies of patients undergoing clinical interviews. One recur-· rent element of behaviour which they observed was 'eye-cover', in which patients briefly passed a hand in front of their eyes, obscuring them from the interviewer and avoiding his gaze. The behaviour was most prevalent among depressed patients, but generally receded as their clinical state improved.

The only experimental reports in the early literature were published by a group working in Bristol. In the first, Hinchliffe, Lancashire & Roberts (1970) studied fourteen depressed patients who had been admitted to the psychiatric wing of a general hospital. The patients were given a 10-minute semi-structured interview about their symptoms, and the interviewer stared continuously and 'gave as much reinforcement as is usual in clinical interview [sic]'. Eye-contact was recorded by an observer who sat in on the interview and observed the subject's behaviour from a distance of 6–8 feet. The depressed patients were compared with surgical controls, who were questioned about their own (surgical) symptoms and were matched individually with the depressed patients for sex, age, and socio-economic status. The depressed group engaged in less frequent periods of eye-contact than their controls, and spent proportionately longer looking away.

Interpretation of the results is difficult, for several reasons. First, the subjects were described in very little detail, and we do not know, for example, how long they had been in hospital or whether the depressed and control groups had been there for a similar length of time. Second, the content of the interview differed for the two groups and may have produced the different results. Third, since looking was not analysed separately for periods of speech and listening, the possibility cannot be eliminated that differences between the two groups in speech patterning may have led to the differences in eye-contact. Finally, the behaviour of the interviewer, which was not recorded, may have differed across groups and produced the differences in gaze, a point which the authors themselves acknowledged.

In their second study, which was concerned with patients who had recovered from depression, Hinchliffe, Lancashire & Roberts (1971) attempted to solve the difficult problem of eliminating the interviewer's behaviour as a source of bias. Sixteen recovered patients were compared with a group who were still currently depressed. After a preliminary 5-minute discussion, the content of which was not described, the subjects were given a standard 7-minute interview about their illness and a number of unrelated topics. The interviewer looked continuously, and the subject's behaviour was recorded for the last 5 minutes of the session. The recovered patients engaged in eye-contact more frequently than the depressed group, and it went on for longer in total, both during speech and overall. There was no difference between the groups in the duration of speech.

As in the first study, the results were difficult to interpret. Little description of the subjects was given, and the reader is left to assume that the recovered patients were interviewed at follow-up, perhaps in an out-patient department, at some unspecified time after discharge. The probable difference between the groups in interview setting, as well as between being in hospital and living at home, may well be sufficient to account for the obtained differences in visual behaviour. Moreover, since the content of the initial 5-minute discussion was not described, the possibility that that produced the differences cannot be eliminated. Furthermore, despite their intention, it was still not possible for the authors to discount the interviewer's behaviour as a source of bias. The only check they made was to count the number of nods, smiles and 'mhmms' she gave in a brief study conducted after the main part of the experiment. Her behaviour there was found to be consistent across the two small groups of subjects who took part in the check, but this need imply nothing, of course, about her behaviour in the main part of the experiment.

The author's work. Although the consensus in the early literature was that many psychiatric patients display abnormal patterns of looking, much of the evidence, as we have seen, was based on the impressions and observations of clinicians, and few experimental reports had been published. To try to examine schizophrenic and depressed patients more closely, therefore, I designed a series of studies myself.

The first was reported by Rutter & Stephenson (1972a), and was conducted at Nottingham. Twenty schizophrenic and twenty depressed patients were given a standard, structured interview within 48 hours of their admission to one of the psychiatric hospitals serving the area. Each group included ten men and ten women, and subjects were selected randomly from all the consecutive in-patient admissions aged 16 to 65 to whom the admitting team had given a provisional diagnosis of either schizophrenia or depression. The forty experimental subjects were matched individually for sex, age, and socioeconomic status with psychiatrically normal chest patients, who were recent admissions to a local general hospital. All subjects, both experimental and control, were given the same interview, which was based on the Symptom-Sign Inventory of Foulds & Hope (1968), and their gaze was recorded on video-tape. The interviewer's own visual behaviour could not be recorded – because we had only one camera – but it was carefully standardized, so that he looked down to read out each question, and then looked up and continued to look until the patient had finished speaking. Facial expression, tone of voice, nodding, and so on were all held constant as far as possible so that interviewer effects would be minimal.

The main findings are reproduced in Figure 1.4. The schizophrenic and depressed groups both spent proportionately less time than their controls looking at the interviewer. Neither differed from their controls in the frequency of looks, but schizophrenic patients were found to look in shorter glances than either their own controls or the depressed group. There were no other differences between the two psychiatric groups. The decrement in looking which they both showed occurred consistently throughout the interview, whether they were speaking, listening, or sitting in silence, and there were no

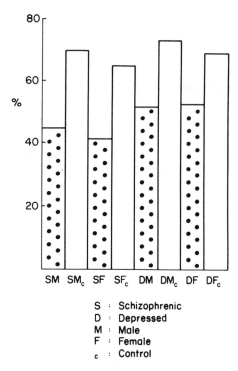

S : Schizophrenic
D : Depressed
M : Male
F : Female
c : Control

Figure 1.4   Rutter & Stephenson (1972a): proportion (%) time spent looking

abnormalities in the relationships between looking and speech. Indeed, except for the single finding that both groups looked less than their controls, their visual behaviour was normal. There was little evidence of prolonged gaze aversion, and patients and controls often overlapped.

Since Rutter and Stephenson (1972a) examined only schizophrenic and depressed patients, there remained the possibility that the decrement in looking would be found among the psychiatric population in general, perhaps the result of stigma or some other non-specific factor. A small follow-up study was therefore conducted (Rutter & Stephenson, 1972b), in which a group of patients who were mostly suffering from alcoholism or anxiety were compared with a control group of chest patients. No significant differences were found between the patients and controls in any of the measures we took. Moreover, the slight differences which did emerge differed significantly from the differences in the first study. Thus, while schizophrenic and depressed patients looked less than normal people, there was no evidence that the abnormality extended to other psychiatric groups.

Clinical descriptions of schizophrenia and depression often include the term 'social withdrawal', by which is meant isolation from social relationships, lack of activity on the ward, and so on. The decrement in looking, Rutter & Stephenson argued, was one aspect of withdrawal, and signalled to other people that the subject was unable or unwilling to interact, and so discouraged them from making an approach. Alternative explanations, based on cortical arousal or some other physiological concept, were unlikely to succeed because schizophrenic and depressed patients are very different in such respects yet their behaviour was similar – a point which emphasizes again how important it is to include appropriate control groups. Social withdrawal offered the more parsimonious account, we believed, and further evidence was to be revealed later.

So far, my own studies, in common with those of most other writers, had concentrated on the clinical interview. The result, as I pointed out in a review paper published in 1973, was that we knew very little about how patients behaved in less constrained encounters and indeed with one another, or even whether the decrement in looking was consistent across partners and settings (Rutter, 1973). These were important issues, and I therefore designed a further pair of experiments. They were published in Rutter (1976).

The first examined acute patients. Twelve recently admitted schizophrenic patients were selected randomly from the two principal psychiatric hospitals serving Oxford, and were compared with three recently admitted control groups: depressed patients; patients suffering from neurotic or personality disorders; and psychiatrically normal chest patients. All four groups included six men and six women aged 18–60, and the sessions were held within 10 days of the patient's admission, the majority within 6 days. Each subject was asked to hold two 5-minute conversations, one with a partner from the same diagnostic category, and one with a member of the hospital staff, who was generally a nurse, and the topics for discussion were adapted from the Choice Dilemmas Questionnaire of Kogan & Wallach (1964). The task was to try to agree a solution. The conversations were recorded in sound and vision on video-tape, and the split-screen technique was adopted so that both subject and partner appeared in close-up (Stephenson, Rutter & Dore, 1973).

Three main predictions were made: first, that the findings of Rutter & Stephenson (1972a and b) would be corroborated; second, that the differences between the schizophrenic and control groups would be greater in both number and degree in the patient partner condition than the normal partner condition; and third, that schizophrenic subjects would show individual consistency across their two encounters. By way of illustration, as well as comparison with Rutter & Stephenson (1972a and b), the findings for the proportion of time spent looking are reproduced in Figure 1.5. The first two predictions received no support. There were very few differences between the schizophrenic patients and the other groups, and those which did occur were quite unexpected. For the most part the schizophrenic patients were very similar to the normal control subjects and, if anything, they looked more than the other two control groups, though significantly so for only a minority of the measures. The differences were distributed evenly over the two partner conditions, and were equally small in both. In contrast, the third prediction received good support. In common with all three groups of control subjects, schizophrenic patients

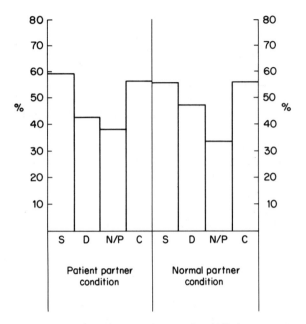

Figure 1.5   Rutter (1976) Exp. I: proportion (%) time spent looking

showed marked individual consistency across encounters, just as Kendon & Cook (1969) had first demonstrated for normal students.

The main purpose of the study was to test whether the transition from the constraints of a structured clinical interview to the freedom of conversations would affect the behaviour of schizophrenic patients, and the evidence is that it did. In interviews, schizophrenics had generally been found to look less than non-psychotic people, while here they behaved quite normally. The obvious implication was that there is something special about the clinical setting which disturbs schizophrenic patients, and that the apparent abnormality in their visual behaviour is not a general characteristic after all but is situation-specific. Further evidence was revealed in the second of the 1976 studies, which turned to chronic patients.

From the records of the two principal psychiatric hospitals serving Oxford, all patients were identified who were aged 18–60, had clear diagnoses of schizophrenia with no known organic complication (including leucotomy), and had been in hospital continuously for 2 years or longer. The available population numbered twenty-four, but thirteen had to be excluded, nine because they were mute or unintelligible when approached, three because they refused to take part, and one because much of his speech during the experimental session proved indecipherable. The remaining nine men and two women were matched individually for sex and age with recently admitted schizophrenic patients, and each subject was asked to hold a 10-minute conversation with a female nurse. Since it was unreasonable to ask chronic long-stay patients to discuss the items used in the first study, television and shared interests were chosen instead.

The results were very straightforward. There was no difference between the chronic and acute groups for any single measure of looking and, once again, this was quite different from the observations of earlier reports. The most interesting aspect of the findings was yet to come, however, and that concerned the acute patients. As Figure 1.5 revealed, schizophrenic subjects in the first study looked on average 56·4% of the time when they talked to the normal partner – but the equivalent group in the second study looked only 37·7% of the time, a value which was very similar to the one obtained in the original interviews in Rutter & Stephenson (1972a). The main difference between the studies was the content of what was said, and the findings began to suggest that that was the critical factor which had disturbed schizophrenic patients in the interview setting. In the first of the 1976 studies, subjects were asked to talk about a relatively impersonal, imaginary problem – and schizophrenic patients looked normally. In the second, although they were encouraged to talk about television and the interests they shared with the nurse, they generally moved quickly on to their personal history and problems – which was, of course, precisely the content of the interview study – and they looked relatively little again.

The final experiment in the series, by Rutter (1977b), was concerned with the origins of abnormal gaze in schizophrenia rather than simply with description, and it explored the following question: is the behaviour a consequence of the disorder, and which appears only when the patient is in the acute phase; or does it occur irrespective of clinical state, even in remission? Put another way, is the disturbance one of competence (a failure to learn the 'rules' of social behaviour), or is it one of performance (a failure to execute the rules appropriately)? If it is competence, abnormalities displayed by acute patients should also be present in remitted patients, but if it is performance, remitted patients should behave normally.

Twenty schizophrenic patients were recruited, aged 18–60. Ten were assigned to be seen on admission, and ten were assigned to be seen on discharge, when remission was assumed to have begun. The control group consisted of chest patients. The acute schizophrenic patients and the control subjects took part in the experiment within a few days of admission, and the remitted group were seen on either the day of discharge or the preceding or following day. Each subject held two 5-minute conversations, each with a female nurse, and one was about an item from the Choice Dilemmas Questionnaire, and was designated 'neutral', while the other was about television and shared interests, and was designated 'personal'.

The results, at first, were puzzling, for there were no main effects of groups, and no interactions with topic, which means that the three groups behaved similarly, and the similarity held for both conversations. There were, however, several main effects of topic, and every one of them indicated that all three groups of subjects looked more in the supposedly personal conversation than the neutral conversation. For acute schizophrenic patients, of course, this was precisely the opposite of the pattern which my previous findings and interpretation had predicted. What seems to have happened, according to a subsequent content analysis of the transcripts, is that patients this time kept to the topic and did not drift onto their own problems, with the result that the two conversations were equally neutral.

Why the supposedly neutral topic should have had these different effects is unclear, but there were two important consequences. First, even though the remitted group were found to behave normally, we were unable to say that abnormalities in acute patients are therefore the result of a failure in performance rather than competence, for the acute patients behaved normally too. Second, since the two conversations produced opposite findings to those I had reported in 1976, we were unable to draw any further conclusions about the role of situational factors. Once again, it was clear that they had important effects, but which particular variables were responsible we still did not know. Topic remained a likely candidate, but a stronger manipulation of the personal–impersonal dimension would have to be used if the issue was to be resolved.

Since the 1977 paper there have been two developments. The first concerns the timing of looks. Although we now had some understanding of the overall level of looking in psychotic patients, we knew nothing at all about how they patterned their looks in relation to speech. As we have seen already, the evidence from normal encounters suggests that visual communication may perhaps play some part in synchronizing transitions from speaker to speaker, and we might expect that the flow of conversation would be impeded if the timing of looks were grossly disturbed. Disturbances of speech had already been widely reported in schizophrenic patients (see the review by Rutter, 1977a, for example), and I therefore went on to explore the timing of their looks, in Rutter (1978).

The paper re-examined the data from all three of my experiments in which patients had taken part in free conversation: the first and second studies from Rutter (1976), on acute and chronic patients, and the study of remitted patients in Rutter (1977b). From transcripts of the sessions, every utterance was identified which consisted of ten words or more, was linguistically complete, and ended in a change of speaker which occurred without overlapping speech, and four measures were scored: the proportion of floor changes which began with the speaker looking at the listener; the proportion which began with the listener looking at the speaker; the proportion which ended with the new speaker looking; and the proportion which ended with the new listener looking. No significant differences between groups were found for any of the four measures in any of the three experiments. That is, schizophrenic patients were indistinguishable from the other subjects. Moreover, their behaviour was very similar to that reported by Rutter et al. (1978) for normal students. Thus, even though schizophrenic patients may sometimes look less overall than other people, there was no evidence that their looks occurred at unusual times.

The second development appeared in a paper by Rutter & O'Brien (1980), which was concerned with maladjusted adolescents. Among clinicians and teachers it is widely believed that two categories of maladjustment can be distinguished – 'withdrawn', and 'aggressive' – and indeed there is experimental evidence to support the distinction (Ghodsian, 1977). Most of the evidence, however, is based on ratings, generally made in the classroom by teachers, and none of the published reports had used direct observation. One objective measure which ought to be important, we argued, was gaze. As we have seen, people who are psychologically disturbed often engage in perfectly normal levels of looking but, when they do not, the abnormality appears simply as an overall decrement and is apparently limited to three groups: psychotic children, schizophrenic patients, and depressed patients. The point which interested Rutter & O'Brien was the one I made earlier, that all three groups are often described as 'socially withdrawn', and what might be expected, we argued, was that withdrawn adolescents too would look less than other people. At the same time, my own previous findings had suggested that gaze disturbance may be restricted to personal enounters, and that a strong manipulation along the dimension 'personal–impersonal' ought to be included. The experiment we went on to design, therefore, compared withdrawn and aggressive maladjusted adolescents, and observed each of them in a personal encounter and an impersonal encounter. It was predicted that the withdrawn group would look less overall than the aggressive group, but that the difference would be substantial only in the personal condition.

Twenty girls aged 12–15 years were selected from two Warwickshire schools for maladjusted children. Five from each school were identified as withdrawn and five as aggressive, and the criterion for selection was agreement across three diagnostic measures: scores at the time of entry to the school on the Bristol Social Adjustment Guides, one of the main instruments for assessing maladjustment; clinical diagnosis, at the time of entry, by the referring agency; and the headmaster's informal classification at the time of the experiment. Each girl took part in two 5-minute conversations with an adult stranger – one on 'personal problems' (which generally meant that the discussion dwelt on why the girl had come to the school), and one on the impersonal topic of 'television programmes' – and all the sessions were video-tape recorded.

Both hypotheses received good support. The first, that withdrawn girls would look less than aggressive girls, was confirmed for both the overall proportion of time spent looking and the proportion of listening spent looking; and the difference was reflected in both our measures of mutual gaze, the proportion of time spent in eye-contact, and mutual focus. Moreover, for two of the three remaining measures, none of which showed a significant difference between the groups, the trend was nevertheless in the same direction. The second hypothesis, that the difference between the withdrawn and aggressive girls would be substantial only for the personal conversation, was confirmed for both the overall proportion of time spent looking and the proportion of speech spent looking, and the findings were again reflected in eye-contact and mutual focus. All three measures which failed to produce a significant interaction tended in the predicted direction. For both hypotheses the group effects represented the majority of cases and not just extreme minorities.

Conclusion. This was an encouraging set of findings with which to conclude. In my original study I had found that schizophrenic and depressed patients, who are often described as socially withdrawn, looked less than other people: but in subsequent experiments they behaved quite normally. By implication their behaviour was situation-specific, and it began to look as if the critical variable might be the content of what was discussed. With the experiment by Rutter & O'Brien (1980) the argument was clinched, for topic produced a marked effect, and it was just as we had predicted: during personal discussions socially withdrawn people tend to avert the gaze; but when the conversation is less arousing they do not. As yet we can only speculate about an explanation, but it is probably very simple: withdrawn people are embarrassed by personal conversations about their symptoms and case histories and, like perfectly normal people who are embarrassed, they respond by looking away.

CHAPTER 2.

THE EXPRESSIVE FUNCTION OF GAZE: EMOTION

Towards the end of his paper, Kendon (1967) suggested that gaze serves three main functions in social interaction: an expressive function; a regulatory function; and a monitoring function. Expression was concerned with how we convey our attitudes and emotions to one another; regulation with how we open and close encounters and synchronize the flow of conversation from speaker to speaker; and monitoring with how we gather information from one another. In this chapter I shall discuss the expressive function and in Chapter 3, the regulatory and monitoring functions.

The literature on the expressive function is vast, and the most useful way to organize it is by methodology. There are two main types of study: encoding and decoding. The encoding approach focuses on the sender, and takes gaze as the dependent variable. The relationship between the sender and receiver is varied in some way, or the sender's emotions are aroused, and measures are then taken of his or her gaze. The decoding approach focuses instead on the receiver, and examines whether variations in the sender's gaze – now the independent variable – have measurable effects upon the other's perceptions. Encoding studies will be presented first and decoding studies second, but the chapter will open with a detailed discussion of one of the few attempts to integrate the approaches theoretically – the intimacy model of Argyle & Dean (1965). Only in the late 1970s, with the attribution models of Ellsworth and Patterson, did any serious alternatives appear, and it is with them that the chapter will close.

The intimacy model of Argyle & Dean (1965)

When research on gaze began in earnest, very few people were concerned with theory. There was, however, a major exception, and that was Michael Argyle. At a time when other writers still persisted in examining gaze in isolation – while agreeing that their approach was 'artificial', and 'multichannel communication' ought really to be their focus – Argyle was studying gaze in context and exploring its relationships with a range of other signals, verbal and nonverbal

31

alike. Some of his research was concerned with encoding, some with decoding, and some with both; and the framework within which he worked was the intimacy model, which he developed in the early 1960s.

The intimacy model

The intimacy model was first presented by Argyle & Dean (1965), and it is probably accurate to describe the paper as the most cited and the most influential in all the literature on gaze. What it said was this:

A. There are both approach and avoidance forces behind EC. The approach forces include the need for feedback . . . and sheer affiliative needs: for example, EC can be used as a reinforcer in the operative conditioning of verbal behavior (Krasner, 1958). It may be innately satisfying. . . . The avoidance components include the fear of being seen, the fear of revealing inner states, and the fear of seeing the rejecting responses of others. . . .

B. If there are both approach and avoidance drives behind EC, Miller's (1944) conflict analysis is applicable, and it would be expected that there should be an equilibrium level of EC for a person coming into social contact with some second person, and that if EC rises above that amount it will be anxiety-arousing. (Of course the equilibrium amount of EC, and the equilibrium distance may not be the same for the two people; they will then work out some compromise solution, more or less satisfactory to both. In the experiments to be reported here, however, [i.e. in the remainder of the paper] we shall hold the behavior of one person constant.)

C. It is supposed that similar considerations apply to other types of behavior which are linked with affiliative motivation. Thus there will be an equilibrium point of physical closeness, of intimacy of conversation, and of amount of smiling. The more these behaviors occur, the more affiliative motivation is satisfied, but if they go too far, anxiety is created.

D. It is suggested that an equilibrium develops for 'Intimacy,' where this is a joint function of eye-contact, physical proximity, intimacy of topic, smiling, etc. This equilibrium would be at a certain degree of intimacy for any pair of people. We deduce that if one of the components of intimacy is changed, one or more of the others will shift in the reverse direction in order to maintain the equilibrium. Thus, Intimacy = f (eye-contact, physical proximity, intimacy of topic, amount of smiling, etc.).

E. Twelve empirical deductions follow from this formulation. For example if amount of smiling is reduced, and intimacy of topic and physical proximity are held constant, EC should be increased to restore the equilibrium level of intimacy.

F. If equilibrium for intimacy is disturbed along one of its dimensions, attempts will first be made to restore it by adjusting the others. If this is not possible because all are held constant, or because the deviation is too extreme, the subject will feel uncomfortable in one of two ways. If the disturbance is in the direction of too much intimacy, the avoidance forces will predominate, and the subject will feel anxiety about rejection or revealing inner states; if in the direction of less intimacy, he will simply feel deprived of affiliative satisfactions (Argyle & Dean, 1965, pp. 292–4).

In summary, the paper argued that eye-contact was part of a system by which we communicate the intimacy of our relationships, and at its core lay a conflict between competing motives. Eye-contact was just one of a set of signals; the model was concerned with both encoding and decoding, and so was truly about communication (Wiener *et al.*, 1972); and it was based on motivation and emotion.

As Argyle & Dean pointed out, a large number of predictions followed from the model – of the form 'if A goes up B will go down' – and many empirical tests have been reported since. By far the largest number have examined the relationship between eye-contact and distance – perhaps because they are the easiest to measure – and the results will be considered shortly. First, however, I shall examine the relationships between gaze and the other components, intimacy of topic and smiling.

Gaze, topic, and smiling

The first two experiments on topic were conducted by Exline, and both supported the intimacy model. In the first, by Exline, Gray & Schuette (1965), students were asked a series of questions by an experimenter who stared continuously. When the questions were personal the subjects looked less during their replies than when they were innocuous, but looking during listening and silence were unaffected. In the second experiment, by Exline *et al.* (1970), subjects were implicated in a confederate's attempt to cheat during an experimental session, and they were subsequently interrogated. The interviewer stared continuously and, when he made the crucial accusation, subjects typically averted the gaze and from then on looked less than before.

A few years later, Anderson (1976) attacked the study by Exline, Gray & Schuette, and argued that it had not provided a proper test of the intimacy model. For Anderson the model implied that compensation must come from the subject himself and not his partner. That is, if a subject raised the level of intimacy by introducing increasingly personal matters, then he and not his partner should be the one to compensate, by adjusting one of the other components. Anderson used a within-subjects design, and asked naive volunteers to form pairs and disclose three levels of personal information to each other – high, medium, and low intimacy. Eye-contact was not affected.

Anderson's criticism raised an important issue, and it pointed to the first of a number of ambiguities in the model. In fact, Argyle & Dean did *not* say who should make the compensation – the subject, the partner, or the pair – and the reader was left to infer that all three were possible. However, the paper did refer consistently to eye-contact – not individual looking – and it seemed that the pair rather than the individual was intended to be the unit of analysis. But there was another complication: Argyle & Dean, and Exline, and others too, used a confederate who stared continuously. Every time the subject looked at the confederate the result was necessarily eye-contact – albeit in an unusual form – and looking and eye-contact could not be distinguished. What the model was really intended to say, and what constituted a proper test, were unclear.

Anderson was not the only writer to argue against Argyle & Dean. Jourard & Friedman (1970) reported two studies, both concerned with self-disclosure. In the first, subjects took part in an interview, and the dependent measure was how long they spent disclosing personal information about themselves. In one condition the interviewer was absent from the room; in another he was present but never looked; and, in a third he was present and stared continuously. Women revealed more about themselves in the first condition than the other two, but men were not affected. In the second experiment the independent variable was psychological distance, and it was found that, if the interviewer touched the subject or revealed information about himself, the subject disclosed more than when the interviewer's behaviour was more remote – the opposite of what the intimacy model was taken to predict. Jourard & Friedman argued that sometimes compensation would occur, and sometimes response-matching or reciprocity, and an important determinant was likely to be the relationship between the people (see also, for example, Baker & Shaw, 1980; Nolter, 1980; Lochman & Allen, 1981). This was another important point to make, because Argyle & Dean often seemed to be writing only about strangers, and whether their model applied to all relationships equally – and, indeed, to all settings – they failed to make explicit.

Schulz & Barefoot (1974) explored both topic and smiling. Subjects underwent an interview, and the interviewer looked at them steadily except when he read out the questions, which ranged from the very intimate to the moderately intimate to the innocuous. The innocuous items produced more looking while speaking than the others, but there were no effects on either looking while listening or smiling. The findings were thus equivocal, and they raised yet another ambiguity: the model did not say which of the components would change first, nor whether one or more than one would be affected. It may be, for example, that gaze was sufficient to compensate for the intimacy of the topic, and that equilibrium was restored without the need for smiling to change as well. Typically, experimenters examine only one dependent variable and, frequently, no effect is found – sometimes, no doubt, because the impact of the experimental manipulation is absorbed by some other aspect of behaviour which the experimenter happened not to measure.

Similar findings were reported in two other papers. In the first, Carr & Dabbs (1974) found that intimacy of topic had no effect on the duration and mean length of periods of eye-contact, though intimate items did lead to a decrease in frequency. In the second, by Goldberg & Wellens (1979), subjects were interviewed either face-to-face or over a videophone, and their gaze and smiling were monitored. As in Schulz & Barefoot (1974), smiling was unaffected by intimacy of topic, but there were several effects on gaze. Subjects spent longer looking overall during the innocuous items than the intimate items and, though the same held for looking while speaking, there was no effect on looking while listening. In both the face-to-face and videophone conditions, looking was defined as gaze in the direction of the interviewer's face.

The two remaining papers both made important theoretical points. The first took gaze as an independent variable, and was by Ellsworth & Ross (1975). In line with their previous work, Ellsworth & Ross suggested that direct gaze served the receiver as a stimulus (for arousal), a reinforcer, and a source of feedback. To act as either of the latter it would have to be contingent upon some aspect of the receiver's behaviour. If it were to act as a stimulus the important factor would simply be how long it lasted, and this would influence whether a positive or negative attribution was eventually made.

Subjects were asked to disclose information about themselves to an experimenter, and each underwent one of four conditions: the experimenter stared continuously; he looked only in response to an intimate revelation by the subject; he looked away continuously; and he looked away contingently. Both male and female subjects were included, and each was paired with an experimenter of the same sex. For women, direct gaze led to more intimate revelations than gaze aversion, whether or not it was delivered contingently; and for men, the effects were reversed, but again they held for both continuous and contingent gaze. In other words, continuous gaze sometimes promoted intimate revelations (the opposite of what the intimacy model would predict), and even relatively infrequent bursts of looking were sufficient, provided they were delivered contingently. Interestingly enough, when the intimacy of the revelations was rated by the subjects themselves, rather than listeners and observers, men and women both said they had disclosed more in the gaze conditions than either of the others. For men, this was the reverse of what the listeners and observers had judged.

The other study was by Sundstrom (1978), and was the first to explore systematically the relationship between the two people. Sundstrom predicted that while an intimate topic of conversation would make strangers uncomfortable and lead them to compensate, friends would feel more at ease and would increase their intimacy – by looking, gesturing, or speaking more. In fact both friends and strangers compensated, at least in their gaze, but the level of compensation decreased over time, presumably as anxiety fell.

One important aspect of Sundstrom's study was that intimacy was imposed by the experimenter and was not allowed to occur naturally and develop spontaneously within the relationship – but whether the model should apply equally in both circumstances is not clear. Furthermore, it may be that, as Ellsworth (1975) and Patterson (1976) were to suggest, the main effect of experimental settings of this sort is simply to arouse people, and the response they eventually make will depend upon how they interpret their arousal. The results also questioned the wisdom of examining only brief encounters. Typically, the intimacy model has been tested on episodes of 3 to 4 minutes. Sundstrom's subjects, in contrast, spent 15 minutes talking to each other, and there were clear changes over time: the first few minutes supported the model, but the rest did not.

Gaze and distance

After presenting their model, Argyle & Dean devoted the remainder of their paper to two experimental studies. Both were designed to examine the relationship between eye-contact and distance, and the second has become very well known. Subjects were recruited for 'an experiment on conversations', and each held three 3-minute discussions with a confederate, who posed as another genuine subject. The task was to make up stories about TAT cards. The speakers sat at 90 degrees across a table (Figure 2.1), and the distance between them, which was manipulated by moving the subject after each conversation, was 2 feet, 6 feet, or 10 feet, measured eye to eye. The confederate stared continuously and, since eye-contact necessarily occurred each time his or her gaze was returned, only the subject's behaviour was monitored. The observations were made 'live', from behind a one-way screen, and one observer scored the number of times eye-contact occurred, while the other scored the overall duration with a cumulative stop-watch. As predicted, the greater the distance the greater the eye-contact, for both the mean length of occurrences and their overall duration. The difference was especially marked between 2 feet and 6 feet, and there were no interactions with sex of subject or sex of confederate. At 2 feet all subjects showed signs of tension.

For some years the experiment went unchallenged but then, in 1970, there appeared a paper which argued that the findings might have been an artefact of the particular method of observation which Argyle & Dean had used. The authors were Stephenson & Rutter, and they were concerned that, as the distance between the subject and confederate increased, so too did the distance between the subject and the observers. The further away the subject sat the harder it became for the observer to distinguish looking from looking away. Since the demand characteristics were such that observers would try not to miss eye-contact, whenever they were in doubt they would record a positive observation. The greater the distance, the greater the doubt, and the greater the tendency to record as eye-contact much that was not (Stephenson & Rutter, 1970).

The paper provoked a considerable debate, and it was clear that alternative methods of observation were necessary (White, Hegarty & Beasley, 1970; Argyle, 1970; Vine, 1971; Cranach & Ellgring, 1973; Knight, Langmeyer & Lundgren, 1973; Patterson, 1975; Martin & Rovira, 1981). Since then, the most popular approach has been to use video-tape recording with split-screen close-up photography (Rutter, Morley & Graham, 1972; Stephenson, Rutter & Dore, 1973; Rimé & McCusker, 1976; Beattie & Bogle, 1982), and many attempts have been made to reproduce the original findings. There are three groups of studies. The first uses a confederate who stares continuously, at least while the genuine subject is speaking; the second uses pairs of naive subjects, sometimes adult strangers, sometimes children, and sometimes people who already know each other; and the third uses a variety of other methods.

Studies using confederates.   It is probably true to say that the strongest support for Argyle and Dean has come from the first group of studies, those which used a confederate who stared continuously. The first was published by Goldberg, Kiesler & Collins (1969). After a short baseline conversation, each subject was interviewed at either 2½ feet or 6 feet, and the interviewer looked away only

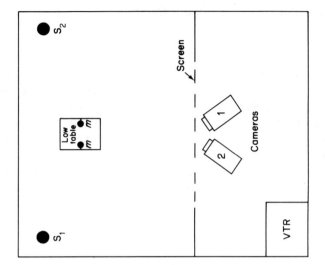

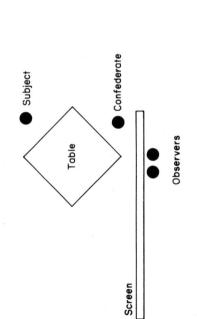

m = Microphone

Figure 2.1   Argyle & Dean (1965) (left) and Stephenson, Rutter & Dore (1973) (right): experimental layouts

when he read out the questions. A strong effect of distance was recorded for duration, but there was no effect for frequency. There were no changes over time, and no interactions between distance and time.

Schulz & Barefoot (1974) used a similar, between-groups, design. Subjects were interviewed at 3 feet or 5½ feet and, at the greater distance, there was more looking while listening in total, but not looking while speaking. As in Goldberg, Kiesler & Collins (1969), the interviewers and subjects were all men. Coutts & Schneider (1975) observed male, female, and mixed-sex pairs of students as they sat in silence in an experimental waiting room. The distance was 2 feet or 7 feet across a table. The duration and frequency of looking and the frequency of eye-contact were all greater at the greater distance, but there was no effect for the duration of eye-contact. Coutts & Ledden (1977) observed female subjects with a female interviewer. After a baseline interview at 1½ metres, the distance was increased to 2·17 metres or decreased to 0·83 metres, and the dependent measure was the difference between the first and second sessions. The duration of gaze was strongly influenced, in the direction predicted by Argyle & Dean, but frequency and mean length showed no effect.

The results from the remaining studies were less supportive. Carr & Dabbs (1974) used an interview, and the interviewer stared continuously whenever the subject was speaking. After some baseline questions on a neutral topic the subjects were moved to 1½ feet or 8 feet for a series of more intimate questions. The dependent measure was the duration of eye-contact during the subject's answers, and there was no effect of distance. The interviewer and subjects were all women. Kleinke, Staneski & Berger (1975), using a different approach, asked male subjects to report their impressions of a female confederate with whom they were asked to chat for 15 minutes. The confederate moved her chair closer or further away during the session – from 45 inches to 29 inches or 68 inches – and she was programmed to look either 10% or 90% of the time. Distance had no effect on how much the subjects liked the confederate, or on how much they looked at her. In the 90% condition she was perceived as more attentive than in the 10% condition, but the most important influence on how she was rated overall was her physical appearance.

Aiello (1972), using a programmed confederate and female subjects, found a curvilinear, not linear, effect, with greater looking at intermediate distances than greater distances. The reason, he suggested, was that gaze is both a response to the 'comfort' of the encounter and a means of regulating it. Women, unlike men, are more comfortable at close distances, because they are 'more oriented toward affectionate and inclusive relationships'. Later, Aiello (1977a) examined both men and women, and observed them in interviews at either 2½ feet, 6½ feet, or 10½ feet. Women, he predicted, should feel uncomfortable at 10½ feet and therefore look less than at the closer distances, while men should show a linear increase with distance. The prediction was supported. The same year, Aiello (1977b) went on to explore greater distances still. Subjects were interviewed at 7 feet, 9½ feet, 12 feet or 14½ feet and, while there was no effect for women, men looked more the greater the distance, during both speech and listening.

Overall, this first group of studies provides only limited support for Argyle & Dean – and, as I suggested earlier, the second and third groups offer even less. Several other comments should also be made. The first is that many writers still employed Argyle & Dean's method of observation. As Patterson (1975) pointed out, several were able to establish good inter-rater reliability between trained observers. But, of course, reliability says nothing about the validity of the data – whether what was recorded really was looking – and very few writers bothered to measure that. The second point is that speech and listening were hardly ever examined separately, even though the patterns of looking are generally very different and any effects of distance may be quite different too.

The third point concerns the size of the manipulations. Argyle & Dean chose their distances from Hall (1955, 1966), who argued that, at least for middle-class western cultures, there are four distances or zones for social interaction: intimate (0 feet to 1½ feet); personal (1½ feet to 4 feet); social (4 feet to 12 feet); and public (12 feet to 25 feet and over). Each zone was divided into a near and a far sector, and 2 feet, 6 feet, and 10 feet fell into the far sector of personal space, and the near and far sectors of social space. Although the majority of subsequent studies used similar manipulations, some did not, and there is no good reason to expect them all to produce the same effects. Furthermore, the dimensions and design of the room may also be important variables, but both were generally ignored. Subjects sitting at 10 feet with their chair-backs pressed against the laboratory wall may behave very differently from others sitting at the same distance in the middle of a large hall. Most papers did not even include a diagram of the layout.

Three further objections were made in a brief but important paper by Bakken (1978). The first concerned the use of confederates who stare. As we shall see later, in the work of Ellsworth, staring has its own peculiar properties, and it is very likely to upset the normal functions of visual behaviour. For example, if the genuine subject looks up for feedback, the confederate's blank stare will be unhelpful and even disturbing. Should the stare have different effects at different distances, this in itself may produce a particular pattern of behaviour in the subject, and any effects of intimacy will be difficult to dis-entangle. There is also the problem I have mentioned before, that, every time the subject looks, eye-contact is necessarily formed – albeit in a contrived way which probably tells us very little about normal visual interaction in everyday life – and looking and eye-contact cannot be distinguished. Bakken also argued that confederates may themselves compensate, in some other aspect of their behaviour, and they as well as subjects should therefore be observed routinely.

Bakken's second and related point was simply that we ought to study real interactions, and not encounters involving confederates or role-playing, or questionnaire responses about how subjects say they would behave under a variety of imagined circumstances. Finally, and this was the third objection, many studies had failed to provide an adequate test of the intimacy model because they had used between-groups designs, in which each subject under-goes only one distance. The model was about compensation and, since one can compensate only after a change has occurred, each subject should experience every condition.

Bakken's third point had already been made by Anderson (1976) and , as I indicated when discussing that paper, Argyle & Dean did *not* say what consti-tutes a proper test of the model. So far as I know, Argyle has never objected to between-groups studies. Nevertheless, the point is important, and it may well be that if the model had been thought out more clearly in the first place, within-subjects studies would indeed have been essential. Unfortunately, though, repeated measures designs do generate their own problems. If people undergo all conditions, the probability is increased that they will guess the purpose of the experiment and respond accordingly. Exactly the same applies to observers, it should be added – unless, of course, some way can be found of disguising the distance so that the purpose of the experiment is not revealed.

Studies using genuine subjects. It was this last point that Stephenson, Rutter & Dore (1973) took up in one of the earliest of the second group of studies, those which made use of pairs of genuine, naive subjects. At the end of their 1970 paper, Stephenson & Rutter had suggested that the best method of observation then available was to score from video-tape recordings made with zoom lenses. The experiment by Stephenson, Rutter & Dore (1973) was the first to use the method. Pairs of subjects sat across a small, low table at 2 feet, 6 feet, or 10 feet (Figure 2.1). Behind a one-way screen were two cameras, one trained on each of the subjects, and their images were combined by means of a split-screen mixer, and were recorded on video-tape. As the distance changed, the camera settings and zoom lenses were adjusted so that the subjects always appeared in head-and-shoulders close-up and were apparently a constant, indeterminate distance apart. Some time after the experimental sessions were over, trained observers scored looking and speech by the method introduced by Rutter, Morley & Graham (1972), and validity and reliability were estab-lished by the method presented by Rutter & Stephenson (1972a). None of the observers knew or guessed the purpose of the experiment, and none realized that the subjects had sat at different distances. When the observations were complete, and the manipulation of distance had been explained, the observers were reshown a sample of the recordings and asked to judge the distance in each case. They were unable to distinguish the conditions reliably.

The results for the five principal measures are reproduced in Figure 2.2 and the findings for 6 feet and 10 feet are shown as percentage deviations from the findings for 2 feet. Neither the duration of looking nor the number of looks was affected significantly by distance, but the mean length of looks, the duration of eye-contact, and mutual focus all showed a significant increase. Mutual focus is the measure introduced by Rubin (1970) to represent the proportion of a pair's looking which results in eye-contact. In addition, the proportions of both speech and listening spent in eye-contact increased with distance, and so too

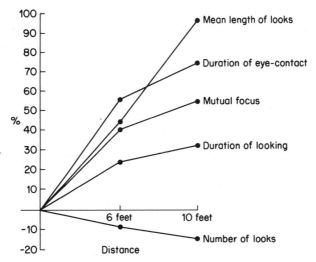

Findings for 6 feet and 10 feet presented as deviations (%) from the findings for 2 feet

Figure 2.2   Stephenson, Rutter & Dore (1973): looking, eye-contact, and mutual focus

did the proportion of speech spent in looking. Male, female, and mixed pairs were all included, but there were no effects of sex, and no interactions between sex and distance.

Overall, our findings provided good support for Argyle & Dean. The effects were a little weaker, but observer artefact was eliminated, and the data were valid and reliable. A year earlier, Argyle had himself reported two experiments with naive subjects (Argyle & Ingham, 1972), and they too appeared to support the model – although, unfortunately, the observers were aware of the manipulation of distance, as were the subjects, and no details of the method of observation and no check on validity and reliability were reported. In both experiments the duration of eye-contact was very close to that expected by chance, and Argyle & Ingham concluded: 'The increase of EC with distance is almost entirely due to the increased amount of individual gaze.'. . . The intimacy model, it will be recalled, had been set up explicitly to describe *pairs* not *individuals*, and the conclusion which Argyle & Ingham had now reached was extremely significant, and I shall return to it in Chapter 3.

More recently, several authors have used children as their subjects, and the results have been mixed. Chapman (1975) was interested in children's responses to humour, and he examined male and female pairs of 7-year olds. In one condition (coaction), both children listened to a humorous tape-recording through headphones and, in the other (audience), one listened and the other looked on. In both, the subjects sat on fixed chairs, 2·7 feet or 5·5 feet apart. The intimacy model received no support. Eye-contact was greater at 2·7 feet than 5·5 feet for the coaction condition, but there was no difference for the other condition; and the same pattern was found for laughing and smiling. The reason, argued Chapman, was that the model assumes that the level of intimacy will remain constant throughout a session, whereas here it rose. The effect of sharing humour was to bring the children closer together, psychologically, and, because a higher degree of intimacy became tolerable, they reciprocated rather than compensated. Eventually, when the arousal produced by the recordings became too great, the children laughed, and their tension was reduced. Chapman also suggested that the effect of distance commonly found in conversations may occur because people are more dependent on information and feedback at greater distances, and not because of their motivational needs. In his own experiment, information and feedback were less important, and that was another reason why reciprocation occurred and not compensation.

Earlier, we discussed a number of methodological comments by Bakken (1978). As well as criticizing much of the previous research, he made a variety of recommendations for the future, and one was to take as many dependent measures as possible:

> Although broadening the range of dependent variables may increase the complexity of the experiment, such an approach would reduce the likelihood that negative results or findings of no difference occurred because the regulatory changes were in some other behaviour and at the same time enable us to learn something about the relative weights of the various immediacy components (Bakken, 1978, p. 302).

A second recommendation was to consider alternative types of approach, including ethnomethodology, and a third was to explore the context in which the experimental session took place: the purpose of the encounter; the relationship between the participants; and so on.

At the time Bakken wrote his paper, very few writers had taken account of his last point, particularly the relationship between the subjects, but one of them was Russo (1975). She examined kindergarten, third-grade, and sixth-grade children, both male and female pairs, and half the pairs were described as friends and half as 'not particularly friends'. Each pair held three 2-minute conversations, one at 1 foot, one at 3½ feet, and one at 6 feet, and they chose their own topics. Only two measures were taken, the proportion of time spent in eye-contact and the mean length of periods of eye-contact, but the reported validity and reliability of the data were high. The proportion of time spent in eye-contact increased with distance, but there was no effect of friendship, and no interaction with distance. For mean length there was no effect of distance and no interaction with friendship, but the value for friends overall was greater than for strangers.

The difference between the two measures, argued Russo – duration and mean length – suggested that they served different functions. Mean length was underpinned by affiliative motivation, while duration was concerned with information-seeking:

> It may be that the greater the distance between interactants, the greater their dependence on visual rather than nonvisual cues, for a variety of complex reasons.

The necessity to increase attention to visual cues and to focus on those cues with high information value, that is, the eyes and face of the other, thus can adequately explain the percentage of eye-contact/distance relationship (Russo, 1975, p. 502).

Once again, as in Chapman (1975), at least part of the effect of distance was explained by information rather than motivation.

The only other study of children was by Pennington & Rutter (1981), and they too examined friendship. The subjects were 11-year-olds, and pairs of boys and pairs of girls were formed, half consisting of 'friends' and half of 'acquaintances' (the equivalent of Russo's 'not particularly friends'). Each pair met for 3 minutes at either 2 feet, 6 feet, or 10 feet, and they discussed their hobbies and interests and a collection of photographs they had seen just before the session. The encounters were recorded on video-tape, by means of our usual split-screen technique, and good validity and reliability were achieved.

The main results are given in Figure 2.3. The proportions of time spent in looking and eye-contact both increased with distance, as did the mean length of

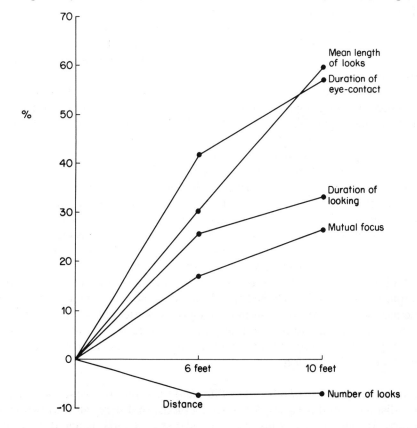

Findings for 6 feet and 10 feet presented as deviations (%) from the findings for 2 feet

Figure 2.3   Pennington & Rutter (1981): looking, eye-contact, and mutual focus

looks during listening and during the encounter overall. There were no other significant effects for either looking or speech, nor were there any effects of friendship or distance × friendship. Though the findings for distance were consistent with the intimacy model for the most part, like Russo (1975) we preferred an interpretation based on information-seeking. If the most important determinant of looking is affiliative motivation, friends should look more than acquaintances – but they did not. If it is information-seeking, however, there should be more looking at a distance than close to, because feedback is harder to collect – and there was.

The two remaining studies of genuine subjects also examined relationships, but this time in adults. The first was by Sundstrom (1978). Female pairs of friends and strangers discussed a selection of intimate and neutral topics at either 2½ feet or 4½ feet, one distance for each pair. It was predicted that the intimate conditions – close promixity and intimate topics – would produce discomfort and compensation in strangers, but the opposite in friends. In the event, the predictions were not supported. Gaze, gesturing, and speech were all measured, but there was only one effect of distance, namely more gesturing at 2½ feet than 4½ feet. Overall, friends and strangers both appeared uncomfortable with the intimate topics, and compensated in their nonverbal behaviour but, as time went on, there was less discomfort and less compensation as the participants adapted.

The second study was by Swain, Stephenson & Dewey (1982), and they examined three groups of people: married couples, opposite-sex platonic friends, and opposite-sex strangers. Married couples and friends, they predicted, should find their level of intimacy relatively undisturbed by proximity, and should therefore compensate less than strangers. Each pair sat at 2½ feet or 6 feet, in a between-groups design, and was asked to prepare a case either 'for' or 'against' British withdrawal from Northern Ireland. The conversations were video-taped in split-screen and lasted 15 minutes. The proportions of time spent in looking, eye-contact, looking while listening, and looking while speaking all increased with distance, and the only measure which did not was the mean length of looks. The relationship between the subjects, however, had only two effects: the proportion of time spent in eye-contact and in looking while listening was greatest for strangers and least for married couples, with friends intermediate. There were no interactions between the two independent variables. As in Pennington & Rutter (1981), the findings for relationship led the authors to interpret all the effects, for distance and relationship alike, as support for the information-seeking function of looking and not affiliative motivation.

Studies using other methods. The third and final collection of studies on gaze and distance used a variety of other methods, and they fall into two main groups. In one, gaze was taken as the independent variable and distance the dependent variable; in the other, personal space and seating position were explored.

The first study to take distance as the dependent variable was published by Argyle & Dean (1965), alongside the other more famous experiment which we have already discussed at length. People were asked to approach, 'as close as is comfortable to see well', one of three stimuli: a life-size photograph of Michael Argyle, with his eyes open and apparently looking at the subject; Michael Argyle in person, seated, his eyes open and again looking at the subject; and Michael Argyle in person, seated, his eyes closed. All the subjects – six adults and six children aged 5–12 years – were acquaintances of the stimulus, and both groups stayed furthest away in the 'in person eyes open' condition. Three years later, however, Cranach, Frenz & Frey (1968) apparently found the opposite, that people approached closest if they were looked at – a result which Castell (1970) was able to corroborate, though only weakly, for both normal and disturbed children, especially when they too were looking.

A rather more extensive series of studies was later published by Patterson (1973b, 1977), and the 1973 paper reported two experiments. In the first, subjects were asked to 'pull up a chair', and then they were given a two-part interview. The closer they sat to the interviewer, the less they looked, and the pattern was constant throughout the session. The second experiment used a similar design, but this time the two parts of the interview were separated by a week. In the first, looking and distance correlated negatively, as before, but there was no relationship in the second. In both experiments there was strong individual consistency across the two parts of the interview in all measures of immediacy – gaze, distance, leaning, and body orientation.

In his 1977 paper Patterson again reported two studies, and he developed the argument that psychological comfort rather than physical distance was the critical variable. Compensation would occur, he believed, when the subject was made to feel uncomfortable by too much or too little intimacy. Once again, subjects were asked to pull up a chair and were interviewed. But then, part-way through, they were asked to move closer or further away, and to sit at the point where they began to feel uncomfortable. A little later, they were asked to move again, to the opposite boundary. The order was balanced across subjects, and the means were found to be 3·1 feet for the near distance, 4·7 feet for the comfortable position, and 9·1 feet for the far distance. From the far to the comfortable to the near position, looking decreased, and subjects also turned their bodies so that they could avoid the direct face-to-face orientation. In the second study, which was conducted in the field, pairs of people were observed as they stood rather than sat, and the indirect orientation at close distances was reported once again, though looking itself was not measured. Overall, concluded Patterson, both the 1973 and 1977 papers offered general support for compensation.

The second group of studies examined personal space and seating position, and useful reviews are to be found in Hayduk (1978), Harper, Wiens & Matarazzo (1978), and Edinger & Patterson (1983). Two of the earliest experiments on personal space were published by Felipe & Sommer (1966). In both, unsuspecting individuals were approached by a confederate as they sat alone, and the first was set in the grounds of a psychiatric hospital, the second in a university library. In general, when the confederate approached very close, subjects eventually got up and left; but before that, they often turned away or 'blocked' the immediate area in some way:

> In the present situation the first reaction to the invasion was accommodation or adaptation: the individual attempted to 'live with' the invasion by turning aside, interposing a notebook between himself and the stranger, and pulling in his elbows. When this failed to relieve the tension produced by the norm violation, flight reactions occurred (Felipe & Sommer, 1966, p. 213).

A few years later, Patterson, Mullens & Romano (1971) conducted another experiment in the library. Readers sitting alone were singled out, and a female confederate approached and took up one of four positions. In decreasing order of immediacy they were the seat adjacent to the subject, directly opposite across the table, two seats adjacent, and three seats adjacent. It was predicted that subjects would compensate, but the prediction was supported only in part. The greater the experimenter's immediacy, the more the subjects leaned away or blocked the invasion by turning away or guarding their space with a hand or elbow – but, also, the more they glanced. The latter finding was the opposite of what was predicted but, as Patterson and co-workers themselves suggested, subjects may simply have been on the lookout for 'danger' in the more immediate conditions, and anxious to monitor what was happening. Mahoney (1974), however, was unable to reproduce the finding, and he even argued that much that is called 'invasion of personal space' is not, and is perfectly tolerable. Finally, Buchanan, Goldman & Juhnke (1977) reported a series of observations in lifts. As they entered, subjects were compelled to violate the personal space of confederates already there. In general, men were reluctant to stand close to someone who stared at them; but whether the confederate looked or looked away had relatively little effect on women.

Like personal space, seating position was first investigated systematically by Sommer, and many of his findings were reported in a book (Sommer, 1969). In one study, for example, people were asked to rate a variety of seating positions for intimacy, and both distance and orientation proved to be important cues: side-by-side was rated the most intimate; the corner position next; and opposite the least. The same was true when subjects were asked to choose positions for a conversation, and Sommer suggested that the attraction of the corner position, which was often chosen, was that it allowed eye-contact to be made and broken easily, so that intimacy could be regulated. Cook (1970), however, found some of Sommer's results impossible to reproduce, and he suggested that motivation was the most important factor, even if more than one position was perceived as very intimate. If subjects were antagonistic to one another, he argued, they would sit opposite; but if their motives were positive, they would sit side-by-side.

Much of the work by Sommer and Cook used questionnaires, but the remaining studies all used experimental methods. Ross *et al.* (1973) observed eight-person discussion groups in either a large room or a small room. The frequency of looking was unaffected by either room size or sex of subjects, and there was no interaction. Scherer & Schiff (1973) asked male subjects to rate photographs showing two men at a cafeteria table. Eye-contact increased perceived intimacy, and distance diminished it. Finally, Muirhead & Goldman (1979) conducted a field study, and observed pairs who were sitting together and appeared to be acquainted. Those who sat opposite each other made eye-contact for longer than those who sat side-by-side.

Conclusion

In summary, research on gaze has produced mixed results for the intimacy model: some supports it; some flatly contradicts it; and the remainder is equivocal. In particular, reciprocation appears to be just as common as compensation. Some of the inconsistency, perhaps, may be explained by methodological problems and differences, but there are other, more fundamental, reasons: the model was imprecise in what it predicted; the encoding and decoding studies were hard to reconcile and integrate; and many of the apparently positive findings could in any case be interpreted in other ways, particularly by introducing the concept of information in place of emotions and motivation. The model had played an important part in focusing and stimulating research, but by the mid-1970s a new impetus was needed. As we shall see at the end of the chapter, eventually it came – in a series of papers by Ellsworth and Patterson – and it was based on attribution theory.

Encoding studies

Three main groups of variables have been explored: attraction and approval; dominance, status, and power; and the emotions of embarrassment, shame, and sorrow.

Attraction and approval

All the studies of attraction and approval have adopted one of three approaches: in the first, natural variations in liking and approval are examined and correlated with gaze; in the second, traditional experimental manipulations are introduced; and, in the third, subjects are asked to play roles.

Correlational studies. The first group of studies made use of natural variations in attraction and approval, and the earliest was conducted by Goldberg, Kiesler & Collins (1969) as part of an experimental replication of Argyle & Dean (1965). Subjects were interviewed by a male confederate, and were subsequently asked to complete a series of scales to say how much they would like him as a colleague for socio-emotional activities and for task-oriented activities. Their ratings were then correlated with their gaze, but only one significant effect was revealed: the more they favoured the interviewer for socio-emotional activities, the greater the proportion of time they spent looking at him. In a similar study, by Strongman & Champness (1968), subjects met a series of partners and, at the end, were asked which three they would most like to have as companions during their leisure time, and which they would least like to have. Again, only one significant effect was revealed: when both members of the pair were attracted to each other a greater proportion of time was spent in eye-contact than when both were unattracted.

The only other correlational study was conducted by Rubin (1970), and he was interested in people who already had an established relationship – dating couples. All subjects first completed a questionnaire designed to measure separately how much they loved their partners and how much they liked them. Each then took part in a short laboratory conversation with either his or her own partner or the partner of one of the other subjects. All couples were opposite-sex and, on the basis of their love scores, four conditions were set up: strong together; weak together; strong apart; and weak apart. The data were not analysed fully but, while the strength of the couple's love had no significant effect upon the duration of their eye-contact, it did influence mutual focus. This was a new measure which Rubin invented to try to take account of the fact that some individuals look very little and so necessarily limit the possible duration of eye-contact in their pair. It provides an interesting index of how much each subject's looking is reciprocated, and is calculated as $100 \times$ (mutual gaze $\div$ A's non-mutual gaze + B's non-mutual gaze + Mutual gaze). Mutual focus was found to be significantly greater for 'strong-together' couples than 'weak-together' couples, which means that, however little each of the two 'strong-together' subjects looked individually, a greater proportion of that looking was devoted to eye-contact than in the 'weak-together' couples. There was no difference between the 'strong-apart' and 'weak-apart' groups. No attempt was made to correlate the subjects' liking scores with their gaze, but it did emerge that liking and loving were independent – as was to be hoped, since the two scales had been designed to be independent in the first place.

Experimental studies. The second group of studies relied on traditional experimental methods, and the first were reported by Exline & Winters (1965b). Unfortunately, like many that followed, the results were very difficult to interpret. The literature on encoding is full of experiments which were poorly designed and poorly executed, and it is frequently impossible to know how to attribute apparently positive results – to the experimental variable, or to some other variable which was not controlled but happened to correlate with it. That was precisely the case with this particular paper.

In their first experiment, Exline & Winters wondered how subjects would respond to being given either a positive or a negative evaluation by the experimenter. After a neutral, baseline interview lasting 5 minutes the experimenter told the subject that he found him intelligent and mature or unintelligent and immature, and then the interview concluded with a further

5 minutes of neutral questions. Subjects given the positive evaluation looked more in the second period than the first, those given the negative evaluation looked less, and a control group given no evaluation at all showed no change. Corresponding differences were found in how the subjects subsequently rated the experimenter, and the authors concluded that the critical variable was liking. But, as they themselves conceded, their interpretation was necessarily tentative:

> the . . . reduction of visual interaction may have been due to subjects' feelings of shame of self as well as feeling of dislike directed toward E. The data do not indicate whether S looked away to hide his shame, express his hostility, or both (Exline & Winters, 1965b, p. 335).

In their second experiment Exline & Winters explored the effects of personal preferences. Midway through a series of creative tasks, subjects were asked to say which they preferred of two assessors who were evaluating them. Before making the choice they distributed their looks equally but afterwards their behaviour changed in a variety of ways, although no consistent pattern was revealed. The authors concluded, as before, that liking was responsible but, unfortunately, there was an additional finding. Some of the control subjects, who were not asked to state a choice, nevertheless developed spontaneous preferences: but they showed no bias in their looking. The behaviour of the experimental subjects, therefore, might well have been the result of some other factor, and committment to a publicly stated choice was one obvious candidate.

Another variable which has received considerable attention is subjects' expectancies for approval. In the first of a pair of studies, Efran & Broughton (1966) asked students to give a 5-minute talk about themselves to two confederates. Before the session they had been introduced to one of the two for a brief, friendly chat, and it was found that they subsequently spent more of their time looking at him than at his colleague. To strengthen the manipulation, the favoured confederate was also allowed to smile more than the other and, in the second of the studies, smiling and nodding were found to be sufficient to reproduce the findings, without a pre-session meeting (Efran, 1968). This time, status was also manipulated, and the effect was particularly strong when the approving confederate was of higher status than the subject.

In a similar study, by Fugita (1974), subjects were again asked to talk about themselves to two confederates, and they were led to believe that their intelligence and personality were under scrutiny. One of the confederates gave signs of approval, while the other frowned and shook his head from time to time. Status was once again manipulated, and it was found that when subjects spoke to low-status confederates their gaze was unaffected by the manipulation of approval but when they spoke to high status confederates they looked significantly more frequently at the approving confederate than his colleague, and for longer in total.

In one final experiment, conducted some years before Fugita's study, Goldberg & Mettee (1969) chose to use just the pre-session meeting for their manipulation, and to hold constant the confederate's behaviour during the session. Subjects were asked to answer a number of printed questions, and there were two conditions: in one they believed they could be seen by the two confederates, and in the other they believed they could not. At the end of the session subjects were asked to rate the two confederates. In the 'Seen' condition, they indicated greater liking for the confederate they had met than for his colleague, but this was not reflected in their gaze. In the 'Unseen' condition they failed to indicate a preference, and the authors' manipulation had simply collapsed. Another feature of the experiment was that, in both conditions, the confederates sat in silence with their heads in boxes. The front panel included a one-way screen, and subjects were told that the confederates' view would be unrestricted in the 'Seen' condition, but obscured by shutters in the 'Unseen' condition. In fact, the confederates could see perfectly well in both.

Another variable on which several experiments have been reported is physical attractiveness. Coutts & Schneider (1975), for example, observed single-sex and mixed-sex pairs of strangers in an experimental waiting room. The attractiveness of the subjects was rated by the experimenters, and measures were taken of visual interaction. Only one significant correlation emerged: in mixed-sex pairs the more attractive the man the more frequently the women looked at him. Although a similar trend was revealed for both the frequency and duration of looks by the man at the women, the correlations were not significant and, in any case, there was no independent check that attractiveness really was the crucial variable. In contrast, Kleck & Rubinstein (1975) used a between-groups design, and systematically varied the appearance of a female confederate, by using make-up. The subjects were men, and it was found that while they looked longer and smiled more at the attractive confederate than the unattractive one when she interviewed them, there were no effects in the less constrained conversation which followed.

Earlier, Kleck had been interested in Goffman's ideas about stigma, and had studied encounters between normal and apparently handicapped people. In his first experiment, subjects took part in two sessions, one with a handicapped person who was confined to a wheelchair and had apparently lost a leg, and one with a normal person (Kleck, 1968). In fact, unknown to the subjects, both partners were physically normal confederates. The subject and confederate each answered a series of questions read to them by the experimenter, who was out of sight behind a screen, and it was expected that subjects would look less at the handicapped person than the normal person. In the event, only one significant effect was revealed, for the mean length of looks while listening to the confederate, and it was in any case the reverse of what had been predicted.

In a similar study, by Kleck et al. (1968), the stigmatized person was this time said to be epileptic. There were no differences between conditions, but there was one significant supplementary finding: the more attractive the subjects found the confederate to be, whether normal or stigmatized, the more they looked overall. The reason, Kleck suggested, was that most of us are unused to talking to handicapped people, and we need as much information and feedback as possible. In other words, the monitoring function of gaze predominated, and any tendency which subjects might have felt to look away more than usual was cancelled out. No attempt was made, however, to look for supporting evidence – for example, subjects' ratings of how they had responded to the confederates – and the interpretation was necessarily speculative.

One last variable, which has received a little attention, is arousal. In the first experiment, by Griffit, May & Veitch (1974), subjects were asked to interview a man and a woman to assess their intelligence. Immediately before the interview, experimental subjects had been sexually aroused by a display of erotic slides, while control subjects watched slides of abstract pictures. Although there were none of the expected effects on subjects' gaze when the whole 5-minute session was analysed, the experimental and control groups did differ in the first minute or so, when arousal was assumed to be strongest. The aroused subjects looked more than the controls at the opposite-sex person, and they also looked more at the opposite sex than the same sex.

In the only other experiment, by Walsh, Meister & Kleinke (1977), subjects were themselves interviewed. Half-way through, they were given false feedback about their heart rate to suggest that they were either normally aroused or highly aroused, and they were told how the interviewers had rated them so far: positive, negative, or neutral. They then returned for the rest of the interview, and their gaze was recorded. Arousal had no effect, but the evaluation by the interviewer did. Subjects given a positive rating looked more than before, while the other two groups looked less – but there was no correlation between gaze and subjects' own ratings of the interviewer.

Role-playing studies. The third and final group of studies on attraction and approval used role-playing methods, and the first and best known were conducted by Mehrabian and his colleagues (Mehrabian, 1968a,b; Mehrabian & Friar, 1969; Mehrabian, 1971; Mehrabian & Ksionzky, 1972; Mehrabian, 1972). Subjects were placed in a laboratory and asked to imagine themselves confronted by a series of people, one at a time, of varying atrractiveness, status, and sex. They were then asked to assume and hold the stance they would take up, and observers seated behind a one-way screen scored their behaviour for orientation, posture, and the presence or absence of looking. All three independent variables proved to be significant sources of variation in one or other of the experiments, but there was no consistent pattern, perhaps because of differences in design. Furthermore, inter-observer agreement was sometimes unacceptably low, especially for looking – but there was good reason. In most of the experiments the imaginary person was denoted by an empty hat stand – the task for the observers was to judge whether or not the subject was 'looking toward an area where the imaginary addressee's eyes would probably be' (Mehrabian, 1968a, p. 303) – and the subjects wore cardboard masks which obscured the whole face and left only small slits for vision.

Subsequent experiments were rather more successful, although it must be stressed that role-playing as an experimental methodology for social psychology has often been criticized (Freedman, 1969; Carlsmith, Ellsworth & Aronson, 1976). Pellegrini, Hicks & Gordon (1970) found that subjects assigned the role of seeking approval from another person looked more frequently and for longer in total than those asked to avoid approval or given no role at all. There was no difference between the latter two groups, but only women were included in the experiment. In a more complex study, Breed & Porter (1972) asked subjects to adopt a positive attitude towards another person – actually a confederate – or a negative attitude. The session lasted 4 minutes. For half the subjects the confederate looked up for the first 2 minutes and then looked away, while for the other half he did the reverse. 'Positive' subjects looked less frequently when the confederate began by looking than when he began by looking away, but 'negative' subjects and control subjects who were given no role did the opposite. When the confederate looked away at the end, the authors argued, subjects may well have felt rejected, especially those in the 'positive' group because they had invested the most. In one final experiment, Lefebvre (1975) examined ingratiation systematically. Male subjects were asked to try to induce a female subject – once again a confederate – to take part in a short additional session after the 'main' experiment was over. In the period leading up to the request they were found to look more frequently, for longer at a time, and for longer in total than control subjects, to whom no role had been assigned.

Status and power

Unlike attraction and approval, status and power have received relatively little attention, and there have been no naturalistic, correlational studies. All the published experiments have relied on traditional techniques or role-playing, and one of the earliest and most extensive was conducted by Exline & Long and reported in Exline (1971). If, the authors argued, power is distributed unevenly between the members of a dyad, the weaker of the two will look more than the stronger – both to signal that he accepts his inferior position or, at least, is behaving appropriately and attending to his partner, and to monitor the other's responses so that he can adjust his behaviour, if need be, to try to secure the most favourable outcome. What is more, the difference between the two people will be greatest when the distribution of power is seen to be legitimate: if it is not, the weaker person will have no particular need to signal his inferiority or to seek feedback.

Forty male subjects were asked to discuss three problems and to agree a solution to each. Power was manipulated by giving one member of the pair the responsibility of allocating rewards at the end of each discussion, and legitimacy was manipulated by varying the composition of the pairs. Half were made up of a senior cadet and a junior from the army training corps, and the power was given to the senior man; and the other half were composed of strangers, and the allocation of power was arbitrary and therefore not legitimate.

Both predictions were confirmed: the less powerful person looked more than his partner in all three discussions, though significantly so during the second and third only; and the difference was especially marked in the legitimate condition. The effects were significant for looking while listening only, but the pattern for looking during speech showed a similar trend. Although the findings were consistent with his predictions, Exline did nevertheless acknowledge that alternative interpretations were possible. In particular, it may be that the powerful person looked less, rather than the weak person looked more, and that he did so because he felt guilty or embarrassed about his power, especially when it was not legitimate.

The remaining studies adopted a variety of experimental approaches and explored a variety of issues (e.g. Rosa & Masur, 1979; Ellyson *et al.*, 1980; Ellyson, Dovido & Corson, 1981; Lamb, 1981). Role-playing was a particularly common technique – Machotka (1965), Mehrabian (1968a), and Mehrabian & Friar (1969), for example – and, in general, it revealed that people with high status were looked at more than those with low status. However, both sex and attractiveness were found to interact with status in Mehrabian's studies and, as we have seen already, the results of role-playing are in any case very difficult to interpret.

Using traditional techniques, Efran (1968) and Fugita (1974) both examined status in conjunction with approval-seeking, as shown in the last section. Efran (1968) found that subjects looked more at people they believed approved of them than at others, and the effect was especially strong if the person giving the approval was of higher status than the receiver. In the experiment by Fugita (1974), subjects were asked to give a talk to two confederates who they believed were to assess them, and one gave signs of approval while the other did the opposite. When both confederates were of low status, subjects failed to discriminate between them; but when both were of high status, the one who appeared to approve was looked at more than the one who appeared not to.

In yet another study which used a confederate, Burroughs, Schultz & Aubrey (1973) found that if a woman gave strong arguments during a discussion she was looked at more than if she gave weak arguments, and she was also more likely to be elected a leader. Interestingly enough, it has also been reported from time to time that leaders choose seating positions which give them the greatest visual access to others in the group, and that people who happen to be sitting in such positions when a new group meets for the first time are more likely than others to be chosen as leaders (Sommer, 1969).

In one final group of studies the variable under investigation was neither status nor power but the related one of competition. Exline (1963) induced competition or co-operation in three-person discussions and found that while subjects with a low need for affiliation looked more in competitive than co-operative encounters, the opposite was true for those with a high need for affiliation. Rutter & Stephenson (1979b), however, could find no effects of competition and co-operation on gaze, despite several for speech, but Foddy (1978) was more successful. In an experimental bargaining game subjects were induced to compete or co-operate. In the co-operative enounters the mean length of looks and periods of eye-contact was greater than in the competitive encounters, and so too was the proportion of looking spent in eye-contact. There were no differences in the frequencies of looking and eye-contact. The findings could not be explained by speech patterning – in some experiments they probably can, but speech and its relationship with gaze are seldom analysed – and Foddy offered an ingenious interpretation, based on ideas from Argyle (1969) and Russo (1975). The frequency of looks, she argued, is a product of the monitoring function, their length the expressive function. Subjects had the same need for information whether they were competing or co-operating, and the frequency of their looks therefore remained constant. The thing which did distinguish the conditions was affect. Subjects presumably were more attracted to each other when they were co-operating than when they were competing, and that was why their looks were longer.

Embarrassment, shame, and sorrow

Several studies have examined embarrassment, and all made use of traditional experimental manipulations. The first was conducted by Exline, Gray & Schuette (1965), and they predicted that when people were made to feel embarrassed, they would try to conceal their feelings and so would avert their gaze. Subjects were given either an embarrassing or an innocuous interview, and the interviewer stared continuously. The embarrassing interview consisted of personal questions about the subject's fears, desires, needs, and impulses, while the innocuous items concerned recreational activities – films, books, sports, and so on. Since concealing any form of information, not just emotions, might lead people to look away, half the subjects in each condition were asked to try to conceal their true opinions and attitudes, while the others were given no special instructions.

The results were inconclusive. Overall, the embarrassed subjects did look less than the controls, but the difference was reflected only in looking during speech and not during listening or silence. Concealment had no effect, and the results therefore did appear to be specific to embarrassment – or, at least, an unpleasant emotion of some sort, since it was merely assumed that the attempt to embarrass subjects had succeeded, and they were not asked. To his credit Exline was cautious in the conclusions he drew, and he acknowledged that other variables might have been responsible – the desire to reduce distractions while recalling forgotten events, resentment towards the interviewer for asking personal questions, or a desire to avoid witnessing another's reactions to one's personal revelations. Indeed, in a subsequent paper, he confessed to considerable doubts (Exline & Winters, 1965a), and wondered whether the embarrassing questions were simply more difficult to answer, cognitively as well as emotionally, and caused people to look away for those reasons.

Some years later, Exline's original hypothesis was taken up again, by Modigliani (1971). Embarrassment, Modigliani argued, was 'a special short-lived, but often acute, loss of self-esteem', which stems from a sense of appearing deficient before other people, and leads us to try to distance ourselves from them, often by averting our eyes. Indeed, he even went so far as to suggest that some of the findings of Milgram (1965, 1974) could be explained by such a mechanism. A substantial majority of subjects were so reluctant to defy the experimenter's authority that they were prepared to obey him almost without question and to administer dangerous, even lethal, electric shocks to other subjects. But when the experimenter gave his instructions from out of sight in another room, almost three times as many disobeyed. Furthermore, many subjects averted their eyes when they pressed the button – though whether to avoid looking at the other person or to avoid seeing him it was impossible to tell.

In his own experiment Modigliani told subjects that they were to take part in a study of teamwork in small organizations. Each was to try to solve a number of anagrams, and failure would mean failure for the whole team. Half the subjects were given very difficult words so that they would inevitably fail, and half were given an easy set. Within each condition, half worked in private and half sat with the rest of the team; and half were given a covering statement to mitigate their failure or success, while the others were not. Immediately before the session, and again immediately after, subjects were interviewed by the experimenter, and it was then that their visual behaviour was recorded.

Unfortunately, as in Exline's experiment, the results were inconclusive. Subjects who had failed in public looked significantly less after the experimental session than before – even if they had received the mitigating statement – while those who had succeeded showed a non-significant tendency in the opposite direction. However, when subjects' self-reports were subsequently examined, no correlations between embarrassment and visual behaviour could be detected. In other words, although the experimental manipulation had affected something, there was no evidence that it was embarrassment. Modigliani's own suggestion was that failure had engendered antagonistic feelings towards the experimenter, and that was why subjects had looked away.

A second group of writers explored deception and shame and, once again, one of the earliest experiments was conducted by Exline and his colleagues. The main purpose of the study – which was originally presented in a conference paper by Exline et al. (1961) but was subsequently published by Exline et al. (1970) – was to explore Machiavellianism. Each subject worked with a confederate on a decision-making task and part-way through the session the confederate cheated, by looking up the answers while the experimenter was out of the room, and so implicated the subject in deception. Later, the subject was interviewed by the experimenter and confronted with what had happened. The experimenter stared continuously and, at the start of the interview, both high and low Machiavellian subjects looked back at him something over 30% of the time. At the point when the accusation was made, both groups responded by looking much less, and this was especially so for the low Machiavellian subjects. Even by the end of the interview they had still not recovered, although the high Machiavellian subjects were by now looking almost as much as at the beginning.

Some years later, Mehrabian reported another of his series of role-playing experiments but, like the results of his work on status, the findings were equivocal (Mehrabian & Williams, 1969; Mehrabian, 1971). Mehrabian & Williams (1969), for example, found that subjects who were instructed to convey a message in a persuasive manner were more likely to look than those who were given different instructions – and were perceived as more persuasive – apparently irrespective of whether or not they believed in the arguments they were asked to use. However, the reliability of the observations was again very low – even though the traditional hat-stand had now been replaced by a human being, albeit a confederate – and the findings were unconvincing.

In the only other published study of which I know, Knapp, Hart & Dennis (1974) asked veterans of the Vietnam War to speak either for or against increases in educational benefits for other veterans like themselves. While there was no difference between the groups in the number of looks, those who spoke against the proposition and so, it was assumed, against their own beliefs, looked less in total. Whether the results could properly be attributed to deception and shame, however, is hard to say. For most people, to argue against one's beliefs for the sake of an experimental exercise is one thing; to deceive is another.

The final group of writers studied sorrow and a mixture of other emotions. Exline *et al.* (1968), for example, asked subjects to tell an experimenter about recent events which had made them happy, sad, or angry, and found that they more frequently looked down in the sad condition than the happy condition. The results for anger were unclear. Fromme & Schmidt (1972) used a role-playing method, and measured how much subjects looked at a confederate as they enacted sorrow, anger, and fear, and how close and how quickly they approached him. In the sorrow condition, subjects looked less than in either of the other experimental conditions as well as a control condition in which no emotion was specified. There were no effects for speed of approach, and subjects kept a greater distance for sorrow than anger, and a greater distance still for fear. Throughout the experiment the confederate wore dark glasses and a fixed, blank expression.

Hobson *et al.* (1973) used a similar procedure to that of Exline & Winters (1965b), and asked subjects to hold a conversation with a confederate. Half-way through they were given feedback on their performance, and were told either that they were doing well or that their behaviour was boring. Even though self-reports confirmed that the manipulation had succeeded in making subjects anxious in the negative condition, gaze was unaffected. Finally, Efran & Cheyne (1974) reported an experiment on personal space. Subjects were required to walk between two confederates who were holding a conversation, and they were compared with control groups who simply passed the couple by or walked between two inanimate objects. It was predicted that the experimental subjects would more frequently use agonistic forms of behaviour, like lowering the eyes and head or even closing the eyes, and the prediction was confirmed. It was also found that the experimental group reported a correspondingly negative mood.

Conclusion

The literature on encoding, it will now be clear, is very difficult to interpret. First, there has been little attempt at theorizing and second, there are serious methodological weaknesses in much of the empirical research. Many of the studies lack ecological validity – especially those, like Mehrabian's, which used role-playing – and many more were so poorly controlled that apparently encouraging results could not be properly understood because it was impossible to know which particular affective state caused them, if any. All one can say empirically, I think, is that if people experience a positive emotion or make a positive attribution about the encounter they will probably look more than if the conditions are negative. As to theory, there is no more to say until the end of the chapter.

Decoding studies

Decoding studies are less easy than encoding studies to classify, but four main issues have been tackled: whether people are aware of how much they are looked at; whether being looked at is arousing; whether gaze is used for making attributions about the sender; and whether the look is a source of social influence.

Awareness

Two main questions have been asked about awareness: do people notice differences in gaze; and, if so, does mere awareness influence how the sender is perceived? The first of the studies, by Kendon (1968), was never published, but was cited by Argyle & Cook (1976). Kendon was concerned only with the first question, and he simply asked what proportion of subjects would mention gaze when they described other people. Eleven of his twenty participants made spontaneous comments when the interviewer's pattern of looking deviated from normal, but none mentioned it when it did not.

In a second and more extensive study, by Cook & Smith (1975), subjects took part in three 5-minute conversations with a confederate, a different one each time. The first was trained to use a 'normal gaze pattern' (which was not defined), the second stared continuously, and the third looked away for the whole 5 minutes. Subjects were later asked to complete a series of rating scales to indicate the impressions they had formed, and also to write free descriptions which were to include comments on how they had arrived at their impressions. Only thirty of the seventy-two mentioned the confederate's gaze in their spontaneous accounts, and there were no differences between the conditions in their impressions. However, when the results were subsequently broken down according to whether the subjects had or had not mentioned gaze, significant effects did emerge. In each case, people who had mentioned gaze formed different impressions across the three conditions, while the others did not, but there was no consistent pattern.

In a third experiment, LeCompte & Rosenfeld (1971) studied observers rather than participants. Two 8-minute recordings were made of someone who was ostensibly an experimenter presenting instructions to subjects. The information he read out was identical in the two recordings, but in one he twice looked up at the camera, for 2 seconds each time, while in the other he failed to look up at all. There was no evidence that subjects noticed the difference.

In two final studies the duration of gaze was manipulated more systematically, but the findings were contradictory. Kleck & Nuessle (1968) filmed two simulated job interviews, using the same trained confederate as the 'applicant' each time. In one condition he looked at the interviewer 80% of the time and in the other 15%. The interviews lasted 5 minutes, and the content of what was said was identical – although the films were subsequently played with the sound turned off. Subjects watched either one version or the other, and afterwards they were asked to say what proportion of time the applicant had looked at the interviewer. Their estimates were very accurate – 70% against 30% – and women were even more accurate than men.

In the other experiment, by Argyle & Williams (1969), subjects appeared on the contrary to be very inaccurate, but there was an important difference in methodology. This time, rather than simply observe, subjects interacted with the other person. Confederates were trained to look 10–20% of the time or 80–90%, and each subject underwent both conditions and was later asked a series of questions including how much the confederate had looked. There was no main effect of actual looking on perceived looking, but there was a curious and unexplained interaction: men correctly said the confederate looked more in the 'high' condition than the 'low' condition, but women said the opposite. There were no differences between the conditions in how much the subjects had felt observed or how comfortable and enjoyable they had found the encounter. Moreover, even when a correlational analysis was subsequently conducted for each condition separately, there were still relatively few significant effects. For both men and women the feeling of being observed correlated positively with the confederate's estimated level of looking, significantly so for all but one of the calculations; but there was no relationship between actual and perceived looking. In fact, though, since the actual level remained constant for all subjects, it is unclear how and why the calculation was made, and what it was expected to reveal.

The most interesting of the findings concerned the subjects' own gaze, for it emerged that people who looked relatively little were often more accurate in estimating the confederate's level of looking than those who looked a lot. In other words, either subjects were somehow able to gauge the confederate's behaviour without looking themselves, or their apparent accuracy was artefactual – in which case many of the other results the authors reported must be treated with caution.

Arousal

Although, as we have seen, many writers have argued that visual interaction is emotionally arousing, there have been very few attempts to explore whether it produces measurable physiological effects. One of the first was by McBride, King & James (1965), and they reported that, when subjects engaged in eye-contact with another person, there was a 'greater G.S.R. response' than when they looked at his or her mouth. Unfortunately, though, no condition of unreciprocated gaze was included, and it was impossible to say whether the effect was due to the subject's or the confederate's behaviour.

A few years later, Kleinke & Pohlen (1971) took as their measure subjects' heart rate, and observed a series of Prisoners' Dilemma games. In one condition the confederate stared continuously at the subject's eyes and in the other he looked away continuously. The former was found to produce significantly higher heart rates than the latter, even though there was no difference in self-reported 'tenseness'. The effect lasted all through the experiment – despite the fact that subjects showed an average decline from start to finish of over five beats a minute – irrespective of experimental condition.

The only other evidence comes from two studies conducted in Britain. The first, by Nichols & Champness (1971), examined GSR (galvanic skin response). Twenty men and twenty women took part, and each underwent twelve 10-second trials with a confederate, who sat 3 feet away. The subject was asked to stare continuously at the confederate's eyes and for half the trials the confederate stared back, and for the other half he or she looked away to a spot 30 degrees from the line of regard. For both frequency and amplitude of GSR, the subject's response was found to be greater in the former condition than the latter, and the authors attributed the result to emotional arousal. However, as they subsequently acknowledged, whether the crucial factor was making eye-contact, failing to break it at the normal time, or holding it too long, the data could not say. Furthermore, there were other uncontrolled variables. In particular, subjects may simply have found the eye-contact condition more complex, interesting, or worthy of attention, rather than more arousing.

It was this last point that Gale et al. (1972) took up in the second experiment. They compared three confederate conditions – smiling and looking, looking, and gaze aversion – and predicted that subjects' arousal would be highest in the first and lowest in the last. The procedure was similar to that of Nichols & Champness (1971) in that the subject was asked to stare continuously at the confederate's eyes, but this time the dependent measure was cortical EEG. In general the prediction was confirmed, and the amplitude of the response was greater for smiling and looking together and looking alone than for gaze aversion, and the greatest difference was between the first and last conditions.

Unfortunately, though, it was again impossible to say whether the critical variable was the emotionally arousing properties of the stimulus or its informational complexity.

Attributions

Almost all the research on attributions has employed traditional experimental manipulations, and only one study, as far as I know, has made use of a more naturalistic approach. Kendon & Cook (1969), whose work we have discussed more than once before, asked subjects at the end of their encounters to complete a series of semantic differential scales to record the impressions they had formed of one another. Three factors were extracted: potency, activity, and evaluation. There were no effects for potency, and only one for activity: the more frequently eye-contact occurred, the less subjects perceived each other as active. For evaluation, however, which probably reflected liking and approval, there were four effects: the longer a subject's looks during speech and listening, and the less frequently they occurred during listening and overall, the more positively he or she was evaluated.

Many experimental studies have been conducted, and most of them fall into one of two categories. In the first, subjects interact with confederates, whose gaze is programmed to vary in systematic ways, and at the end of the encounter they record the impressions they have formed, generally by completing rating scales. In the second they merely observe, and the stimulus material is typically presented in the form of video-tape recordings or films. Very few studies have combined both approaches, even though there is little reason to assume that participants and observers will behave in the same way.

Participants.   One of the earliest experimental studies of participants was conducted by Exline & Eldridge (1967), and was concerned with credibility. If, the authors predicted, an experimenter looked as he commented on the subject's behaviour, his words would be perceived as more authentic than if he looked away. In the event the results were unclear. Each subject received two sets of comments, and it was found that, if the confederate looked away as he gave the first, but stared continuously during the second, he was perceived as having greater confidence in both messages than if the pattern of gaze was reversed. In other words, a recency effect appeared to operate. A second prediction, that Machiavellians would be less willing than other people to accept direct gaze as a mark of sincerity, was rejected altogether.

In the only other study, Beebe (1974) reported that the more a public speaker looked at the audience, the more honest he was perceived to be, as well as skilled, informed, experienced, friendly, and kind. Since then, no further experiments have been published – which is a pity for, as Ellsworth (1978) pointed out, sincerity is a particularly interesting issue for gaze, and one which highlights the problems of interpretation for experimenters and subjects alike:

We might ask whether some . . . deep gazers deliberately *use* their gaze to create an impression in their companions, on the lines of a con man trying to convey sincerity. Here we are asking whether people can trade on the cultural assumptions about gaze as a signal. This case is interesting, because the gazer is *also* trading on the cultural assumption that the gaze, like many other 'expressive' behaviors, is not generally used deliberately as a signal; it is a trustworthy sign in part because it is assumed to be unintentional (Ellsworth, 1978, p. 343).

At the same time as Exline was reporting his results with Eldridge, Ellsworth herself was beginning to work on gaze, and one of her earliest studies was concerned with impression formation (Ellsworth & Carlsmith, 1968). Female interviewers were programmed to look 'very frequently' or 'hardly at all', and the content of the discussions was devoted to research findings on the supposed effects of birth order on personality. 'Looking hardly at all', it should be noted, meant looking at one or other of the subject's ears and, although this may sometimes be mistaken at a distance for genuine looking, at 4 feet, the distance which Ellsworth & Carlsmith used, it probably was not (Vine, 1971; Cranach & Ellgring, 1973). Each individual's birth position was known to the experimenter, though not the interviewer, and half the subjects were exposed to findings which were unfavourable to them, and half the opposite. Afterwards they all completed a series of evaluative scales, and it was found that when the content of the interview was favourable, the interviewer was rated more negatively if she looked hardly at all, but when it was unfavourable, the opposite was true. A positive message, the authors concluded, was attenuated by gaze aversion, and a negative message was mitigated.

Some years later, Scherwitz & Helmreich (1973) made a successful attempt to replicate Ellsworth & Carlsmith (1968), but using a different method. Subjects were asked to hold a conversation with another person over a 'video-phone' but, in fact, what they saw and heard through the television monitor was a pre-recorded tape of a confederate whose gaze and comments were programmed. In the first experiment there were three levels of looking: high, intermediate, and low (where looking was gaze directed into the camera), and three levels of content: favourable, mixed, and unfavourable. At first sight the findings appeared to contradict Ellsworth & Carlsmith, since unfavourable content this time led to positive ratings when the confederate looked, and the opposite was true for positive content. However, the comments in the present experiment were much more personal than before – the partner's first impressions of the subject's intelligence, personality, and so on – and Scherwitz & Helmreich were able to demonstrate in a second study that this was the critical variable and that the conclusions of Ellsworth & Carlsmith were valid as far as they went. When we are given a positive personal evaluation we prefer someone who looks away; but when the message is unfavourable we prefer the speaker to look if it is personal but to look away if it is relatively impersonal.

Several other writers made use of rather more dramatic manipulations. Thayer (1969), for example, asked subjects to sit facing a confederate for 3 minutes in an 'impression formation' task. The confederate stared almost continuously or looked away almost continuously – three 58-second stares with three 2-second breaks, or three 2-second looks with three 58-second breaks – and staring led to higher ratings of dominance. Neither participant was allowed to speak. Later, Breed (1972) asked subjects to tell a story in front of a confederate who stared continuously, looked intermittently, or looked only twice. The confederate was perceived as more interested in the first condition than the others, and subjects responded with greater looking.

In the first of two rather more persuasive studies, by Cook, subjects were asked to talk to a series of trained confederates, each of whom used a different pattern of gaze: total gaze aversion, looking during speech only, looking during listening only, normal gaze (undefined), and continuous staring (Argyle, Lefebvre & Cook, 1974). After each encounter the subject rated the confederate, and the normal pattern led to the most liking, and gaze aversion the least. The same held for activity and potency, but here the findings for gaze aversion were significantly different from the others. Interestingly enough, continuous gaze produced very similar ratings to the normal pattern, and the only condition which appeared to violate the subjects' expectations to an intolerable extent was gaze aversion.

In his second experiment Cook again used repeated measures, but this time subjects who mentioned their partners' gaze were examined separately from those who did not. There were three levels of gaze – 'averted', 'normal', and 'continuous', and, as we have seen already, there were no clear differences for the 'unaware' subjects (Cook & Smith, 1975). There were, however, several effects for the 'aware' group and, in particular, they appeared to regard gaze aversion as a sign of nervousness, uncertainty, unpleasantness, and impotence, the latter measured by the semantic differential technique. Unfortunately, though, it may be that subjects who noticed gaze simply guessed the purpose of the experiment and responded to its perceived demand characteristics. If so, the results are very difficult to interpret and, by implication, so too are many others in the literature.

The remaining studies of participants were all conducted by Kleinke, whose theoretical interest was Bem's ideas about self-perception. The first experiment, which we have discussed briefly already, was by Kleinke & Pohlen (1971). Subjects played a Prisoners' Dilemma game with a confederate who was programmed to look continuously or look away continuously, and to adopt a co-operative, competitive, or mixed strategy. The ratings which subjects gave him were affected only by his strategy and not his gaze, but those they gave themselves were affected by both. When the confederate played competitively and stared, or co-operatively and looked away, subjects saw themselves as friendly and co-operative; but, when he did the opposite, their ratings were reversed. An analysis of the game itself revealed that, while subjects generally matched the confederate's strategy, their behaviour was unaffected by his gaze.

The second experiment, by Kleinke et al. (1973), made use of false feedback.

Volunteer students met for 10 minutes in mixed-sex pairs to get to know each other and to discuss any topic they chose. At the end they were told that one of them had been under observation from behind a one-way screen and had looked an average amount, less than average, or more than average. The information was false – or, at least, random – and was introduced to test the hypothesis that both the subject (the person whose gaze had apparently been monitored) and the partner would use it to arrive at their impressions of each other, in the way that Bem (1967, 1972) would predict. In the event there were no main effects for the impressions subjects formed of partners, and only one for the impressions partners formed of subjects: those who had apparently looked very little were described as inattentive. There were, however, several interactions with sex and, in general, men and women were influenced in opposite ways, and the effects for women were the stronger. Unfortunately, the paper did not report whether the participants believed the false information they were given and, presumably, that may make a difference.

In his third experiment, Kleinke used an experimental interview (Kleinke, Staneski & Berger, 1975). Male subjects were interviewed by female confederates, who gazed constantly, intermittently, or not at all. Experimental subjects were reinforced by a system of coloured lights each time they looked, and were punished when they averted their gaze for 6 seconds or longer. Control subjects received non-contingent feedback. Experimental subjects were found to look more and more as time went on, and control subjects looked less and less, but the ratings they gave to the interviewer were unaffected by their own visual behaviour. The interviewer's gaze, however, did have a significant influence, and gaze aversion produced the most negative evaluations, especially in the case of unattractive interviewers, who were perceived as disproportionately inattentive unless they looked. Attractiveness was rated by independent judges. In the authors' words:

> interpersonal attraction is related to gaze and physical attractiveness through a number of mediating variables which will have to be isolated more specifically in future research (Kleinke, Staneski & Berger, 1975, p. 115).

Observers. The first of the studies of observers was conducted by Kleck & Nuessle (1968). As we have seen already, a confederate was trained to spend either 80% or 15% of the time looking at his partner, who was said to be interviewing him for a job, and the encounters were video-taped. The recordings were subsequently played to observers, with the sound turned off, and there were many differences in the impressions they formed. In the 'high' condition the interviewer and applicant were perceived as more attracted to each other than in the 'low' condition, and their relationship was seen as less tense. The applicant was perceived more positively overall, and by female observers as more potent but by men as less. Fourteen items from an adjective checklist also revealed differences – but eighteen did not, even though all thirty-two had been chosen as likely candidates.

Subsequent experiments used a variety of approaches. LeCompte & Rosenfeld (1971) recorded a confederate 'experimenter' giving instructions to subjects. In one condition he looked up twice at the camera, for 2 seconds each time, while in the other he averted his gaze for the whole 8 minutes. When he looked, he was perceived as less tense and less formal. Haase & Tepper (1972) made video-tape recordings of counsellors working with their clients, and asked a group of experienced practitioners to rate them for empathy. The counsellors were genuine, but they were programmed either to give a variety of nonverbal signals, including looking, or to withhold them. The nonverbal cues accounted for twice the variance of the verbal content, and there was a significant effect for gaze, which was the most important cue. Thayer & Schiff (1974) made films of two 'students' (in reality, actors) reading together in the college library, and asked observers to guess how long they had known each other. After a few seconds one of the two looked at the other for 1 second or 5 seconds, and the look was either reciprocated or not. Male, female, and mixed-sex pairs were used, and each observer watched all the films. A long look, it was found, was taken to signify a long relationship, especially when it was reciprocated. The sex of the pair produced no main effects for any of the variables, but several interactions, and the same was true for sex of observer. In a follow-up experiment, which appears from the authors' description to have used the same recordings, observers were asked to say whether there was 'any evidence of sexual interest between the individuals' (Thayer & Schiff, 1977), and long and reciprocated looks were both perceived as signs of involvement. Gaze has also been associated with dominance and power (e.g. Abele, 1981; Dovidio & Ellyson, 1982), and with anxiety and depression (e.g. Waxer, 1979).

The final group of experiments used role-playing. In the first, by Holstein, Goldstein & Bem (1971), subjects interviewed actors who were trained to appear expressive – by looking, smiling, and gesturing – or unexpressive. Although the interviewers subsequently rated the former more positively than the latter, observers did not. Indeed, in both cases, observers gave lower ratings than interviewers. In the second experiment, by Kleinke, Meeker & Fong (1974), actors played an engaged couple, and they were trained to look at each other, use each other's names, and touch each other, or to avoid all three. The couple were supposedly being interviewed by a psychologist, and the recordings were shown to observers. Looking led to a more positive evaluation than looking away, and gaze was a more important cue than the others. In the final experiment, by LaCrosse (1975), the setting was again a psychological interview. Confederates role-played counsellors, and were programmed to use either affiliative or non-affiliative forms of behaviour, which included looking at the client 80% or 40% of the time. Observers' ratings were found to be more positive in the affiliative condition than the other, and frequency of looking was cited as the most important cue.

The look as a source of social influence

Most of the work in this section has examined the effects of staring, and much the most important contribution, both empirically and theoretically, has come from Ellsworth and her colleagues. The first of their papers was published by Ellsworth, Carlsmith & Henson (1972), and reported a series of field studies designed to test the hypothesis that staring elicits avoidance. A stare was defined as 'a gaze or look which persists regardless of the behaviour of the other person', and was considered to be a threat to the receiver. If escape were impossible at first, tension and arousal would mount, and the response when it finally came would be exaggerated.

The first experiment was conducted at a road junction controlled by traffic lights. The experimenter, riding a motor scooter, pulled up next to the target and stared at the driver until the light changed to green. The dependent measure was the time it took the target to cross the intersection, and experimental subjects were found to cross more quickly than controls. Subsequent experiments demonstrated that the same happened when drivers were stared at by a pedestrian; pedestrians at pedestrian crossings were affected in the same way; and the sex of the starer was immaterial. The results could not be explained by saying that staring violates the norms of everyday experience since an equally unusual, if asocial, stimulus had no effect – a young woman sitting hammering and picking at the pavement. Instead, Ellsworth offered two other interpretations, and she appeared to favour the second:

> The first is that staring is generally perceived as a signal of hostile intent, as in primates, and elicits avoidance or, in some circumstances, counterattack. The second is that gazing at a person's face is an extremely salient stimulus with interpersonal implications which cannot be ignored. The stare, in effect, is a demand for a response, and in a situation where there is no appropriate response, tension will be evoked, and the subject will be motivated to escape the situation (Ellsworth, Carlsmith & Henson, 1972, p. 311).

Elman, Schulte & Bukoff (1977) attempted to reproduce the findings. In their first experiment they found, against Ellsworth, Carlsmith & Henson, that staring did not lead subjects to walk faster at a pedestrian crossing. However, the stare lasted on average only 5 seconds, and the authors argued that this might have been too short to be perceived as a threat. In their second experiment, therefore, duration was varied systematically, and the stare lasted either 2 seconds or more than 15. The observations were made on people coming out of a lift and this time subjects walked faster in response to the long stare but more slowly in response to the shorter stimulus. In both experiments the effect of staring was cancelled out if the confederate also smiled.

A number of other studies were subsequently reported by a variety of authors, and all of them took the invasion of personal space as their setting. Smith, Sanford & Goldman, (1977), for example, asked confederates to go to the college library, select unaccompanied readers, sit opposite them, and stare for 15 minutes. The people who were stared at – 'starees', in the language of Smith *et al.* – got up and left sooner than the controls. For male starers, more women than men left, while for female starers, there was no difference. Men, unlike women, sometimes stared back. The same year, Buchanan, Goldman & Juhnke (1977) found that if passengers in a lift stared at men about to come in, they were more likely to preserve their personal space than if they did not; but there was no such effect for women. Finally, there appeared a paper – 'The effects of staring and pew invasion in church settings' – by Campbell & Lancioni (1979). Confederates approached people sitting at the ends of pews, and either stared as they tried to get in, or did not. Those who were stared at were more likely to move away or return the gaze than those who were not, but few did both. Whether the invaders worked alone or in pairs made no difference. Like Ellsworth, the Campbell & Lancioni study argued that the stare was an agonistic signal, and also served to involve the receiver so that the stimulus could not be ignored and a response had to be made.

The next theoretical advance came in two papers, one by Ellsworth & Carlsmith (1973) and the other by Snyder, Grether & Keller (1974). Both invoked the concept of 'de-individuation', developed by Zimbardo (1969). In sub-human primates it is well established that gaze aversion acts as a signal of appeasement (Tinbergen, 1960; Lorenz, 1966; van Hooff, 1967; Exline & Yellin, 1969), and Ellsworth & Carlsmith wondered whether the same might be true of humans. Alternatively, might gaze aversion actually increase the probability of an aggressive attack – the prediction which Zimbardo would make? In the authors' words:

> According to this hypothesis, the easier it is to treat the victim as an object, lacking humanity and individuality, the easier it is to overcome inhibitions to hurting him. If we assume that lowering the face and averting the gaze dehumanize a person to some extent, it follows that victims who employ this tactic should be subject to *more* aggression than victims who establish direct eye contact with the aggressor (Ellsworth & Carlsmith, 1973, p. 281).

The experiment which Ellsworth & Carlsmith designed to test the rival theories was complex and consisted of two phases. In the first, half the subjects were aroused to anger by a confederate, and half were not. In the second phase both groups were given the opportunity to administer electric shocks to the same confederate and, just before each shock was due, the confederate either looked up at the subject or continued to look down. Subjects were instructed not to look away, and half of them in the main design always received a look, while the other half were always confronted by gaze aversion. There was also another condition in which each subject sometimes received a look and sometimes did not – that is, a within-subjects condition.

In the 'between-groups' part of the experiment the results supported the de-individuation hypothesis: victims who looked were less likely than those who looked away to be shocked by the angry subjects, and there was no difference between conditions for the unaroused group. In the 'within-subjects' part of the design, however, subjects were more likely, not less, to administer a shock when eye-contact had occurred than when it had not, and this was true for both the angry and the unaroused groups.

Neither of the original hypotheses could accommodate both sets of findings, but Ellsworth & Carlsmith were nevertheless able to offer an ingenious interpretation. Each subject completed a questionnaire after the experiment, and it was clear that eye-contact had indeed been an aversive stimulus, just as for the 'victims' in the studies by Ellsworth, Carlsmith & Henson (1972), it was assumed. One way to try to remove the aversive stimulus was to administer electric shocks to punish the victim, and so 'teach' him not to look. When the subject had reason to believe that he could change the victim's behaviour (that is, in the 'within-subjects' part of the design), he tried to. Otherwise, he did not, and instead he simply decreased the number of shocks and avoided eye-contact that way. The only thing which the interpretation could not explain was the finding that unaroused subjects in the 'between-groups' part of the design were unaffected by eye-contact, even though they had found it aversive.

Snyder, Grether & Keller (1974) took a quite different position, and argued that the stare need not always act as a threat and lead to avoidance: what mattered was the context. Consider, for example, the case of a hitch-hiker who is trying to attract a lift. If he or she stares then, according to Ellsworth, the driver will feel uncomfortable or tense, and the simplest way to get rid of the aversive stimulus will be to drive on. At the same time, however, if the stare 'individuates' the target then, since our cultural norms say that people who request help should be given it, to drive on would be to induce guilt. In this particular context, Snyder and co-workers argued, the second factor is likely to outweigh the first, and drivers who are stared at are more likely to offer a lift than those who are not. The prediction was supported – though fewer than 10% of drivers stopped in any condition – but the authors did acknowledge that the precise mechanism by which the stare enhanced compliance was unclear.

Two years later, Ellsworth responded to this last point, and used it to develop her theory further (Ellsworth & Langer, 1976). If staring is sometimes aversive and sometimes not, she argued, perhaps it is simply a 'non-specific activator'. When I stare at you, you become aroused – perhaps because my behaviour forces you to interact with me – and you cast around for an explanation and a suitable response. If you succeed, your arousal falls; if not, you eventually take flight. The stare has no particular meaning of its own, and we have to attribute one – by using the context – before we can make a behavioural response.

To test their ideas, Ellsworth & Langer made use of an experimental paradigm which by now had become very popular in social psychology: by-stander intervention. In a shopping centre, a confederate crouched by a wall with her head down. Another confederate approached shoppers and asked them to help. In one condition she gave a clear message, saying that the woman had lost a contact lens; in the other the message was ambiguous, and the woman was described as 'not feeling well'. For half the subjects in each condition the confederate who needed help looked up as they approached, and for the other half she looked down. The expectation was that:

> when the nature of the victim's plight and the required remedy are clear, the victim who stares at a potential helper should elicit approach and assistance. The more ambiguous the victim's problem, the less likely it is that staring will elicit a helpful response; as the appropriate response becomes more doubtful, the tendency to avoid involvement becomes relatively stronger (Ellsworth & Langer, 1976, p. 118).

The prediction was supported. When the message was clear and the victim looked up, 83% of subjects offered to help, and this was significantly more than in any of the other three conditions. As Ellsworth & Langer concluded:

> Whatever the exact mechanism involved, the stare is a powerful stimulus, powerful despite, or perhaps because of, its lack of a specific and invariant meaning. Although the stare does not serve as a releaser for any particular behavior pattern in humans, it may well serve as a releaser for a diffuse emotional arousal. The arousal is interpreted or altered in context, and the particular behavior that is motivated varies accordingly (Ellsworth & Langer, 1976, p. 122).

For Ellsworth & Langer the stare elicited attention, arousal, and a sense of involvement with the other person, and at the heart of their interpretation lay emotion and motivation.

If gaze was one non-specific activator then, wondered Kleinke (1977), might touch be another, and might their combined effect on compliance be additive? In Kleinke's experiment a confederate left a dime in a telephone box and, each time someone found it, she approached and asked, 'Did you find it?' A two by two design was used, with look/no look and touch/no touch the independent variables, and the dependent variable was whether the coin was returned. Touching was successful, but gaze had no effect and there was no interaction. In a second experiment, in which the subject was asked to lend the confederate a dime rather than simply return it, both gaze and touch produced main effects, but again there was no interaction. Similarly mixed results have often been reported since (Valentine & Erlichmann, 1979; Valentine, 1980; Kleinke, 1980; Bull & Gibson-Robinson, 1982).

Only two other experiments have been published, as far as I know, and both were concerned with conformity. Davey & Taylor (1968) replicated the procedures of Asch (1956), but asked confederates either to stare at the subject as he was about to state his opinion, or to look away. About a quarter of the responses showed conformity, but there was no difference between conditions. The other study was conducted by Goldman (1980), and he was interested in verbal reinforcement and the extent to which it could be used to induce subjects to conform to an interviewer's inferred attitudes. Students were interviewed about inter-collegiate sports. In the first half of the encounter no reinforcement was given but, in the second, favourable attitudes were reinforced with words like 'good', 'all right', 'OK', and the interviewer was programmed to look at half the subjects and look away from the others, and to stand a distance of either 4–5 feet or 2–3 feet. The degree of attitude change from the first set of questions to the second was measured, and it was found that looking and the 4–5 foot distance both led subjects to converge upon the interviewer's attitudes, while looking away and the close distance had the opposite effect. There was no interaction between gaze and distance. The interviewer's look, argued Goldman, signalled that he liked the subject, and his approving comments signalled his own attitudes. The look motivated the subject *to* conform, and the words indicated *how*.

When Ellsworth began her work on staring, although there already existed an extensive literature on the encoding and decoding of gaze, there had been very few attempts to integrate the findings, either within or between the two areas. It was this which concerned Ellsworth most, and so she began to develop her own theoretical ideas. Although her empirical work had focused on the stare – an unusual and specific form of visual behaviour which may ultimately tell us relatively little about normal looking – her theoretical account in its later forms was concerned with gaze in general. In 1978, in a review of *Gaze and Mutual Gaze* by Argyle & Cook (1976), she argued as follows.

Gaze is a salient stimulus, which arouses the receiver and is difficult to ignore. The look has no intrinsic meaning, and the receiver has to resort to contextual information to try to interpret it:

> In simplified terms, the argument is that the arousal produces the need to interpret, and the context provides the specific content of the interpretation. The context may be as small as the accompanying facial expression, or as large as the history of the relationship, the social norms governing the social setting, or a cultural belief system, such as the belief in the evil eye (Ellsworth, 1978, pp. 347–8).

The range of possible interpretations, however, is limited, and the initial inference is almost always that the sender is simply attending. If gaze continues, the next inference is often that the sender is trying to involve the receiver in an encounter, and the latter will probably feel compelled to respond. In other words, the receiver:

> will be motivated to do two things: (1) interpret the gaze itself in terms of the type of involvement it signals, and this inferred involvement may be positive or negative; and (2) figure out how to respond, and his or her attitude toward the response called for may also be positive or negative (Ellsworth, 1978, p. 349).

For Ellsworth, the key properties of gaze were thus salience, arousal, and involvement (Ellsworth, 1975). However, the precise relationships and their sequence were not yet clear, and she foresaw three possibilities, each of which involved arousal, but in different ways. The first was the one I have just outlined, and arousal was located early in the chain: A looks at B → B becomes aroused → B tries to interpret the arousal → B infers A's attention → B interprets A's attention by means of contextual cues. The second possibility was that the effects of gaze might be independent: A's gaze → B both becomes aroused and infers that A is attending → together these two effects lead B to make an interpretation based on the context. The third possibility was that arousal follows rather than precedes B's attribution of attention: A's gaze → B infers that A is attending → B becomes aroused → B tries to interpret A's attention by means of contextual cues.

Conclusion

Like the literature on encoding, the literatutre on decoding is very difficult to summarize. First we examined awareness, then arousal, and then attributions, and there were many inconsistencies and many occasions when the findings were quite different from those for encoding. Once again, weaknesses of methodology were often to blame but the more fundamental problem was the lack of theory. Then, in the final section, we turned to gaze as a source of social influence, and now a theory began to emerge. The look, it was argued, is a salient, arousing, and involving stimulus, which it is difficult for the receiver to ignore, and which demands an explanation. Seldom is there any intrinsic meaning to discover and, instead, the receiver must make an attribution. The context, the person's motives and set, and the timing and contingency of the behaviour all play their parts, as well as the look itself, and what matters most is the relationships between them.

Conclusion: Ellsworth, Patterson, and attribution

As we saw at the start of the chapter, the only serious attempt at theoretical integration in the early literature was the intimacy model of Argyle & Dean (1965) and for a decade or more there was little else. But now a new approach had begun to develop. It came from Ellsworth and Patterson, as we have seen, and it was based on attribution theory.

The first formulation was by Patterson (1973a). Whereas Argyle & Dean had spoken of 'intimacy behaviours', Patterson used the term 'immediacy behaviours' taken from Mehrabian (1969). The immediacy behaviours were touch, distance, eye-contact, body lean, and body orientation, and probably encompassed all the indices of intimacy which Argyle & Dean had proposed, including those in their category, 'etc.'. Indeed, many experiments on intimacy had incorporated Mehrabian's additional behaviours already – for example, Libby (1970); Watson, (1970); Patterson, Mullins & Romano (1971); Breed (1972), Schultz & Barefoot (1974); Coutts & Schneider (1976); Coutts & Ledden (1977); and Lesko (1977) – and Argyle himself was later to acknowledge their importance (Argyle & Cook, 1976). In general, Patterson believed, the evidence supported the intimacy model, and compensation was the rule. However, immediacy behaviours served other functions too (Patterson, 1982; Edinger & Patterson, 1983), apart from indicating intimacy, and, since their roles were sometimes in conflict, the results were inconsistent.

By 1976 Patterson was able to account for the inconsistency. Like Ellsworth, he argued that arousal was the key factor and, indeed, Ellsworth (1978) wrote that Patterson's approach was simply one version of the 'general theoretical point of view' at which she too had arrived. Patterson was concerned with interpersonal changes only, and he argued that a change in A's intimacy behaviours would sometimes arouse B and sometimes not. When arousal did occur, B would make an attribution and if it was negative he would compensate, but if it was positive he would reciprocate. If there was no arousal there would be no attribution and no change in behaviour. Most experiments, Patterson went on to say, had found evidence of compensation rather than reciprocation, but there were good reasons:

> The vast majority of subjects or subject-confederate pairs sampled in most of these experiments are strangers to one another. The settings used are often either relatively sterile laboratory rooms or places where interaction is often inappropriate such as libraries. In addition, in the laboratory setting, individuals often know or suspect that they are being observed. Finally, if a confederate is programmed for expressing different levels of intimacy, the manipulations are often relatively extreme and potentially threatening – at least between strangers. The combination of these circumstances probably makes it very easy for an aroused subject to label his experience as discomfort or anxiety and consequently show compensatory reactions. In more benign (i.e. less threatening and less reactive) settings involving acquainted individuals, reciprocity of increased intimacy may be more commonly found (Patterson, 1976, p. 242).

In subsequent papers in 1978 and 1981, Patterson raised a number of additional issues and added a number of refinements to his model (Patterson, 1978; Patterson et al., 1981). Before, he had concentrated on increases in arousal, but now he acknowledged that decreases were equally important. Moreover, like Ellsworth (1978), he too conceded that where arousal should be located in the chain from stimulus to attribution to behavioural response was uncertain. What determined whether an attribution would be positive or negative was also not yet understood, but individual differences and contextual factors, including the history of the relationship, were likely to be important.

Meanwhile, Argyle & Cook (1976) had also been refining the intimacy model. Many more signals, they acknowledged, contributed to intimacy than had been envisaged originally, and so too did social norms. Moreover, compensation could occur in more than one dimension, and an almost infinite number of combinations was possible – with the result, unfortunately, that predictions were even harder to make than before. Furthermore, the model was now explicitly about interpersonal and not intrapersonal change, and the authors allowed that the 'agreed' level of intimacy might change during the encounter. Most important of all, Argyle at last conceded that reciprocation as well as compensation could occur – though when he did not say.

So significant were the changes – particularly the introduction of reciprocation – that one wondered what remained. For some, the answer was nothing, but for Ellsworth (1978), intimacy had always been just a 'special case' of the theory which she and Patterson had proposed, and the introduction of reciprocation was to be regarded as a strength:

> By adding compensation *and* reciprocation to the general theoretical framework
> involving affective response to the gaze and other non-verbal cues, as Patterson has
> done, equilibrium theory falls out as a special case, and the research is integrated,
> not disintegrated (Ellsworth, 1978, p. 350).

To date, the work of Ellsworth and Patterson is much the most successful attempt to integrate the literature on decoding – and, what is more, their approach can readily be extended to encoding, though that is not something they have suggested themselves. The literature on encoding consisted of discrete empirical areas – attraction and approval; status and power; embarrassment, shame, and sorrow – and there were no apparent links. But now there was an explanation, and it was very simple: when we become aroused (for whatever reason), we make an attribution, and if the attribution is positive we look more, but if it is negative we look less. Encoding and decoding are *both* underpinned by attribution, and the literature at last had found a framework.

CHAPTER 3.

THE REGULATORY AND MONITORING FUNCTIONS OF GAZE: INFORMATION

In Chapter 2 we examined the expressive function of gaze, and we saw that, by looking and looking away, we are able to communicate our attitudes and emotions to one another. A vast amount of empirical research has been published, and substantial progress has been made in the last few years towards integrating the literature theoretically. At the heart of the theorizing lies emotion, as we saw – for emotion, it is claimed, is what determines our looking and eye-contact and shapes our attributions and responses.

For Kendon (1967), however, the expression of emotions was only one function of gaze, and there were two more. The first was regulation, which was concerned with how we use visual signals to help us open and close encounters and synchronize transitions from speaker to speaker; and the second was monitoring, which was concerned with how we gather feedback from one another. This time, emotion played no part, and gaze was seen instead as a means of exchanging information.

Despite Kendon's paper, emotion has dominated the literature for many years, particularly the literature on eye-contact. By tradition, of course, eye-contact is endowed with an almost mystical emotional significance and, until very recently, it was assumed to be driven by emotional forces alone, which were beyond the control of the individual and operated at the level of the pair. But then, in the late 1970s, a very different interpretation was proposed: namely that eye-contact might be a mere accident, a chance product of how much each of the two people happened to look individually. Already we knew that regulation and monitoring could be understood without recourse to emotion and now, it appeared, so too could eye-contact.

The regulatory function

Beginnings and endings of encounters

Perhaps the simplest function of the look is to seek and offer attention. Cranach (1971) argued that gaze is the first in a hierarchy of signals by which we declare that we wish to communicate and that the channel is open. First we look and turn our head towards the other person, then we turn our whole body, and only then do we speak. Averting the eyes serves the opposite function and, for sender and receiver alike, gaze and gaze aversion are important signals which are difficult to ignore. As Ellsworth (1975) put it:

> a direct gaze is a salient element in the environment. Unlike many nonverbal behaviors having a potential cue value which is rarely realized, such as foot movements, changes in pupil size, and subtle facial or postural changes, a direct gaze has a high probability of being noticed. For a behavior that involves no noise, and little movement, it has a remarkable capacity to draw attention to itself even at a distance. . . . People often use a direct gaze to attract another person's attention in situations where noise or gesticulation are inappropriate. The fact that we expect others to be responsive to our gaze is illustrated by our exasperation when dealing with people who have learned immunity to the effects of a stare, such as waiters (Ellsworth, 1975, pp. 56).

In many settings there are implicit norms for gaze, and what is appropriate and what is not are well defined. Sometimes, however, there is ambiguity, and a particularly good example is the waiting room. According to Goffman (1963), the fundamental 'rule' for gaze among strangers is 'civil inattention': first look briefly, then look away to signal that the other person is of no special concern. Should you wish to venture a conversation, proceed cautiously, and first establish whether the other person will be willing to join in: simply break the rule of civil inattention and look a second time.

Goffman's speculations were based on naturalistic observations, but they subsequently received good experimental support from Cary (1978). Pairs of unacquainted students were recruited, and one member of the pair was asked to sit in an experimental waiting room. The second was then also sent in to wait, and gaze was recorded at four points: as the door opened, as it closed, as the newcomer moved away from the door into the room, and as he finally sat down. Of the newcomers, 99% looked at the person already in the room as they opened the door, and the values were 46%, 88%, and 94% for the other three points. The corresponding values for the other person were 91%, 69%, 48%, and 61%, and eye-contact resulted for 84%, 35%, 41%, and 50% of the pairs. A verbal greeting occurred in 78% of the pairs, and both gaze and greeting were found to predict whether or not a conversation ensued. Of the thirteen pairs who did not make eye-contact as the door opened, only one spoke for any appreciable time, against twenty-three of the sixty-seven who did make eye-contact and twenty-two of the sixty-two who gave a verbal greeting. The most important effect concerned eye-contact at the time when the newcomer moved away from the door. Of the twenty-nine pairs who had made eye-contact when the door opened and who now did so again, all but four struck up some sort of conversation. For fifteen of them, it continued for the whole session.

As well as signalling attention, gaze plays an important part in greetings. The ethologist, Eibl-Eibesfeldt, for example, described what he believed was a culturally universal pattern, consisting of a series of very brief acts, which together lasted only one-third of a second or so: a look, a smile, a raising of the eye-brows, and a nod. He called the sequence 'eye-brow flash', and normally the receiver would respond in the same way (Eibl-Eibesfeldt, 1972). Detailed observations were also reported by Kendon & Ferber (1973), who filmed an outdoor birthday party. There were several regular phases as people met, and two involved eye-contact. The first occurred during the 'distant salutation', when hostess and guest first spotted each other. Next, the guest would approach, averting the gaze and preparing to shake hands or embrace, and the second mutual glance would occur in the 'close phase', as she reached her target. When guests met one another, rather than their hostess, there was greater flexibility. The pressure to make contact was less and, after the initial sighting and mutual gaze, further advances would be made only if both people indicated that that was what they wanted. The signal was often another mutual glance.

A regular pattern of gaze is also to be seen at the ends of encounters. Steer, Charles & Lake (1973), for example, found that, as couples changed tasks in the course of an experimental session, eye-contact would increase as the transition was negotiated. When one of the people was asked to leave the room, looking was more likely if the pair were friends than if they were strangers (Summerfield & Lake, 1977). Sissons (1971), in a field study conducted at a railway station, reported social class differences. An actor, dressed in 'middle-class' or 'working-class' clothes, asked passers-by the way to a well-known landmark. At the end of the encounter the people least likely to give a look, a smile, or a nod, were working-class respondents leaving the supposedly middle-class man. Status differences, however, and degree of acquaintance, had no effect in a study reported by Knapp et al. (1973). They video-tape recorded a long series of two-person interviews, monitored the final 45 seconds very closely, and reached the following conclusion:

> 'proper' leave-taking seems to consist primarily of a combination of reinforcement, professional inquiry, buffing [short words serving to change the discussion, e.g. 'ah', 'er'] and appreciation on the verbal level, and the nonverbalisms of breaking eye contact, left positioning, forward lean, and head nodding. (Knapp et al., 1973, p. 194).

Transitions from speaker to speaker

The published research on transitions from speaker to speaker is much more substantial and, as we saw in Chapter 1, it was pioneered by Kendon (1967). Kendon reported that long utterances began with the speaker looking away and ended with him looking up, and from this he concluded that gaze helps to synchronize turn-taking. There were, however, as we saw, two principal objections to what he said: his data referred only to the beginnings and endings of utterances and could not properly be extrapolated to turn-taking; and, in any case, his findings were not supported by subsequent studies. Thus, Levine &

Sutton-Smith (1973) observed that speakers often looked not just at the end of their turns but at the beginning as well, as Nielsen (1962) had also reported; Cegala, Alexander & Sokuvitz (1979) found that speakers were more not less likely to begin a turn with a look than a look away; and Beattie (1978) and Rutter *et al.* (1978), in the only studies designed especially to replicate Kendon, both concluded against him. The supposed role of gaze in turn-taking was simply not supported by the evidence.

How, then, *do* we manage to make smooth transitions from speaker to speaker? Kendon himself suggested that a variety of signals were used (Kendon, 1978) and, indeed, there is a wealth of published research. Some of the most important has been by Duncan, and useful reviews of both his and others' work are to be found in Siegman & Pope (1972), Sacks, Schegloff & Jefferson (1974), Kendon, Harris & Key (1975), Duncan & Fiske (1977), Harper, Wiens & Matarazzo (1978), Hedge, Everitt & Frith (1978), Duncan, Brunner & Fiske (1979), Goodwin (1981), Kendon (1982), and Beattie (1978, 1981, 1982).

In the first of his papers on the subject, Duncan (1972) identified three principal sets of signals for turn-taking: turn-yielding signals by the speaker; attempt-suppressing signals by the speaker; and back-channel signals by the listener. All three were sent and received in a relatively structured way, and could be said to be rule-governed. The data were based on detailed analyses of two clinical interviews, the first 19 minutes from each.

Turn-yielding signals, by which the speaker signalled that he was about to stop talking, included rising and falling changes in intonation; drawling on the final syllable or the stressed syllable of the final clause; bringing the hands to rest; 'sociocentric' verbal sequences such as 'but uh', 'or something', and 'you know'; a drop in pitch associated with a sociocentric sequence; and syntactic cues such as the completion of a grammatical clause. Turn-yielding signals were often given in combination. Attempt-suppression signals (or 'gesticulation signals' as Duncan called them in later papers), by which the speaker over-ruled attempts by the listener to interrupt, were usually gestures, typically a raised hand. Back-channel responses, or 'accompaniment signals' in Kendon's terms, denoted attention or assent by the listener, and were not attempts to intervene. Most commonly they were head-nods, or expressions such as 'mhmm', 'yes', 'that's right', and so on.

Most transitions from speaker to speaker were accomplished smoothly. Provided the listener waited until the speaker had given a turn-yielding signal, overlapping speech was usually avoided, especially if several signals had been given together. On the few occasions when overlapping speech did occur, it was generally because the listener had interrupted without an invitation, or because the speaker had offered the floor but had then continued to speak nevertheless. If, instead of a turn-yielding signal, the speaker emitted a turn-suppression signal, the listener almost always acceded. Considerable power still rested with listeners, however, for, on as many as half the occasions when they were offered the floor, they declined to take over.

In later papers the model became more complex. Duncan (1974) isolated the 'speaker continuation' signal, by which the speaker indicated that he intended to continue and the listener should not interrupt. The same year, Duncan & Niederehe (1974) presented a correspondingly more detailed analysis of the *listener's* behaviour. Once he had decided to bid for the floor, they argued, the listener would abandon simple back-channel responses and change to the 'speaker state' signal – head movements away from the speaker, audible drawing of breath, raising the hand, and overloud delivery of back-channel responses – which signalled that he intended to speak. The system was elaborated still further in Duncan & Fiske (1977), and, by 1979, Duncan had moved on to make an additional distinction, between 'organization' signals and 'strategy' signals (Duncan, Brunner & Fiske, 1979). Organisation signals, which denoted the structure of turn-taking, included all those we have discussed so far; and 'strategy' signals were cues which subjects used to reinforce organisation signals and to strengthen their effect on the partner. In the 1979 system, for the first time, gaze at last played some part, for it was one of the three strategy signals which Duncan identified. If a turn-yielding signal was accompanied by a look – or, more precisely, a turn of the head in the listener's direction – it was more likely to provoke a change of speaker than if it was emitted in isolation.

Throughout his work Duncan relied on correlational methods rather than experimental manipulation, and the number of encounters he analysed was very small. Moreover, he made no attempt to calculate the relative weights of the signals he identified, or to take account of the semantic and syntactic verbal context in which they occurred. Nevertheless, his work was a major achievement, and it made one very important point about gaze – namely that looking plays almost no part in turn-taking. Some of Duncan's signals were verbal, some were vocal, and some were nonverbal, but it was only as a strategy signal that gaze was finally introduced, in 1979. As Duncan said, in excluding gaze as a turn-taking cue:

> it failed to differentiate smooth exchanges of the speaking turn from instances of simultaneous claiming of the turn by the two participants (Duncan, 1975, p. 206).

If looking is unimportant, what, then, can we say about signals like nodding, and gestures of the hands? Are they not transmitted visually and, if they are to have the effects which Duncan claimed for them, do they not have to be seen? The answer is that indeed they do, but *seeing* and *looking* are different. Looking is gaze directed at the eyes, and seeing we might define as visual contact with the whole person, the thing we are denied when we talk over a telephone, for example. When we look, all we can do is monitor the other's eyes, and that tells us very little: only seeing can give us the information we need. Visual communication does play an important part in regulating social encounters, but SEEING not LOOKING is generally what matters.

The monitoring function

At the same time as sending signals to express our emotions and attitudes, and to help us regulate the flow of conversation, the eyes take in information, enabling us to monitor the other person's behaviour and responses, and so to correct and control our own performance (Argyle & Kendon, 1967). It was this that Kendon called the monitoring function of gaze:

> In looking at q [the listener], p [the speaker] can gather information about how he is behaving . . . we have seen how p appears to 'place' his q-gazes at those points in his discourse where he may well be expected to be looking for a response from his interlocutor, by which his subsequent behaviour may be guided. Thus, towards the ends of long utterances, q-gazes are found more often than at the beginning of such utterances . . . and it is presumably at the ends of long utterances, that p will look for guidance in q's response to him, for what to do next. Similarly, at the ends of phrases, within a long utterance, p is found to look up, and at these points he may be said to be checking to see that q is still attending. Consonant with this interpretation, that p looks at points of uncertainty in his discourse, is the finding that p looks at q when he asks him a question (Kendon, 1967, p. 53).

Since Kendon first drew attention to the monitoring function of gaze, there have been three main developments. The first attempted to devise experimental methods for separating the expressive, regulatory, and monitoring functions; the second explored the consequences of over-loading the subject with information; and the third examined more closely the particular sorts of information we monitor.

The separate functions of gaze

As we saw in Chapter 2, it is often possible – albeit in retrospect – to interpret findings which apparently support the expressive function of gaze as actually supporting the monitoring function. The clearest example, perhaps, is the case of distance, where it has sometimes been argued that people look more at a greater distance not to reinforce the affiliative aspect of the encounter, as Argyle & Dean (1965) and others had supposed, but because distance makes it harder to gain feedback (Russo, 1975; Chapman, 1975; Pennington & Rutter, 1981; Swain, Stephenson & Dewey, 1982). Furthermore, Russo (1975) and others have argued that conclusions about the functions of gaze should, in any case, never be based on single measures, such as duration, because the frequency and length of looks may serve quite different functions. What was needed, it became clear, was a systematic experimental approach, in which a wide range of measures could be taken and the various functions of gaze could be examined separately.

The first two experiments of this sort were published by Argyle and his colleagues – one in 1973, the other in 1976. The later paper, by Argyle & Graham (1976), proposed a straightforward, perhaps trivial, hypothesis: if we are given an interesting object or background to look at while we are in conversation, we will probably look at our partners less than would otherwise be the case. Subjects held a conversation about either a topic of their choice or planning a holiday in Central Europe. For some of the pairs a map of the area was provided; and for some the blinds were drawn so they could not look out of the window. To no-one's surprise, the greatest amount of looking at the partner was found when there was no distraction and the least when the map was provided and the blinds were open. Even if gaze did serve a monitoring function, it seemed, there were other more powerful influences on where people looked.

The earlier experiment, by Argyle *et al.* (1973), was more substantial but was also very difficult to interpret, despite the authors' intentions. One way to examine monitoring, it was argued, was to set up an encounter in which one subject could see his partner but the other could not. If monitoring predominates, the one who can see should look normally, because he is still able to monitor his partner; but if the main function of gaze is to send signals, he should not look, because he is invisible and looking would serve no purpose. Since some of the looking which occurs during conversations may be attributable to the regulatory function, monologues should also be examined because they do not necessitate synchronization with the partner, and any looking which occurs must be concerned with the other functions.

Pairs of subjects communicated through a one-way screen, by means of microphones and loudspeakers. One subject sat in darkness and the other sat in normal lighting, with the result that the first could see the second but could not be seen himself. A white circle drawn on the screen marked the approximate position of the invisible subject. Each pair underwent four conditions – first one subject and then the other sat on the dark side of the screen, and the distance between them was 3 feet or 6 feet – and, within each condition, first one subject and then the other gave a monologue, and then the pair held a conversation. The order of trials was balanced. The results showed that subjects who could see looked more than those who could not, whether they were speaking or listening, and the effect was especially strong for conversations. Those who could not see their partner still looked about 25% of the time, however, and there were no effects of distance.

The main finding, that subjects who could see looked more than than those who could not, was taken as evidence for the monitoring function; the lack of effect for distance was seen as evidence against affiliation and the expressive function; and the lack of difference between conversations and monologues for subjects who could not see was considered to be evidence against regulation. However, as the authors acknowledged, the results were very hard to disentangle. The setting was unusual, to say the least, and some of the looking may simply have resulted from habit: even though we cannot see the other person or we are invisible ourselves, that does not mean we can readily 'switch off' our gaze. Furthermore, there was no way of knowing whether subjects were trying to look or to see as they gazed in the direction of the other person. Nevertheless, Argyle and his colleagues remained confident, if indecisive:

We conclude that amount of gaze is a joint product of a number of approach and avoidance forces. However, the different components do not appear to add up in any simple way, and it seems likely that two or more can operate simultaneously. For example, A might look at B primarily for affiliative reasons, but he would also receive information. Or A might look up at the end of an utterance to collect immediate feedback, but this look will act as a synchronising signal to B. And A cannot look at B to collect information without sending signals about his attitude to B (Argyle *et al.*, 1973, pp. 30–1).

The remaining experiments adopted a different approach, and examined the relationship between the two people, generally comparing friends with strangers. One of the papers was by Rutter & Stephenson (1979b), and we argued as follows:

> If Looking is primarily affective, friends should Look at each other more than strangers, since liking and approval have generally been said to be associated with greater Looking (Argyle & Cook, 1976). If, on the other hand, Looking is more concerned with collecting information, friends should Look less than strangers since they are familiar with each other's responses and should need to check them less frequently (Rutter & Stephenson, 1979b, p. 203).

Since we expected the monitoring function to be the more significant, we predicted that friends would look less than strangers.

The design of the experiment has already been described in Chapter 1, where findings for the timing of looks were presented (Rutter *et al.*, 1978, Experiment 1). Twenty-four subjects were recruited, and each was asked to bring a friend of the same sex to the laboratory. Twelve pairs of friends were formed, and twelve pairs of strangers, and each held a 20-minute discussion about items taken from a sociopolitical questionnaire completed shortly before the experimental session. Only items which had revealed a difference of opinion were used, and half the pairs held a competitive discussion in which the object was to persuade the partner to one's point of view, and the remainder

Table 3.1.   Rutter & Stephenson (1979b): effects of friendship

	Friends		Strangers		
	Mean	SD	Mean	SD	F
Time spent looking (%)	62·7	24·2	78·4	9·8	5·8*
No. looks per minute	6·6	1·8	6·3	2·3	<1
Mean length looks (%)	6·3	3·8	9·8	6·3	5·6*
Time spent in eye-contact (%)	40·5	23·2	59·0	9·4	6·0*
Speech spent looking (%)	57·1	22·3	65·9	12·7	2·0
Listening spent looking (%)	66·7	26·1	87·8	6·3	9·2**
Mutual silence spent looking (%)	19·4	12·5	16·0	7·7	3·6

*$P<0·05$; **$P<0·01$.
Note. d.f. = 1,20 throughout.

held a co-operative discussion, in which the object was to find common ground in preparation for later trying to persuade a third party to the shared view.

The results are given in Table 3.1. As predicted, friends looked less than strangers, and the differences were significant for the proportions of time spent in looking and eye-contact, the mean length of looks and, especially, the proportion of listening spent looking. There were no effects of task or time, and no interactions with relationship. Looking, we concluded, did serve predominantly as a means of collecting information rather than expressing emotions and attitudes, and there were two additional pieces of supporting evidence. First, the largest difference between friends and strangers occurred for the proportion of listening spent looking, while the proportions of speech and silence spent looking failed to distinguish between the groups. Listening is the most convenient time to look for information because we are free from the preoccupation of planning what to say and avoiding distraction. Had looking been primarily affective, friends should not only have looked more than strangers, but consistently so, whether speaking, listening, or sitting in silence.

The second piece of evidence came from an analysis of speech patterning. Friends used significantly shorter but more frequent utterances than strangers, with the result that they spent significantly less time speaking than strangers, and considerably more time in silence. Because they knew each other's beliefs and attitudes before the conversation started, friends needed less time to explore them. In other words, just as they had looked less than strangers because they needed less information, so they spoke less.

Previous studies had not always reached the same conclusion. Rubin (1970), for example, found that whether a couple were in love or were strangers had no effect on the proportion of time they spent in eye-contact or the length of their looks. For those who were strongly in love, however, a greater proportion of looking resulted in eye-contact than for those whose love was weaker, a finding which argued for affiliation. Moreover. Coutts & Schneider (1976) reported a pattern of findings which was almost the reverse of our own, and argued strongly in favour of affiliation and against monitoring. In a test of the intimacy model, pairs of female friends and strangers were observed as they discussed TAT cards. There were many differences in immediacy and, in particular, friends looked more frequently than strangers and for longer each time and in total. The same was true for eye-contact.

Other findings were different again. Russo (1975), testing the intimacy model, examined children in conversations at different distances, and took just two measures, the proportion of time spent in eye-contact, and the mean length of periods of eye-contact. For the former there was no difference between the two groups, but for the latter there was: periods of eye-contact were longer for friends than strangers, though only for female pairs. Finally, Sundstrom (1978) argued that while strangers should respond to increases in intimacy with discomfort and a reduction in affiliative signals, friends should experience no discomfort and should become more affiliative, using a more direct facial regard, among other things. In the event, both groups showed signs of discomfort and became less affiliative, but friends and strangers alike adapted as time went on. No main effects of friendship were presented, but the report was not exhaustive.

On balance, the studies of friendship have produced inconsistent results, and it cannot be said that the approach has produced clear support for the monitoring function. Some of the strongest evidence had come from Rutter & Stephenson (1979b) and in two recent experiments my colleagues and I tried to replicate and extend the study. Both were concerned with the effects of distance and were outlined in Chapter 2, and the first was by Pennington & Rutter (1981). Eleven-year-old children were recruited from a community college, and fifteen pairs of friends and fifteen pairs of casual acquaintances – little more than strangers – were formed. Each pair was observed during a 3-minute discussion about the subjects' hobbies and interests and a collection of pictures they had been shown just before the experimental session. None of the measures of gaze and speech was affected by the manipulation, and there were no interactions with distance.

The second experiment was by Swain, Stephenson, & Dewey (1982). Three types of pair were recruited – married couples, opposite-sex platonic friends, and opposite-sex strangers – and each pair held a 15-minute discussion about British withdrawal from Northern Ireland. There were several effects for distance, and two for relationship: the proportions of time spent in eye-contact and looking while listening were much greater for strangers than married couples, and friends were intermediate. There were no interactions between relationship and distance, and the interpretation of Rutter & Stephenson (1979b) received good support: strangers spent longer than married couples in eye-contact and looking while listening because they were unfamiliar with each other's responses and needed feedback; and the effects of physical separation, though apparently consistent with the affiliative hypotheses of the intimacy model, were attributable to the increased difficulty which subjects experience when they try to monitor their partners at a greater distance.

Information overload

According to both Nielsen (1962) and Kendon (1967), one of the reasons we look away from time to time during social encounters is to shut out information and avoid distraction. As shown in Chapter 1, people sometimes avert their gaze as they begin a long utterance, and the explanation, said Kendon, was as follows:

> In looking away at the beginning of a long utterance, p [the speaker] is shutting out one important source of input from his interlocutor, and it may be that he is actually withdrawing his attention from him, as he concentrates on what he is going to say . . . we imply here that paying attention to one's interlocutor and planning what to say, are incompatible activities. Analyses of the relationship between sensory input and motor action in serial tasks such as tracking, and studies of selective listening to speech, support the hypothesis that the human being is to be

regarded as capable of dealing with only limited amounts of information at once, and this imposes upon him the necessity of distributing his attention among the several facets of the situation where his activity depends upon processing large amounts of information from several sources simultaneously. This is likely to be the case in social interaction. See the discussion in Broadbent (1958) and Welford (1960) (Kendon, 1967, pp. 34–5).

A similar pattern is to be observed during hesitations:

Hesitations . . . are marked by a decline in the extent to which p looks at q and, unlike the phrase boundary pause, p tends to look back at q as he begins speaking fluently again. The hesitations once over, p has worked out a phrase to express what he wants to say, and he can run it off, watching q's response to it as he does so (Kendon, 1967, p. 41)

Very few attempts have been made to examine Kendon's suggestions experimentally, but such evidence as there is generally supports what he said. The first study was by Exline & Winters (1965a). Exline, Gray & Schuette (1965) had found that subjects who were asked embarrassing questions looked less as they spoke than those asked innocuous questions, and Exline & Winters wondered whether the cognitive demands of the task might be responsible. That is, perhaps embarrassing questions placed a greater load than other sorts of question on memory and information-processing generally, and that was why people looked away. Two predictions were made: the harder the cognitive task, the less the speaker would look at the listener; and cognitively abstract people would look more than those who were cognitively concrete, regardless of the task. Subjects were asked to tell a story to a listener who stared in silence, and it was to include as many names as possible from three categories, said to be ranked in ascending order of difficulty: four-legged animals, makes of car, and European cities. Both predictions were confirmed.

The second experiment was by Allen & Guy (1977), and they examined the pattern of looking in a more descriptive way, which resembled Kendon's own approach. If we look away to avoid overload, they argued, we should do so most of all when we face the greatest uncertainty or stress – while we are processing information or making judgments, for example. When we are sure of ourselves, and the cognitive demands are lower – when we are making affirmations, or agreeing, for example – we should look away much less. Thus, as we utter 'mental process' words and 'judgemental' words we should look away, but when we utter 'affirmation' words we should not. 'Mental process' words included 'believe', 'enjoy', 'guess', 'hope', and so on; 'judgemental' words included 'all', 'any', 'bad', and 'every'; and 'affirmation' words included 'uh-huh', 'yeah', and 'yes'.

Both predictions were supported, and there was also good evidence that the more speakers said, and the more dysfluencies they produced, the more they looked away. In the authors' words:

The findings presented here provide support for Kendon's proposition that the speaker breaks eye contact to reduce stimulus load as he concentrates on what he is

84

going to say. As the speaker continues, we can identify nine elements of his task: (1) plan, compose, and emit a syllable string; (2) monitor his own speech; (3) evaluate what he hears against his intention; (4) edit and correct as he exceeds the limits of the intended effects; (5) monitor partner visually; (6) monitor partner aurally; (7) suppress environmental noise; (8) suppress internal noise; and (9) maintain somatic posture and somatic outputs. Overload appears to occur when the speaker encounters uncertainty, faulty memory, slips of the tongue, logical or grammatical contradictions, and errors in sequence (Allen & Guy, 1977, p. 94).

The final experiment was by Cegala, Alexander & Sokuvitz (1979), and they too examined the pattern of looking away during 5-minute conversations. There were three sets of findings. During filled pauses and complex sentences subjects generally looked away; during sentence fragments, conjunctions, fillers like 'you know', and at the beginnings of turns, they generally looked; and during simple sentences, sentence changes, and repetitions, looking and looking away were equally likely. Complex sentences impose the greatest demands on information-processing, and filled pauses are generally taken as an index of planning (Maclay & Osgood, 1959; Rochester, 1973; Beattie, 1981). Both were associated with gaze aversion, and Kendon's argument was supported once again. The same was true for subsequent work by Erlichman (1981) and Beattie (1981).

The information sought

In Chapter 2 we examined the expressive function of gaze, and we saw that the look serves as an emotional *signal*. By looking and looking away we communicate our emotions and attitudes, and the signal influences both the attributions our partners make and the way they respond to us. In Chapter 3 we have moved on to the regulatory and monitoring functions, and here the emphasis has been on gaze as a *channel* through which information is exchanged, information which allows us to synchronize the flow of conversation and to find out how we are being received.

The question which remains – and it is one I have raised from time to time already – is what particular sorts of information we seek when we glance at our partners. Do we look simply to find out whether they too are looking; or is the information we seek something else? Here are the views of some of the leading writers we have considered:

> In looking at q, p can gather information about how he is behaving. He can check on where q is looking, how his face looks, and on his bodily posture. He may observe, for example, whether or not the anticipatory changes that presage a 'floor take-over' have occurred. We have not, in this study, done more than compare 'looking at' with 'looking away', and we have not been able to explore what of the other person p sees, or is on the look out for, when he looks at him. The presumption has been that when p 'looks at' q, he looks at him in such a way that, were q to 'look at' him, their eyes would meet. But this is only a presumption, and it might be very informative to investigate exactly where p does look when he 'looks at' q. (Kendon, 1967, p. 53).

when A looks at B he can pick up information about him. He can see whether or not B is looking at him; he can also observe B's facial expression, posture, movements, and so on (Argyle & Kendon, 1967, p. 77).

Argyle and Kendon (1967) have put forth a model of social interaction as a serial motor skill. The social skill performer uses the verbal and nonverbal cues of others in the interaction to change and correct his performance, in much the same way as the motor skill performer uses perceptual feedback from the environment to correct his performance. In social interaction each person is continually looking for feedback from the others in order to modify his behavior. . . . While a person is speaking, most of the feedback he receives typically comes through nonverbal channels (Ellsworth & Ludwig, 1972, p. 386).

According to all three extracts, gaze is only one of the sources of information we seek, and facial expression, posture, gesture, and so on are equally important. But now we are faced again with the problem which arose in the case of the regulatory function: if looking is defined as gaze directed 'in the eye' (Argyle & Dean, 1965), in such a way that the two individuals' 'eyes would meet' if they looked simultaneously (Kendon, 1967), then most of the information we seek is simply not accessible to us until we stop looking and move our eyes to scan the rest of the body. Access to the whole person, not just the eyes, is what we require, and that is something which only SEEING and not LOOKING can give us.

Eye-contact: A chance product of individual looking?

Strongman & Champness (1968)

The recent findings on regulation and monitoring had dealt heavy blows at looking and eye-contact, and had begun to undermine their significance for social interaction. Now a third attack was mounted. One consequence of the early emphasis on gaze – or perhaps it was a cause and not an effect – was that many writers had concentrated on eye-contact and had all but ignored individual looking. Subjects were typically paired with confederates who stared continuously, with the result that eye-contact, however oddly contrived, was the only available measure to take. Argyle & Dean, indeed, had even gone so far as to base their whole intimacy model on eye-contact rather than individual looking. For poets and others, the purpose of the look had always been to search out the other's gaze, and the meeting of the eyes was something very special. The early experimentalists, it seemed, agreed.

Then, in 1968, there appeared a paper by Strongman & Champness. Imagine, they said, that the two participants were robots, and each was programmed to look and look away at random, independently of its partner. Sometimes, merely by chance, both would happen to be looking, and eye-contact would occur. If A was the duration of the first robot's looking, B the duration of the second, and T the duration of the encounter, then the duration of eye-contact would be AB/T. Could it be, they asked, that real people operate in the same way – that, in everyday encounters in which each subject is free to look and look away at will, eye-contact occurs simply because the two individuals happen, by chance, to be looking at the same time? (Strongman & Champness, 1968).

In their own experiment, Strongman & Champness observed a series of forty-five conversations. Ten subjects each interacted for 2 minutes with every other subject, and their actual and expected durations of eye-contact were compared. For every single conversation the formula underpredicted – from as little as 22% to as much as 110% – so that only some of the behaviour could be explained by chance. The excess was said to signify approach forces or affiliation and, had the formula overpredicted, avoidance forces would have been held responsible.

A little later the issue was taken up again, this time by Argyle & Ingham (1972). As we have seen already, their principal interest was distance, and they reported two experiments, the first a comparison of 2 feet and 10 feet, the second a comparison of 3 feet and 6 feet. The formula appears to have been reasonably successful in both cases. In the first experiment the ratio between observed and expected eye-contact was 88.2% at 2 feet and 96.9% at 10 feet; in the second it averaged 86%. Unfortunately, though, the authors did not apply statistical tests to examine the differences between the actual and expected values or the correlation between them, but they did show that the ratios were unaffected by distance.

The Strongman & Champness formula allows one to establish two things: the extent to which eye-contact is determined by the chance overlap of the two individuals' looks; and the extent to which approach or avoidance forces predominate in the encounter. According to Argyle & Ingham, however, the formula was too crude, for it took no account of the fact that people look more when they listen than when they speak. What was needed was a more elaborate version – but when they devised one themselves, and applied it to their own data, they found that the actual and estimated values were even closer than before.

In fact, Argyle & Ingham were mistaken in their criticism of the Strongman & Champness formula, and their revision was unnecessary. All that matters for the calculations is how much each person looks, not when the looks occur or what determines them. In any event, the conclusion still held: eye-contact was a chance product of individual looking.

The author's work

Strongman & Champness had made a substantial contribution, and the results which they and Argyle & Ingham had reported were very important. For several years, however, the implications were ignored but then, in 1977, we took up the issue ourselves (Rutter *et al.*, 1977). The paper was very brief, and it simply re-examined every one of our studies in which pairs of naive subjects had been asked to hold a conversation and their visual behaviour had been

	No. pairs	Subjects	Topic	Duration of encounter (minutes)
Stephenson, Rutter & Dore (1973)	27	Strangers	First impressions of City and University of Nottingham	5
Rutter et al. (1978) first experiment	18	Strangers	Selves and interests	20
Rutter et al. (1978) second experiment	24	12 = strangers, 12 = friends	Divisive social/political issues	20
Lazzerini & Stephenson (1975)	16	8 = strangers, 8 = friends	Weather or sex	5
Rutter (1976) first study	12	Schizophrenic × schizophrenic pairs	Choice Dilemmas Questionnaire items	5
Rutter (1976) second study	11	Chronic schizophrenic × nurse pairs	Television and shared interests	10

Figure 3.1 Rutter *et al.* (1977): outline of the experiments

monitored. There were six studies altogether, and the details are given in Figure 3.1. All six have already been described at some point in the book.

A wide variety of subjects, relationships, and tasks was represented, and the experiments had been designed originally for a wide variety of purposes. Stephenson, Rutter & Dore (1973) were interested in distance, and they examined pairs of strangers at 2 feet, 6 feet, or 10 feet, as they sat for 5 minutes discussing their first impressions of the City and University of Nottingham. The two experiments by Rutter *et al.* (1978) were designed to examine the precise timing of looks, and this time the conversations lasted 20 minutes and involved friends as well as strangers. Lazzerini & Stephenson (1975) likewise examined friendship and, in addition, some of their discussions were designed to be intimate and personal, the remainder neutral and innocuous. The two experiments by Rutter (1976) were part of an investigation into social behaviour in schizophrenic patients.

For each set of data, two calculations were made: the difference between the actual and expected durations; and the correlations between them. The results were very clear, and they are given in Table 3.2. In every case the actual and expected values were almost identical; the correlation between the two values was at least $+0.97$; and the proportion of variance explained by the formula was 95% or more. A subsequent analysis of all 108 pairs combined revealed that the formula was as likely to overpredict as underpredict. Thus, in every one of our experiments, the findings were consistent with the chance prediction: the duration of eye-contact appeared to be nothing more than a chance product of individual looking.

Despite the clarity of the results, a little caution was still necessary. For one thing we had to face the familiar problems of interpreting correlation: although chance may appear to account for the findings, some other factor which happens to mimic the chance pattern may actually be responsible; and while we assumed that the level of eye-contact was determined by individual looking, it

Table 3.2. Rutter *et al.* (1977): actual and predicted eye-contact

	Actual EC (seconds)		Predicted EC (seconds)		
	Mean	S.D.	Mean	S.D.	*r*
Stephenson, Rutter & Dore (1973)	116·3	54·5	120·7	56·8	0·99
Rutter *et al.* (1978) first experiment	216·3	82·2	215·8	81·5	0·99
Rutter *et al.* (1978) second experiment	279·8	108·6	283·0	108·0	0·97
Lazzerini & Stephenson (1975)	54·0	27·0	50·8	26·0	0·97
Rutter (1976) first study	109·5	55·0	106·5	55·7	0·98
Rutter (1976) second study	167·6	132·4	164·3	132·2	0·99

is conceivable that the opposite was really the case, although how such a mechanism would operate is difficult to imagine. Moreover, we did not know how far the findings would generalize. Though Dabbs *et al.* (1980) supported our conclusion, Strongman & Champness (1968) and Argyle & Ingham (1972) had both found that chance fitted less well than here, and Exline & Fehr (1982) were sceptical too. Rubin (1970) had reported that lovers spent a greater proportion of their looking in eye-contact than did less intimate couples, something which appeared to defy chance. All our experiments had used relatively unemotive settings and tasks, and it may be that sometimes, in more arousing encounters, for example, we do not operate independently of each other as the formula assumes, but instead actively seek eye-contact or try to avoid it. What appeared to be true for our subjects might not be true for lovers, for example, or strangers in trains.

In two of our subsequent experiments we were able to examine the issue of arousal more closely, because both were designed to compare emotive and innocuous encounters. The first was a study of schizophrenic patients (Rutter, 1977b), the second an examination of withdrawn adolescent girls (Rutter & O'Brien, 1980) and, once again, the correlations were very high. Even when subjects were embarrassed, it seemed, or were socially withdrawn, still the chance prediction was supported. Whatever the setting, the findings were the same, and neither arousal nor emotional tone was significant.

Since the publication of our 1977 paper there have been two important developments in the area. The first was by Lazzerini, Stephenson & Neave (1978), and they took up the issue of independence: is it really the case that subjects look independently of each other as the formula assumes? From the raw data collected by Lazzerini & Stephenson (1975), the authors took a random selection of values for the length of looks by the two individuals in each pair. They then ran a computer simulation which plotted the number and length of periods of eye-contact which chance would predict if the two sets of values were genuinely independent. Both number and length proved indistinguishable from the values found in the original experiment, and it was concluded that indeed subjects did behave independently, and the pair was an inappropriate unit of analysis for research on gaze.

The second development appeared in two very recent papers, one by Wagner, Clarke & Ellgring (1983), and the other by Hargreaves & Fuller (in press). The point which concerned them both was our use of correlation for, as they were able to demonstrate very clearly, the range of possible values for eye-contact was considerably restricted, given the range of values for looking, and our correlations might therefore be spuriously high. Eye-contact could not, for example, exceed the lower of the two values for looking, and our results might simply be a statistical artefact.

Consider the argument more closely, however. From the very beginning the literature on gaze had assumed that eye-contact and looking were independent of each other, that one could build theories of eye-contact which took no account of looking, and Argyle & Dean, for example, had done just that. What

Strongman & Champness had done, and then we ourselves, was to challenge that assumption and *either way*, it seemed to us, the outcome was the same. If chance was responsible, then eye-contact was dependent upon looking; and if the results were an artefact, then still the dependency remained. *Statistically* there might be a debate, but *theoretically* there was not: looking predicted eye-contact, and the one was dependent upon the other.

That was the issue as we saw it, but what mattered most was the implications, and perhaps the most serious concerned intimacy itself. Explicitly, the intimacy model was built on eye-contact, not looking, yet if eye-contact were no more than a chance event, what status could the model pretend now? Suppose, even, that the relationship between eye-contact and distance – the classic effect – were shown to be the product of chance. What then?

In 1977 our analysis had included a range of studies, but by now we had conducted three on distance itself – Stephenson, Rutter & Dore (1973), Pennington & Rutter (1981), and Swain, Stephenson & Dewey (1982). All have been described elsewhere in the book and for present purposes we simply applied the chance formula to each in turn, with the results given in Table 3.3. For each distance, in each experiment, the correlation between actual and expected eye-contact was at least $+0.96$, and over 90% of the variance was explained. The nature of the relationship between the two subjects was immaterial, and the findings held for all types of people examined. Where

Table 3.3. Supplementary studies: actual and predicted eye-contact

	Distance (feet)	Actual eye-contact (seconds)	Predicted eye-contact (seconds)	r
Stephenson, Rutter & Dore (1973)				
Strangers	2	80·9	85·5	0·99
Strangers	6	126·6	131·6	0·99
Strangers	10	141·6	144·8	0·98
Pennington & Rutter (1981)				
Friends	2	44·9	37·1	0·97
Friends	6	64·5	64·3	0·99
Friends	10	70·7	69·3	0·99
Acquaintances	2	43·7	39·3	0·96
Acquaintances	6	60·7	56·0	0·99
Acquaintances	10	68·6	65·9	0·99
Swain, Stephenson & Dewey (1982)				
Married couples	2½	140·0	156·9	0·99
Married couples	6	156·3	152·4	0·96
Friends	2½	99·7	100·0	0·98
Friends	6	239·3	248·9	0·99
Strangers	2½	170·2	168·7	0·99
Strangers	6	369·5	382·5	0·99

significant differences did occur between the expected and actual values the discrepancies were small though consistent across subjects, and the chance formula was as likely to overpredict as underpredict. All three experiments had earlier confirmed that eye-contact increased with distance, as the intimacy model predicted – but now we knew that the finding could be explained almost wholly at the level of two individuals responding independently. Intimacy, it seemed, was beside the point, and the model was misconceived.

Conclusion

As we saw in Chapter 2, most of the early research on gaze was concerned with emotion and motivation, and much of it was guided by the intimacy model of Argyle & Dean. There were two types of investigation: encoding studies, which focused on senders and how they used gaze to express their attitudes and emotions; and decoding studies, which focused on receivers and how the attributions they made, and their own behaviour, were influenced by the partner's gaze. In decoding studies the subject was often required to stare at a confederate whose gaze was programmed; in encoding studies he was typically stared at himself, with the result that eye-contact, of a sort, was the only available measure to take. Looking by individuals was assumed to be an independent measure, but it provoked relatively little interest, and eye-contact predominated.

Then came the chance formula and the finding that looking and eye-contact were not independent after all. The duration of eye-contact was simply the chance product of how long each of the two individuals looked at the other. Indeed, as early as 1976, even Argyle had noted that 'Mutual gaze is often no more than the co-occurrence of individual gaze patterns' – but, sadly, he seemed not to appreciate the significance of what he was saying (Argyle & Cook, 1976).

The debate about chance was very important, and there were many implications. The first was methodological, and concerns the use of confederates who stare. As the work of Ellsworth suggested, staring is a powerful means of influencing people, both the attributions they make and the way they behave. It is relatively uncommon in everyday life, and there is good reason to believe that it will lead laboratory subjects to display unusual patterns of looking. For that reason alone the procedure should be avoided, one might think, but now, from the chance data, there came an additional objection. If eye-contact is normally a chance event, dependent upon the free responses of two independent individuals, then programming one of them to stare continuously will interfere with the natural mechanism and allow the genuine subject complete control over eye-contact. That, we now know, is quite different from what happens normally, and the outcome is likely to be a deviant, unrepresentative pattern of findings which will tell us little if anything about everyday behaviour.

The remaining implications are theoretical, and the first concerns the intimacy model. For Argyle & Dean, intimacy was a function of the pair, of the two individuals acting together, and it was signalled by eye-contact and not individual looking. Anything which threatened the status of eye-contact as an independent measure would therefore threaten the model itself: and that, of course, is precisely what the chance findings did, for they showed that eye-contact is controlled not by the pair acting as a unit, but by the two participants acting as independent individuals. That was something which the intimacy model could simply not accommodate. The only solution appeared to be to recast it in individual terms – but to do that would be to destroy its very foundation.

The second implication concerns the supposed emotional significance of eye-contact, and the argument is very straightforward. If eye-contact is a chance event it simply cannot have emotional significance, whatever people may believe to the contrary. Certainly, I may look in order to encode positive emotions towards you, and you may decode my look as a positive sign, but that is looking not eye-contact. All that eye-contact can communicate is a simple piece of *information*: I am looking at you, you are looking at me, and we have each other's attention. *Emotion* is irrelevant. In Kendon's words:

> when one perceives that another is looking at one, one perceives that the other intends something by one, or expects something of one. In a word, one perceives that one is being taken account of by another . . . we can only be sure that we are being effective in what we do if we know that the other is taking account of it . . . it [eye-contact] will be rewarding to him [the speaker] not because through eye-contact any particular 'need' is gratified, but because through eye-contact *p* knows that he is affecting *q* in some way and that he is, thereby, making progress in whatever he is attempting to do (Kendon, 1967, pp. 59–60).

The third and final implication leads on from the second, and it concerns the nature of the information we seek. Looking is gaze directed at the eyes, yet, as shown earlier in the chapter, information from the eyes is not generally what we seek. Facial expression, gestures, posture, and so on – visual access to the whole person – are our real concerns and, for them, looking cannot help. To SEE, not to LOOK, is what we try to do – and, at last, the literature had realized.

CHAPTER 4.

SEEING AND BEING SEEN

By the early 1970s the literature was changing, as we saw in the first three chapters. Originally, interest had centred on the structure of gaze: how much did people look and make eye-contact; was there a detectable pattern; did each individual behave consistently from encounter to encounter; did people differ from one another and, if so, what was responsible? By the early 1970s structure had given way to function: why did people look and make eye-contact; was it to express their emotions and attitudes; was it to help synchronize the flow of conversation; was it to monitor the responses of the other person? At first emotion predominated but, gradually, information began to take over: emotion played no part in regulation and monitoring; and eye-contact, the cornerstone of the emotional approach, was about to be revealed as nothing more than a chance product of individual looking.

Then, in the mid-1970s, came the most important turning-point of all. If information rather than emotion was to account for looking and eye-contact, it had to be properly established that the information people seek comes from in or around the eyes. Looking is defined as gaze in the eye, in such a way that the two individuals' eyes would meet if they looked simultaneously and, if the information came from anywhere else, looking could not be the means by which it was collected. In fact, it did come from somewhere else – from gesture, posture, and so on – and it was soon clear that, to synchronize their encounters and to monitor one another, people needed access to the whole person, not just the eyes. What mattered, in other words, was SEEING not LOOKING.

Although the most important developments were to come in the 1970s, research into seeing had already begun in the 1960s. Some of the earliest work was by Moscovici and his colleagues (Moscovici, 1967), and the most important of their experiments for present purposes was one conducted by Moscovici & Plon (1966). Pairs of lycée students from Paris were asked to spend 20 minutes discussing the cinema, and there were four experimental conditions: face-to-face; back-to-back; side-by-side facing the front; and face-to-face with a screen between, so that visual communication could not take place. There were four pairs in the first two conditions, and five in the other two, and each subject was used only once.

Different channels of communication, the authors argued, require different linguistic codes, and the crucial variables were familiarity and formality. Face-to-face, subjects are able to converse spontaneously, but in an unfamiliar setting such as back-to-back, or a restricted, formal one such as side-by-side, they have to take great care in planning and organizing what they say, and their language will resemble written text, with a high ratio of nouns and connectives to verbs. In the screen condition, however, there should be no difference from face-to-face, because the removal of visual communication is not in itself sufficient to make the setting either unfamiliar or formal. Back-to-back and side-by-side, therefore, should both differ from face-to-face, but screen should not.

The predictions were confirmed. In both the back-to-back and side-by-side conditions the ratio of nouns and connectives to verbs was higher than face-to-face, but in the screen condition it was not. Just as the authors had argued, the removal of visual communication appeared to be unimportant in itself, and unfamiliarity and formality were sufficient explanations. In Moscovici's words:

> On the whole, verbal output of the back-to-back and side-by-side participants resembled written language, whereas language emitted in the face-to-face and screen discussions was generally like spoken language. The specificity of the two major kinds of linguistic behaviour, speaking and writing, results from the emitter's familiarity with the setting in which the message is produced and from the psycho-sociological connotations of that setting. . . . Purely physical factors that affect the visibility of non-linguistic stimuli are not the only important ones (Moscovici, 1967, p. 259).

and

> the grammatical differences between two channels or languages – written and spoken, for instance – *are not due to the conditions of physical stimulation*, but to the relation these channels create between sender and receiver (Moscovici, 1967, pp. 258 and 259; Moscovici's emphasis).

The only other early paper to make a significant impact was by Argyle, Lalljee & Cook (1968), and this time the focus was on linguistic style rather than content, and the way the subjects perceived the encounter. There were three experiments and, in each case, the setting was manipulated in a variety of ways so that the degree of visual communication was varied systematically. In one condition, for example, subjects wore dark glasses so that the eyes were invisible; in a second they wore a mask which obscured the face so that only the body could be seen; in a third they wore a different mask, with slits for the eyes so that the face was hidden but not the eyes; and in a fourth a screen was placed between them, obscuring the whole body so that there was no visual contact at all. Sometimes both subjects were treated in the same way, but sometimes more of one was hidden than the other, so that the arrangements were asymmetrical. Subjects were required to undergo as many as seven interactions, lasting perhaps 90 seconds each.

Conclusions proved very difficult to draw. The results differed from experiment to experiment, in ways which had not been predicted and, in any case, it is hard to know how far one can generalize from experiments which are so obviously contrived and have such transparent demand characteristics. Nevertheless, two findings did merit attention. First, reports of discomfort, and difficulty in monitoring the other person and maintaining communiction, were greatest when the setting was asymmetrical and not when the overall level of visual communication was lowest. Second, visual communication did appear to influence the style of speech – pauses were longest when only the face was visible, and interruptions were most frequent when visual communication was absent altogether – but it was difficult to discern any pattern.

Although it was not generally recognized at the time, both papers had made a significant contribution, albeit in rather different ways. Moscovici has often been dismissed by later writers because he chose unusual experimental manipulations and his results could apparently not be explained by visual communication. But that, of course, was precisely the point: the grammatical changes which he revealed were produced not by the physical conditions directly but by the effects they happened to have upon the relationship between the participants. Given one set of relationships people spoke spontaneously, but given another, their language resembled written text. By implication, if the relationship were manipulated in other ways – quite apart from physically – the result would again be changes in language. What mattered was how the manipulation affected the subjects' 'psychosociological connotations'.

The main value of the paper by Argyle, Lalljee & Cook – apart from illustrating how difficult it can be to interpret results if experimental procedures are contrived beyond reasonable limits – was that it moved away from the content of what people said to the linguistic style they used and the outcomes they reached: in this case their perceptions of the encounter. All three dimensions of social interaction – content, style, and outcome – appeared to be affected by whether or not the speakers could see one another; and Moscovici and Argyle, Lalljee & Cook between them had provided an invaluable framework for what was to follow – and, indeed, for this particular chapter. For the sake of clarity, I shall examine the three types of research separately – outcome, then content, then style – but by the end of the chapter I hope it will become clear that they can, and should, be integrated theoretically. How to integrate them will be the subject of Chapter 5.

Outcome

Outcome studies have been much the most numerous, and four main areas have been investigated experimentally: negotiation and conflict; attitude and opinion change; transmission of information and problem-solving; and person perception.

Negotiation and conflict

The first extensive research on negotiation and conflict and, indeed, on outcome generally, was by Morley & Stephenson (1969, 1970a). The setting they chose to explore was a simulated plant-level negotiation between a union representative and a management representative. The subjects were male students, and the two roles were assigned at random. Each negotiator read a detailed description of the dispute, which was based on a genuine case and, unknown to the subjects, the descriptions were so worded that one side was given a stronger case than the other – the management side in Morley & Stephenson (1969) and the union side in Morley & Stephenson (1970a). There were twenty pairs in each experiment, and they were given 30 minutes to try to reach a settlement. Half the pairs negotiated face-to-face, and half communicated over an audio-only link, in which subjects sat in separate rooms and spoke to each other over a microphone–headphone intercom without visual communication.

The results are given in Table 4.1 and, taken together, they were clear: the audio condition gave a noticeable advantage to the side with the stronger case,

Table 4.1   Morley & Stephenson (1969, 1970a): outcomes for Experiment I (1969) and Experiment II (1970a)

Outcomes of negotiations in Experiment I (in scale points)

	Face-to-face/ free	Face-to-face/ constrained	Telephone/ free	Telephone/ constrained
	4	4*	6	7
	5	5	3	6
	4	3*	6	4
	4	4	2	6
	1	6	2	6
Mean	3·6	4·4	3·8	5·8

* Denotes deadlock

Outcomes of negotiations in Experiment II (in scale points)

	Face-to-face/ free	Face-to-face/ constrained	Telephone/ free	Telephone/ constrained
	1	4	6	4
	3*	4	5	7
	4	3	5	3
	4	3	5	4*
	3*	4	5	5
Mean	3·0	3·6	5·2	4·6

* Denotes deadlock

so that there were more settlements in favour of that side in the audio condition than face-to-face, and the most common finding in the latter condition was compromise.

The likely interpretation, the authors argued, was as follows. The audio condition lacked social cues, among them those transmitted visually, and so could be characterized as 'formal'. Negotiations include both interpersonal and interparty dimensions (Douglas, 1957, 1962; Stephenson, Kniveton & Morley, 1977; Stephenson, in press), and the effect of 'formality' is to upset the normal balance, in such a way that interpersonal considerations are disregarded, relatively speaking, and interparty issues predominate. 'Formality' encourages one to behave impersonally, to disregard the subtleties of self-presentation, and to concentrate on putting one's case as thoroughly as possible and pursuing victory for one's side. As the participants focus on the issues, the relative merits of the case come to the fore and are evaluated objectively, and the stronger case simply carries itself. Face-to-face, where visual communication is free to occur and the setting is less 'formal', interpersonal considerations are less easy to ignore, the objective merits of the case are less prominent, and the most likely outcome is compromise.

In 1977, Morley & Stephenson went on to report a series of replications Morley & Stephenson (1977). In the original experiments each negotiator had been given a minimum point below which he must not settle, but the procedure was such that the two points were incompatible (so that one side necessarily 'lost' if an agreement was made), and neither side knew the other's instructions. In the first replication the procedure was modified so that half the pairs were given compatible goals and half were not and, within each condition, half the subjects were told their opponent's target and half were not. The result was that strength of case no longer had any effect, not even in the condition which most closely reproduced the original. There was, however, a confounding factor. The material for the replication was more complex and detailed than before, and subjects may not have been given sufficient time to prepare. Perhaps with more time the original findings would return.

That indeed proved to be the case. In the second replication the same material was used, but more time was allowed, and the original effect was confirmed: when subjects had incompatible goals and incomplete information about the other side's instructions, the audio condition gave a distinct advantage to the stronger case. However, now came a crucial finding, for when subjects did know their opponent's goal, the difference between face-to-face and audio was cancelled out and, in fact, almost reversed. That is, when negotiators were told the point below which their opponent was forbidden to settle, the audio condition no longer held an advantage for the stronger case, and a trend in the opposite direction emerged instead. When the original 1969 and 1970a materials were used in another of the 1977 replications, exactly the same was found again. Thus, simply by giving the participants additional information about each other's goals, Morley & Stephenson produced a significant change in outcome – but what the mechanism might be they did not speculate. By implication, something had happened to the 'interpersonal–interparty' balance.

There was just one other important replication, and that was concerned with the properties of the two media. Although the audio condition had been designed as a means of precluding visual communication, it also isolated the subjects physically, because they sat in separate rooms. Face-to-face, subjects were together in one room and they could see each other; in the audio condition they were in separate rooms and visual communication was precluded. Either factor might be responsible for the findings, and some means of disentangling them had to be found.

The solution which Morley & Sephenson chose was to introduce a third condition, closed-circuit television, in which subjects sat in separate rooms, but remained in visual contact, although not to quite the extent that the face-to-face condition permitted. The original materials and procedures were used, and the original findings for face-to-face and audio were reproduced successfully. CCTV, as the authors had hoped, was very similar to face-to-face and significantly different from audio. 'Formality', it was concluded – or, more precisely, visual communication – had indeed been the crucial factor all along, and physical presence was unimportant. If negotiators have incompatible goals, and they do not know their opponent's target, the side with objectively the stronger case will probably win if the setting is 'formal'; but if the settlement points are common knowledge, the advantage will probably disappear, and may even be reversed.

Morley & Stephenson had based their work on simulated negotiations, and subsequent studies using similar techniques were to produce very similar conclusions (Pruitt & Lewis, 1976; Stephenson & Kniveton, 1978). Other writers, however, approached the issues differently. Smith (1969), for example, set up a simulated law-suit, and the litigants were assigned to communicate either face-to-face or by written notes only. Sometimes they failed to reach a settlement at all but, when they did, it was generally face-to-face, and the solutions were more varied than in the other condition. The explanation, Smith argued, was that the face-to-face condition gives greater scope for negotiators to use their own powers of persuasion. Neither the time to reach a settlement nor satisfaction with it were affected by the experimental manipulations.

In another experiment, Wichman (1970) moved away from negotiation altogether, and instead used the Prisoners Dilemma, a mixed-motive game in which subjects may choose to adopt either a co-operative or a competitive strategy. There were four experimental conditions: no communication; vision only without sound; sound only; and face-to-face. As more cues were added, so co-operation became more common, and when the two vision conditions were combined and compared with the two no-vision conditions together, a large significant difference was revealed. Increasing the number of cues, Wichman argued, increased the feeling that the partner was capable of being influenced, and so made co-operation more worthwhile. Similar findings were also revealed by Laplante (1971) and Gardin *et al.* (1973) who likewise used the Prisoners Dilemma game. Morley & Stephenson's conclusions, it appeared, extended well beyond experimental negotiations.

The only other substantial contribution has come from Short (Short, Williams & Christie, 1976), and he, like Morley & Stephenson, examined simulated negotiations. He too suspected that a failure to reproduce the original findings might sometimes mean that subjects had been given too little time to prepare and in his first study he therefore attempted to replicate the first of Morley & Stephenson's own replications, but allowing more time (Short, 1971a). Thirty pairs took part, half face-to-face and half over an audio link, and subjects were assigned at random to the union and management roles. The union side was given the stronger case, and the original 1970a finding of Morley & Stephenson was reproduced successfully, as in their own second replication: the audio condition gave a clear advantage to the stronger case. What is more, it also produced significantly more failures to reach an agreement.

Short next turned his attention to the concept of 'strength of case' itself. For Morley & Stephenson a strong case was one in which a large number of supporting arguments was available to the negotiator, and the arguments were of good quality. Alternatively, Short argued, it might be preferable to measure whether the arguments produced a successful outcome and, on this index, there was no difference between Morley & Stephenson's cases, since victories were evenly distributed. Yet a third approach might be to say that a strong case is simply one which the negotiator himself accepts. If so, then perhaps the subjects in previous experiments who had been randomly assigned a weak case had lacked the strength of their convictions and this, rather than the objective merits of the material, was responsible for the results.

It was this last suggestion that Short went on to test in Short (1974). The subjects were civil servants, and forty-eight pairs (seventy-nine male and seventeen female subjects) were recruited to discuss departmental budget cuts. A variety of proposals were on the agenda, and the negotiation was so arranged that one member of the pair was able to argue a case which was consistent with his or her beliefs ('consonant' condition), while the other was not ('non-consonant' condition). The purpose of the manipulation was to make inter-personal factors salient, and it was predicted that the individual who was personally involved would be relatively more successful face-to-face, while the other subject would be more successful in the audio condition.

The prediction was confirmed. What is more, a condition in which subjects communicated over closed-circuit television proved to be very similar to face-to-face so that, once again, the effects could be attributed with confidence to visual communication rather than physical presence. By manipulating the interpersonal dimension, Short had produced a very different pattern of findings from the originals. Interpersonal factors had been made salient at the expense of interparty considerations; and face-to-face rather than audio was now the favourable medium to the 'stronger' side.

Having taken issue with the concept of strength of case, Short now turned to 'conflict'. This was the last experiment in the series and, although it was reported in Short (1971b), the data were collected some time after the experiment described in Short (1974) had been conducted. Conflict in negotiations is not unitary, Short argued. We may have a conflict of interests, a conflict of values, or a personal conflict, but all three have generally been subsumed under 'interpersonal' and 'interparty'. Suppose the 1974 experiment were repeated, but in such a way that the individuals' beliefs were irrelevant because both negotiators were assigned to the 'non-consonant' condition. Neither should have the 'strength of his convictions', and interpersonal factors should now be relatively unimportant. The only conflict should be a conflict of interests, and differences in outcome between face-to-face and audio should disappear. The prediction was confirmed.

To summarize, then, what we have is this. Morley & Stephenson drew attention to the fact that negotiations include both interpersonal and interparty dimensions. If the setting is made 'formal', they argued, the normal balance is disturbed, interparty considerations predominate, and the side with objectively the stronger case generally prevails. However, if the negotiators are given a little more information about each other, and are made aware of their opponents' minimum settlement target, the effect disappears.

Morley & Stephenson did not speculate why this should be, but Short's findings provided the answer. When one subject was asked to negotiate a case to which he was committed, while the other was assigned at random, the person with the 'strength of his convictions' was found to hold an advantage face-to-face; but if neither subject was committed, there was no difference between conditions. The balance between interpersonal and interparty considerations remained the crucial variable. If the setting lacks visual cues, and so can be characterized as 'formal', interparty factors will normally predominate, and the side with objectively the stronger case will prevail; but if the experimenter intervenes and changes the balance by promoting interpersonal considerations – by asking subjects to argue for their own beliefs, for example, or by giving them more information about the other person – the differences between 'formal' and 'informal' settings will be removed or even reversed. By telling subjects their opponents' minimum settlement points, Morley & Stephenson had increased the salience of interpersonal factors, just as Short had done with his own manipulations; and when the balance changes between interpersonal and interparty factors, the effects of formality change too.

Attitude and opinion change

Most of the early research on attitude and opinion change was concerned with mass communication and advertising, in which a 'sender' tried to influence a 'receiver' over one medium or another, and the sender and receiver had no opportunity to interact. In the 1970s, however, the field began to widen to include two-way communication and interpersonal influence, and some of the earliest work was once again by Short and his colleagues of the Communications Studies Group at the University of London (Short, Williams & Christie, 1976).

The first experiment was by Short (1972a). Most people, Short argued, believe that the best medium for persuasion is face-to-face. To change someone's mind, we need personal contact, the opportunity to bring our social skills to bear, and the impersonal nature of the telephone imposes too many restrictions. Opinion change should therefore be greater face-to-face than over an audio link, and CCTV might well be intermediate. Sixty subjects took part in the experiment, and they first completed a questionnaire about controversial social issues. Thirty pairs were then formed and assigned to meet face-to-face, over a loudspeaker audio link, or over CCTV, and each underwent two conditions. In the 'real disagreement' condition the subjects were genuinely divided, and they were asked simply to try to reach an agreement; while in the 'false disagreement' condition there was actually no division of opinion, but one subject was asked to play devil's advocate. The discussions lasted 15 minutes and, at the end, the agreements were recorded and the subjects were given an opportunity to report their own private opinions as well.

Against prediction, medium of communication had no effect upon the agreements in either condition. However, it did have a significant effect upon private opinions, but in the opposite direction to that predicted: there was more not less change in the audio condition than face-to-face, and CCTV was in between and significantly different from neither. The finding held for both the 'real' and the 'false' conditions, and for genuine and devil's advocate subjects alike, and opinions generally converged towards the middle. Neither side could be said to have had the stronger or weaker case – not even in the 'false' condition since the devil's advocates, no doubt, were as strongly committed as the genuine subjects to their roles – and the literature on negotiation appeared unable to explain the outcome. Short could offer no satisfactory interpretation, and he therefore went on to a series of replications.

There were four experiments altogether, and three of them used very similar procedures to the original (Short, 1972b and 1973; Young, 1974b). The fourth, however, was slightly different (Short, 1972c), in that subjects were asked to rank-order the seriousness of eight social problems, and then to try to reach an agreement on the ranking. In all four experiments the agreements and private opinions were both recorded, and the original pattern was confirmed: private opinions changed more in the audio condition than face-to-face, and CCTV was intermediate. In fact, the effect was significant for only two of the experiments (Short, 1972c and 1973) but, when all five sets of data were combined statistically, both audio and CCTV were found to have produced significantly more change than the face-to-face condition.

Two possible interpretations suggested themselves, and the first was this. Face-to-face, I believe that I can influence you by my skill, irrespective of the objective merits of my arguments. Since you, presumably, can do the same to me, I have to be wary, and so I resist and try not to change my mind. In the audio condition, however, I believe there is less scope for personal powers of persuasion, and I allow myself to relax and concentrate on the issues, with the result that I am more likely to be swayed by the merits of your case.

The second interpretation went as follows. Because the encounters were tense and embarrassing, people were more relaxed in the audio condition because it removed some of the more threatening and personal features of the confrontation. They were therefore able to concentrate better on the issues and devote more attention to the task, and it was this which accounted for the results.

Despite its attractions, the first interpretation was not supported by the data, for when subjects who had changed their opinions were compared with those who had not, only the face-to-face and CCTV conditions showed a positive association between trusting one's partner and changing one's mind. The audio condition revealed exactly the opposite and, although there was no obvious reason for the reversal, it did mean that the second interpretation was the more likely. Audio, Short argued, was more impersonal than face-to-face, and subjects were able to devote more attention to the task, and so were more likely to be influenced by the arguments – in much the way that Morley & Stephenson had suggested for negotiations. In Short's words:

> Medium can affect the likelihood of reaching agreement, the side which is more successful, the nature of the settlement reached, the evaluation of the other side and the individual opinions after the discussion. Understanding these effects is therefore important. All the results can be reconciled with the underlying hypothesis that . . . discussions over that medium [audio] are more task-oriented, less person-oriented than face-to-face discussions (Short, Williams & Christie, 1976, p. 109).

Since the work of Short and his colleagues, only two experimental studies have been published, as far as I know; one by Tysoe (in press) and the other by Rutter et al. (1984). Tysoe's study was concerned with labour relations. Twenty-four subjects were recruited, all male students, and they first completed a questionnaire designed to find out whether their views were broadly pro-union or broadly pro-management. Each subject was then assigned to the role of union negotiator or management negotiator, consistent with his beliefs and attitudes, and was asked to spend 30 minutes with another representative of his own side preparing for a negotiation. The purpose of allowing subjects to plan together was to increase commitment to their side and so to maximize interparty considerations in what was to follow. The negotiation was to be about an industrial dispute, and there were to be a number of financial issues to resolve. Once the 30 minutes were up, the subjects were separated, and were then paired randomly with a representative from the other side to spend 50 minutes negotiating an agreement on five specific issues. Each pair met either face-to-face or over an audio link.

A variety of measures were taken, and they included attitude change. At the end of the session, subjects were asked to complete the union–management questionnaire a second time, and it was found that, while the audio subjects showed no change on average, the face-to-face subjects showed a significant degree of polarization, which was defined as movement towards one or other extreme. Some moved one way and some the other, and the fact that the greatest change occurred face-to-face and not in the audio condition was quite the opposite of what Short and his colleagues had reported. There was, however, an intriguing explanation, and it came from an analysis of the negotiations themselves.

Face-to-face, it was found, the discussions were protracted and wide-ranging, while in the audio condition they kept to the specific issues, and agreement was typically reached in less than half the allotted time. When the discussions were task-specific, general attitudes were unaffected; but when they were wider-ranging, and perhaps included some of the broader issues, changes did occur. Had change been measured for the specific issues – which more closely resembled Short's approach – the pattern might well have been reversed. The apparent contradiction with Short's findings was thus, it seemed, resolved.

The second paper, by Rutter et al. (1984), brings us to an important theoretical issue. As we have seen, the early literature on outcomes was dominated by simulated industrial negotiations, and the crucial explanatory concepts proved to be 'interparty' and 'interpersonal'. But then, as interest moved away to non-industrial settings and to attitude and opinion change, 'interparty' lost its relevance, for subjects were no longer representing sides or parties but themselves. Instead, as we have just seen in the work of Short and Tysoe, 'interparty orientation' began to be replaced by the concept of 'task-orientation'. For Morley & Stephenson, however, task-orientation had been merely one *index* of interparty orientation. What we might well expect to find, therefore, is that the relationship between 'formality' and 'task-oriented/ interpersonal' will be weaker than that between 'formality' and 'interparty/ interpersonal'. Indeed, if we follow Morley & Stephenson's model strictly, there might not be a relationship at all. So far, the transition from one concept to the other had been implicit; with the paper by Rutter et al. (1984) it was brought into the open.

Ninety-six subjects took part in our experiment, forty-eight men and forty-eight women, and half were university students and the remainder were people who responded to a newspaper advertisement. Within each sample, subjects were allocated to same-sex groups of two or four, giving eight groups of each size from the student sample, and the same from the other sample. Two or three days before the experimental session, subjects had been asked to complete a questionnaire about abortion, and now the task for each group was to discuss the topic for 20 minutes, and to try to reach a consensus as to what the law in Britain should be. Half the groups held their discussion face-to-face, and half conversed from behind cloth screens which precluded visual communication. At the end of the session each subject was asked to complete the questionnaire again.

The experiment tested three main predictions, and the first, in line with

Short's finding, was that there should be more attitude change in the screen condition than face-to-face, because the subjects could not see one another. Secondly, we predicted that group size, which had not been explored before, would also influence outcome. The larger the group, the more 'formal' the setting in Morley & Stephenson's terms, because the harder it is to take account of each member as a person, and so the more attitude change there should be. We also expected an interaction with medium of communication, so that the greatest change would occur in four-person screen groups, and the least in two-person face-to-face groups. However, thirdly, we expected that the first two hypotheses would be supported only to the extent that verbal content was affected by the manipulations. If content were 'depersonalized' and 'task-oriented' – the chief explanatory concepts we chose to use – there would be a considerable degree of attitude change; if it were not, there would be very little.

Four measures of attitude change were taken: movement, which was the overall amount of change, in whatever direction; polarization, which was movement in the direction of one or other extreme; social progression, which was polarization in the direction of the extreme nearest which the subject had started; and agreement, which, unlike the other three, was a group measure, and represented the variability or lack of variability among the members of the group. All four measures were based on the individual subjects' final questionnaire responses, and group consensus – which, in any case, was often not achieved – was excluded from the analysis.

The results are given in Table 4.2. The first two hypotheses were both rejected, for there were no effects of medium or group size and only one, unpredicted, interaction between them. The third hypothesis concerned the content of the discussions, and here too there was relative stability across conditions, with little evidence that medium or group size had affected either depersonalization or task-orientation. 'Outcomes', it is true, behaved as predicted; but 'information' behaved in the opposite way, and the interactions suggested that, in both cases, much of the variance was attributable to just one cell. Given that we expected attitudes to change only if content changed, the negative findings were thus explained. Why, though, had content not changed?

Table 4.2   Rutter *et al.* (1984): outcome means

	Face-to-face		Screen		F Ratios		
	2	4	2	4	FF/S	2/4	Interaction
Movement	8·1	8·1	9·6	8·1	0·4	0·9	0·5
Polarization	0·3	0·6	0·6	0·0	1·9	0·1	6·3*
Social progression	0·7	0·8	0·7	0·8	0·6	1·7	0·0
Agreement	0·6	0·7	0·4	0·8	0·0	4·1	1·0

* P < 0·05.

There seemed to be three possible explanations, and the most likely was this. Abortion is a personal and emotive topic, and it produces a particularly interpersonal type of discussion. Even in the literature on negotiation, where the task was generally impersonal, differences between media were cancelled out if the experimenter introduced additional interpersonal considerations – and here, interpersonal considerations were salient from the outset. In other words, if the topic is already highly personal, or subjects perceive that their task is to behave in an interpersonal way, the distinction between depersonalization and task-orientation breaks down, and predictions are hard to make.

The second possibility was that the beliefs and attitudes with which this particular experiment was concerned were deep-seated and strongly held, and therefore unlikely to be influenced by a brief laboratory discussion. Indeed, it is a common criticism of attitude research in general that almost all of it centres on trivial, superficial opinions and, if more salient attitudes and values were explored instead, experimental manipulations would have little success in bringing about change.

The third possibility was that our manipulation of the experimental setting was not sufficiently strong. The previous literature had compared face-to-face and audio conditions, and so had varied both visual communication and physical presence. Here, we removed only one set of cues – just as closed-circuit television removes the other – and we could detect no effect. Thus, what matters, perhaps, is not just visual cues but the aggregate of available social cues altogether. As will be seen later, that is indeed the central issue.

Transmission of information and problem-solving

Most of the early research on the transmission of information was concerned with whether visual communication affects the ease and accuracy with which factual information is communicated. The earliest experiment was by Champness & Reid (1970) of the Communications Studies Group, and they asked people to convey the contents of a business letter face-to-face, over an audio link, or from behind an opaque screen. The time the task took, the accuracy with which it was accomplished, and the subjects' perceptions of accuracy were all measured, but no differences were detected.

Several other studies, all of them unpublished, unfortunately, have produced similar outcomes, and Short, Williams & Christie (1976) were able to suggest that differences between media are likely to occur only when social interaction is necessary. If one subject transmits, the other receives, and feedback is not required, there will probably be no differences. It is important to note, though, that the argument assumes that the information is purely verbal and could be conveyed in writing (diagrams, for example, are not needed), and that the medium reproduces speech faithfully. If the medium is noisy, or the information to be transmitted is unpredictable, lip-reading may well be needed (Sumby & Pollack, 1954) and this time visual contact will probably improve communication.

The other main area of investigation has been problem-solving, and here social interaction does take place. One of the earliest experiments was by Champness & Davies (1971). Pairs of subjects were asked to co-operate in finding a solution to an industrial problem, namely that an old but loyal worker was impeding production on a conveyor belt. The discussions took place either face-to-face or over an audio link, and 12 minutes were allotted. The nature of the solution, subjects' satisfaction with it, and the extent of agreement between them were all measured, but no differences were detected. However, measures of process did reveal effects. Face-to-face, the solutions concentrated on the individual worker, and the conversation was generally divided equally between the two subjects; while in the audio condition there was less concern with the particular employee (perhaps signifying a degree of depersonalization), and the tendency for speakers to match each other in the length of their utterances disappeared.

In two follow-up experiments, Davies (1971a, b) moved on to a closed, deductive task, in which the quality of the solution could be measured objectively and precisely. Once again, there was no difference between conditions in outcome, but there were two effects for process, namely that the face-to-face discussions were longer, and a wider range of possible solutions was aired before a choice was finally made. Whether the wider range of solutions caused or was caused by the length of the discussions it is impossible to say and, of course, there may have been no causal link at all. Nevertheless, Tysoe (in press) found similar effects, as seen already, and it is well established that telephone interviews tend to be shorter than their face-to-face counterparts (Short, Williams & Christie, 1976). In everyday life, expense and physical discomfort may be partly responsible; but under laboratory conditions such considerations are unlikely, and the findings suggest genuine differences in the process of social interaction.

The remaining studies of problem-solving have all been concerned with communication between people and computers and, unfortunately, many of the findings are available only in unpublished company reports (e.g. Woodside, Cavers & Buck, 1971). Of the published work, the most important is that of Chapanis and his colleagues (Chapanis, 1971; Chapanis et al., 1972). A variety of co-operative tasks was used and in each case the subject was given only part of the information he needed to solve the problem; the rest had to be elicited from the partner. Face-to-face, audio, and a variety of written modes of communication were explored, and the principal measure was how long it took to reach the correct solution. Face-to-face and audio, it was found, did not differ, but the written media were noticeably slower, perhaps because of the physical constraints. The strongest effect, however, was that audio subjects exchanged ten times more messages than those who communicated in handwriting, and face-to-face subjects exchanged more still. Thus, the media which were rich in cues promoted interaction, but the others were in some respects more efficient. Interpersonal factors were relatively unimportant, and social cues were of no great significance to the outcome but, once again, they did affect the process.

Person perception

Although it is widely believed that visual cues play an important part in person perception (Argyle, 1978; Harper, Wiens & Matarazzo, 1978; Cook, 1979), the experimental literature, though extensive, is far from conclusive. Two main types of study have been conducted. In the first, subjects interact, and in the second, they observe other people interacting. In both cases the partner or target is visible under some conditions and invisible under others, and the dependent measure is the impressions subjects report at the end of the session. Some of the studies have examined the evaluative quality of the impressions – whether we perceive people more or less favourably when we can see them – and the remainder have examined the accuracy of the impressions and the confidence with which they are held.

Interaction studies: evaluative quality.   Interaction studies first began to appear around 1970, and the majority were concerned with the evaluative quality of impressions. Some of the earliest made use of the Prisoners Dilemma paradigm, and the first was by Wichman (1970). As shown earlier, subjects were asked to play the game under conditions of no communication, video without sound, audio without vision, and face-to-face. The more cues available, the more the subjects co-operated with each other but, unfortunately, evaluative ratings were not collected. However, in another Prisoners Dilemma experiment, by Gardin *et al.* (1973), ratings were taken throughout, and the results were positive. Subjects sat side-by-side or opposite, and visual communication was either allowed or prohibited (by a screen). Co-operation and positive evaluation were both greater in the vision condition than the non-vision condition, but significant interactions showed that the effects occurred only when the subjects sat opposite – that is, when the potential for visual communication was strongest.

The most extensive of the Prisoners Dilemma studies was by Laplante (1971). Subjects played with an invisible partner who they believed to be a genuine subject but who was actually a programmed confederate. At three points during the game the confederate delivered a short message to the subject, either face-to-face, over closed-circuit television, by telephone, or in writing. For some of the subjects the message was friendly, while for the others it was unfriendly. All were then asked to evaluate the confederate on a series of scales which were subsequently factor-analysed, and the most important effect proved to be a significant interaction between medium and message on the factor, 'pleasant/friendly'. While the friendly message produced increasingly positive ratings from writing to face-to-face, the unfriendly message produced increasingly negative ratings, and the difference between the messages was greatest face-to-face and least in writing. A medium which is rich in cues serves, it appeared, not simply to produce positive evaluations of the partner but to intensify whatever emotion is being expressed.

Another of the early approaches was concerned with the 'observer–observed' effect. Manipulations of visual communication are sometimes asymmetrical, so that more of one subject is visible than the other. The more exposed subject often comes to regard himself as the observed and the other as the observer, and the asymmetry produces discomfort. Argyle, Lalljee & Cook (1968) conducted some of the earliest work, and Argyle & Williams (1969) went on to examine in more detail the conditions under which the perceptions arise. Interviewees, they found, generally perceive themselves as more observed than interviewers, and women feel more observed than men, as do young people talking to older people. Moreover, subjects who look relatively little feel more observed than those who look more, and the whole effect, Argyle & Williams concluded, has more to do with set than realistic impressions.

The approach was later taken up again, by Levine & Ranelli (1977), and they chose to concentrate on observers. How would observers feel, they asked, if they were made to watch someone 'losing face'? Sometimes the observers were visible to the target person and sometimes they were concealed behind a screen; and their beliefs were manipulated too so that, irrespective of whether they were actually visible, sometimes they were led to believe that they were and sometimes that they were not. The dependent variables were the degree of comfort or discomfort which the observers reported, and their perceptions of the target.

The main result was a sex difference. Men felt more comfortable when they were actually hidden than when they were not, but less comfortable when they were psychologically hidden than when they were not. Their ratings of the target followed the same pattern. For women there were no main effects, but face-to-face they felt more comfortable in the psychologically visible condition than the other, with a slight opposite tendency in the screen condition, a pattern which was repeated for their perceptions of the target.

The sex difference was not easy to explain but overall, Levine & Ranelli suggested, the most important factors were a desire to minimize the target's embarrassment and a concern not to spy. Thus, it would not always be the case that subjects would favour reciprocal visual communication in the way that Argyle and his colleagues had suggested. An important consideration was the nature of the encounter.

Apart from the work on the Prisoners Dilemma and the 'observer–observed' effect, much the most important contribution has come from the Communications Studies Group. In the first of their studies, by Reid (1970), a confederate was interviewed by a series of civil servants for a travel scholarship. The encounters took place either face-to-face or over the telephone, but no differences were found in the way the interviewee was perceived. Unfortunately, though, the findings were difficult to interpret because the same confederate was used for all the sessions, and he may have varied his behaviour systematically from condition to condition. In a follow-up study, Young (1974a) therefore examined genuine interactions between civil-service interviewers and students who had come for vocational guidance. Face-to-face, closed circuit television, and a loudspeaker audio system were compared, but again there were no clear effects. Likewise, Klemmer & Stocker (1971) of Bell Laboratories reported that impressions over the new Picturephone were very similar to those over an ordinary telephone.

Given the widespread belief in the literature that visual signals ought to make a difference to our impressions, the early results from the Communications Studies Group were disappointing. But then Williams (1975a) offered a possible explanation, namely that the precise task the subjects were given might be an important source of variance – the point which Levine & Ranelli (1977) were to take up again later, as seen already. One hundred and forty-four civil servants, mostly strangers, were recruited for Williams' experiment, and each took part in two conversations, one a free discussion about the problems of everyday life, the other a debate about how those problems should be rank-ordered in importance. Each conversation was with a different partner, and over a different medium: face-to-face, CCTV, or telephone. Afterwards, subjects completed forced-choice questionnaires to evaluate both partners and conversations, and the responses were factor-analysed.

Overall, the order of preference for both partners and conversations was found to be face-to-face, CCTV, telephone. However, only some of the comparisons attained statistical significance, and several of them were affected by the task variable. Thus, in the free discussion, partners were evaluated more positively over CCTV than the telephone; in the other encounter CCTV partners were preferred to those in both the other conditions. The evaluations of the conversations themselves produced rather more effects. In the free discussion there was a straightforward rank-ordering from face-to-face to CCTV down to telephone, while in the debate, CCTV conversations were preferred to both the others, the same pattern as for partners. Task, it began to appear, *was* a crucial variable.

According to the Communications Studies Group one of the most important properties which distinguishes between media is the extent to which they are perceived to allow psychologically close encounters. Those which do are said to have high 'Social Presence', and those which do not are low in 'Social Presence'. 'Social Presence' was the most important concept to emerge from the group's work, and it is one to which we shall return in Chapter 5. For Williams, Social Presence, together with Argyle & Dean's concept of intimacy, offered the most parsimonious interpretation of his 1975a findings. Resolving a conflict, he argued, was an intimate task, and a medium which was rich in Social Presence – such as face-to-face – might upset the subjects' equilibrium because it would increase intimacy still further. A medium less rich in Social Presence – CCTV, for example – was therefore preferred, as were the partners. In contrast the free discussion was much less intimate and, this time, greater Social Presence was preferred. What mattered most was the interaction of Social Presence with task.

Unfortunately, Williams' analysis could not account for all the findings (for example, CCTV is intermediate between face-to-face and telephone in Social Presence, but was not always intermediate in subjects' ratings), and the main problem, as he acknowledged, was that the interpretation was retrospective and the intimacy of the topic could not be defined or quantified in advance. A further study was therefore needed, and the results were published in Williams (1972) – a paper which, despite the dates, appeared after the material for Williams (1975a) had been collected. This time, only two media were examined, videophone and audio (the videophone with the picture turned off). Each subject had two conversations, one with a stranger and one with a friend, and one was held over each medium. Each subject had only one type of encounter: free discussion, debate (as in Williams, 1975a), or persuasion, in which the subjects' task was to persuade their partners to their own viewpoint, something which was assumed to be especially intimate.

Partners were evaluated as more positive and more formal in the videophone condition than the audio condition, and the former conversations were seen as more interesting and co-operative. The videophone condition was rated as the more efficient and complex. There was a little evidence for individual differences between subjects, in that the partner and conversation in the videophone condition, and indeed the medium itself, were evaluated more favourably by 'person-oriented' people than 'thing-oriented' people, but there were few effects of either friendship or type of encounter. The findings could therefore not be said to have confirmed Williams' 1975a interpretation, but a proper comparison could not be made because the 1972 experiment for some reason omitted the face-to-face medium.

The remaining experiments by the Communications Studies Group were all concerned with persuasion and opinion change. Short (1972b), in a study discussed earlier, asked subjects to try to persuade each other to their own point of view, either face-to-face, over CCTV, or over an audio link. They then evaluated each other on the scales which Williams (1975a, 1972) had used, and five factors emerged, but only the first distinguished between the conditions. Audio subjects were perceived as more trustworthy than the other two groups, and the results thus fitted Williams' earlier interpretation rather better than his own.

The importance of the task was also demonstrated by Tysoe (in press), who compared face-to-face and audio negotiations. In the audio condition, as shown earlier, the discussions were brief and very task-specific and although the media did not differ in the impressions subjects formed of each other, differences did emerge in self-evaluation, in that people saw themselves more favourably face-to-face than in the audio condition, and the process of the encounter spilled over into the subjects' self-ratings.

In two concluding experiments Williams explored the possibility that certain settings may encourage subjects to form coalitions. In the first, by Williams

(1973), three-man groups played a mixed-motive game, in which each took the role of a departmental manager, one of whom the group was to select to dismiss a member of his staff. Two of the subjects sat together face-to-face, and the third communicated with them by CCTV or telephone, and it was predicted that the two would form a coalition against the third. In the event they did not – perhaps because the demand characteristics of the experiment were so strong and transparent – and there were no differences, either, in subjects' impressions of one another. In the second study, by Williams (1975c), four-man groups were examined, and this time coalitions did form – in the CCTV and audio conditions, but not face-to-face – but there were few reliable effects for impressions.

Interaction studies: accuracy and confidence.   Very few studies of accuracy and confidence have been reported, and most of them have come from the Communications Studies Group once again. In the first, by Reid (1970), groups of three were formed, and one subject spoke while the other two listened, one of them face-to-face, the other over an audio link. The speaker was asked to spend 5 minutes describing his life at school and college, and another 5 minutes describing the furniture in his home. Each block was divided into 30-second periods, and sometimes the subject spoke the truth and sometimes he was programmed to lie. The listeners' task was to detect which he was doing when. No significant effects were found. Accuracy was scarcely greater than chance in either condition and, although face-to-face subjects reported greater confidence than audio subjects, the difference was not reliable.

Reid (1970) in his second experiment was more successful. Civil servants were monitored as they interviewed a candidate for a scholarship, and face-to-face interviewers were found to be significantly more confident than audio interviewers that their impressions were accurate. Accuracy itself was not measured, unfortunately. Moreover, as we saw earlier, Reid's method relied on role-playing, and only one confederate was used as the applicant, making interpretation very difficult.

The remaining experiments at the Communications Studies Group were all conducted by Young, and the first was an attempt to overcome Reid's methodological weaknesses. This time civil servants interviewed genuine applicants and, although differences were detected in the quality of impressions, and CCTV subjects were perceived as more 'predictable' than either face-to-face or audio subjects, there were no differences in accuracy. Unfortunately, the findings were once again very difficult to interpret, for accuracy was measured by comparing interviewers' evaluations of the subjects with the subjects' evaluations of themselves – a method which has been criticized many times because it lacks an external criterion (Cook, 1979).

Young's other studies were both concerned with metaperceptions – subjects' perceptions of their partners' perceptions. In an earlier, unpublished study, Weston & Kristen (1973) had examined group discussions, and they had compared face-to-face, an audio-visual teleconferencing network, and an audio-only teleconferencing network. Ratings of perceived understanding were taken, and subjects who were deprived of visual communication reported considerable difficulty in gauging one another's responses. Furthermore, they believed that there was much misunderstanding and little agreement on the issues under discussion – academic courses. Young (1975) was able to confirm the result for perceived misunderstanding; but when genuine accuracy was measured rather than perceived accuracy (Young, 1974b), there were no effects. Subjects interacted face-to-face or by telephone, and then rated each other and how they believed they had been rated themselves. Accuracy was generally only slightly above chance, and there was no difference between conditions in the discrepancy between genuine accuracy and perceived accuracy. Thus, just as accuracy and confidence do not have to correspond, so perceptions and metaperceptions may be quite different too.

Observation studies: evaluative quality. Observation studies of evaluative quality fall into two main groups, and the first is similar to interaction studies, except that subjects merely observe social encounters and do not take part themselves. The earliest examples were concerned with emotion (Levitt, 1964; Williams & Sundene, 1965; Byrne & Clore, 1966), and, by the 1970s much of the literature had come to concentrate on warmth and empathy, and several studies of psychotherapy had appeared. In the first, by Dilley, Lee & Verrill (1971), therapists met their clients face-to-face, through a 'confessional' screen, or over a telephone. From audio tapes, experienced counsellors then rated the therapists for empathy, but no differences between conditions were found.

In a second study, by English & Jelenevsky (1971), the counselling sessions themselves took place face-to-face, and now it was the observers who underwent different experimental conditions – sound, vision or sound and vision. Again the dependent variable was ratings of empathy, and while the absolute values were not reported, inter-rater agreement was found to be almost constant across conditions, ranging from 63% for face-to-face to 68% for audio.

In one other study, by Strahan & Zytowski (1976), undergraduates were asked to rate just one target, namely Carl Rogers. The material came from the last 5 minutes of one of Rogers' films, and subjects made their evaluations under one of five conditions: transcript only; filtered soundtrack so that vocal cues were audible but verbal content and vision were absent; unfiltered soundtrack; film without sound; and film with sound. For women, verbal content and not visual signals proved to be especially important in producing a favourable impression, and subjects who simply read the transcript often made the most positive judgements. For men there was no clear pattern.

In the only other major study, Berman, Shulman & Marwit (1976) again took warmth as their independent variable, but this time not in a therapeutic setting. Instead, actors were asked to portray warm or cold experimenters, and observers made judgements from sound, vision, or sound-and-vision. In contrast to the findings of English & Jelenevsky, sound-only produced more disagreements between observers than the other conditions. Moreover, significant interactions were revealed between actor and medium, suggesting that some actors conveyed emotion through sound predominantly, while others relied more on vision.

The second main group of observation studies adopted a quite different approach, and tried to assess the relative importance of visual and verbal information by combining them in various ways, so that sometimes they were consistent and sometimes they conflicted. The earliest studies were by Mehrabian and his colleagues (Mehrabian, 1971). Mehrabian & Ferris (1967), for example, recorded speakers uttering a single, neutral word ('maybe') in three tones of voice – positive, neutral, and negative. Facial expression was varied in the same way – positive, neutral, and negative – and each subject was asked to decode all nine messages. Facial expression was found to account for about 40% of the variance while vocal cues accounted for under 20% – even though vocal cues are themselves more important than verbal content, according to Mehrabian & Wiener (1967).

The earliest British study of this sort was by Argyle et al. (1970), and they examined the way in which we form impressions of people's attitudes towards us. Three verbal messages were prepared – one to make the source appear superior to the receiver, one equal, and one inferior – and each was delivered on video-tape in three different nonverbal manners: superior, equal, and inferior. 'Nonverbal' here included anything which was not part of verbal content, and nonverbal cues were found to carry much more weight than verbal content – so much so that, when the two conflicted (as happened when a superior verbal message was delivered in an inferior manner, for example), the observers were overwhelmed by the nonverbal information and all but ignored the verbal content. 'Hostility–friendship' revealed a similar pattern of findings (Argyle et al., (1971).

By the mid-1970s many similar studies had been reported – among them, Bugental, Kaswan & Love (1970); Domangue (1978); Hagiwara (1975), and Walker (1977) – and useful reviews are to be found in de Paulo et al. (1978) and especially Furnham, Trevethan & Gaskell (1981). The majority had reached the same conclusion as Mehrabian and Argyle but, more recently, a number of criticisms have been levelled at the approach, and rather different findings have begun to emerge. Friedman (1978), for example, argued that previous studies had wrongly assumed that communicated meaning is unidimensional, and he went on to demonstrate that whether or not nonverbal cues carry more weight than words depends upon the particular response the observers are asked to make – that is, their particular task.

High-school students were presented with photographs of teachers who were said to be addressing a student. The teacher's facial expression signified happiness, surprise, anger, or sadness, and below the photograph were typed the words the teacher was said to be speaking. The words denoted a positive or negative attitude, coupled with dominance or submission. All subjects saw all combinations and were asked to make two responses in each case: how positive was the teacher towards the student, and what course grade would he or she probably award. Nonverbal cues had a greater impact than words for the first question, but the reverse was the case for the second. Furthermore, there were large individual differences, and Friedman was led to conclude as follows:

> the present demonstration suggests what should be obvious: words do matter. . . .
> The prepotency of nonverbal cues is a myth. Even worse, the issue is a red herring.
> It will likely prove more profitable to ask not which cues matter more, but rather
> 'Which mean what, and when?' (Friedman, 1978, p. 149).

The same year, 1978, saw the publication of an extensive piece of work by de Paulo *et al.* They wondered whether, although visual cues may carry more weight than verbal cues overall, the effect may weaken as the discrepancy increases. The greater the discrepancy, the more the message is likely to be perceived as an attempt at deception and so, perhaps, the more likely it is that the observer will attend to the words. The prediction was supported, and it was also found that visual information had a greater influence on women than men, was more significant for discrepancies involving the face than discrepancies involving the body, and was more important for some emotions than others (de Paulo *et al.*, 1978). One especially attractive feature of the work was that video-tape recordings were used, rather than photographs.

The most recent paper of all was by Furnham, Trevethan & Gaskell (1981) and, in an excellent review of the paradigm, they pointed to two principal weaknesses. First, the stimulus material was often contrived so that verbal and nonverbal components were made to convey equal weights when received individually – something which may well be uncommon in everyday life. Second, potentially important distinctions between different nonverbal cues, vocal versus visual in particular, had often been disregarded, and experimenters had confined themselves to crude comparisons between verbal and nonverbal. Moreover, the presentations were typically brief and unrealistic, and the response measures too were questionable. Repeated measures had frequently been used, for example – possibly leading subjects to form accurate hypotheses about the experiment, as well as to lose motivation and concentration – and rating scales had often been constructed in an arbitrary way. To generalize from study to study was most hazardous.

In Furnham *et al.*'s own experiment, 5-minute video-tape recordings were made of two laboratory interviews, and each was then shown to observers under one of four conditions: verbal (script only); vocal (soundtrack only); visual (picture only); and sound-and-vision. The interviewee behaved consistently from condition to condition, but the interviewer changed: in one recording he behaved positively towards the interviewee, both verbally and nonverbally, and in the other he behaved negatively. There was thus no discrepancy between verbal and nonverbal information; and, as in previous studies – which Furnham *et al.* had criticized – pilot work ensured that the verbal and nonverbal components carried equal weight when received alone.

Despite a variety of analyses no clear pattern was detected, either for interview condition or for mode of observation, and the authors concluded that psychologists had simply been asking the wrong question.

> It is not a case of whether verbal or non-verbal channels carry more information relative to each other, because they act differently in different situations depending on the nature of the message, the people communicating and the situational constraints of the social episode in which the communication occurs. . . . It may well be that verbal, vocal, and visual cues operate quite differently in different situations and are integrated in different ways depending on the nature of the interaction, wider aspects of the situation, the personal characteristics of the people being perceived and finally the personalities of the perceivers. It is completely misleading to maintain that non-verbal cues are more important than verbal cues in impression formation and attraction across all persons and all situations (Furnham *et al.*, 1981, pp. 14 and 15).

Observation studies: accuracy and confidence. Very few observation studies of accuracy and confidence have been published, and the majority of those which have are difficult to interpret because of methodological weaknesses. Giedt (1955) and Cline, Atzet & Holmes (1972), for example, were interested in perceptions of personality and took 'experts' ratings' as their criterion against which to assess subjects' accuracy. Both papers argued that verbal signals were the most important – but, needless to say, the opinion of experts may not always be a valid criterion; nor, indeed, is it easy to imagine one which would be. Much the same problem has arisen in judgements of emotion (Burns & Beier, 1973).

Of the remaining early experiments, only one produced unambiguous results, and that was by Maier & Thurber (1968). Students were asked to role-play lying or telling the truth, and observers were asked to judge which was which, by reading the transcripts, listening to audio recordings of the proceedings, or watching and listening to the sessions 'live'. Unexpectedly, accuracy was found to be significantly lower for the 'live' condition than either of the others, but confidence was slightly higher. Thus, even if visual signals do not in fact promote accuracy, people may still believe that they do, just as we saw for interaction studies (Reid, 1970, Young, 1975).

The two remaining studies were both published in response to the Mehrabian/ Argyle paradigm, in which discrepant verbal and nonverbal messages were paired. One was by Furnham, Trevethan & Gaskell (1981) and, as well as the quality of impressions discussed already, it examined the confidence with which they were held. One or two scales revealed significant differences between media, but when confidence was measured over all the scales combined there were no significant effects.

The other study was by Archer & Akert (1977). Like Furnham and his colleagues (1981), Archer & Akert were critical of the Mehrabian/Argyle paradigm: adequate context was seldom included; the presentations relied on posed discrepancies which are comparatively rare in everyday life; subjects were almost always asked to make judgements about emotion, and other possible measures were ignored. One such measure was accuracy, and it was this which Archer & Akert set out to explore, using a simple and effective technique. Twenty real, everyday scenes were video-tape recorded and, after each one, subjects were asked a straightforward question to which there was an unambiguous right answer. One episode, for example, showed two women playing with a baby, and the question was which was the mother; another showed two men discussing a game of basketball they had just completed, and subjects were asked which had won; another showed a young woman on the telephone, and the question was whether the person at the other end was male or female. Half the subjects simply read the verbatim transcript of the encounter, and the other half were presented with the full video-tape recording in sound and vision.

The findings were very clear: subjects in the sound-and-vision condition were significantly more accurate than those in the transcript condition; and, while the former performed significantly better than chance, the latter were significantly worse than chance. The authors concluded as follows.

> Words alone are not sufficient for accurate interpretations. . . . In fact, the current study provides no indication that verbal transcripts of interactions provide any independent contribution to accurate interpretation (Archer & Akert, 1977, p. 449).

A study of interaction and observation: Kemp et al. (in press). As has been shown, neither interaction studies nor observation studies have produced conclusive evidence, and there are, perhaps two main reasons – one theoretical, the other methodological. The theoretical reason is the importance of task, and one of our own current aims is to explore the variable more thoroughly (Clark & Rutter, 1983; Elwell, Brown & Rutter, 1983). The methodological reason is simply that many of the experiments were conducted very poorly. Several weaknesses have been touched upon already – short presentations of posed, unfamiliar stimulus material; repeated measures, from small samples of subjects; limited, insensitive dependent variables – but there remain two over-riding deficiencies which we have not yet discussed. The first is that participants and observers have never been compared directly in one experimental design, with the result that we still cannot say confidently whether visual information affects the two groups similarly or differently; and the second is that almost every experiment has restricted itself to only one or two dependent measures, and none has yet examined quality, accuracy, and confidence together. Both are major weaknesses and, to try to overcome them, we set up an experiment of our own. Participants and observers were combined in one design, and measures of quality, accuracy, and confidence were taken from every subject.

The experiment was published by Kemp *et al.* (in press), and it was conducted in two parts. In the first, subjects were recruited by means of a newspaper advertisement. Twenty-four respondents were selected at random, and they first completed two questionnaires: one autobiographical, the other about their sociopolitical opinions. Twelve single-sex pairs were then formed, and each held a 10-minute discussion based on differences of opinion revealed by the second questionnaire. Half the pairs met face-to-face, the remainder over a loudspeaker audio link, and all the sessions were recorded on video-tape in split screen and sound. Immediately after the discussion, subjects completed five more questionnaires: ratings of their own behaviour during the session; the biographical and sociopolitical questionnaires as they believed their partner would have answered them; their partner's behaviour during the discussion; and their partner's personality. For every item on all five questionnaires they also recorded their level of confidence in making the judgement.

The recordings from the first part of the experiment now became the stimulus material for the second. This time the subjects were seventy-two students recruited by word-of-mouth. Each was assigned to one of three conditions – sound-and-vision, vision only, and sound only – and was asked to observe one discussion. Half were assigned a face-to-face encounter, the remainder an audio encounter, and each recording was used three times during the experiment. In the sound-and-vision condition the tapes were played normally through a television monitor; in vision only, the sound was turned off; and, in sound only, the picture was turned off. Observers sat in pairs, and one was responsible for monitoring the speaker on the left of the screen, the other the speaker on the right. As soon as the playback had finished the observers were asked to complete the questionnaires the participants themselves had answered: the biographical and sociopolitical questionnaires as they believed their speaker would have answered them; and ratings of behaviour and personality. Once again, confidence scales were included for every item.

	Participants[1]	Observers[2]		
		Sound and Vision	Vision only	Sound only
Face-to face conversations (6 pairs)	Pair 1	Pair 7	Pair 13	Pair 19
	2	8	14	20
	3	9	15	21
	4	10	16	22
	5	11	17	23
	6	12	18	24
Audio conversations (6 pairs)	Pair 25	Pair 31	Pair 37	Pair 43
	26	32	38	44
	27	33	39	45
	28	34	40	46
	29	35	41	47
	30	36	42	48

[1] Participants: $n = 24$
[2] Observers: n = 72

Figure 4.1   Kemp *et al.* (in press): experimental design

The experiment was designed to examine three sources of variance and their interactions – participants versus observers; observation condition; and medium of conversation – and three sets of predictions were made: (a) participants will form qualitatively different impressions from observers, and the impressions will be more accurate and more confidently held; (b) for observers, impressions will be qualitatively different, more accurate, and more confidently held in sound-and-vision than vision only and sound only; and (c) impressions formed of face-to-face participants will be qualitatively different from those formed of audio participants, as well as more accurate and more confidently held. The first prediction was tested by comparing face-to-face and audio participants with sound-and-vision and sound only observers of face-to-face and audio participants, and the design formed a two-by-two analysis, with face-to-face/audio and participants/observers the two independent variables. The second prediction was tested by examining observers alone, in a two-by-three analysis, with face-to-face/audio the first factor and sound-and-vision/vision only/sound only the second. The third prediction was tested by examining the effects of face-to-face/audio in both the previous analyses.

The results are given in Tables 4.3 and 4.4. Table 4.3 presents the main effects and interactions for participants against observers, and Table 4.4 presents the findings for observers alone. The evaluative quality of impressions was assessed from the sociopolitical beliefs which subjects attributed to targets and the behavioural and personality impressions they formed, and the means in the tables are based on summary scores from factor-analyses of the raw data. Accuracy was assessed by taking the discrepancies between targets' and subjects' responses to the biographical and sociopolitical questionnaires, and then averaging across items. Confidence was assessed by examining the subjects' confidence ratings on all four types of impression and then, once again, averaging across items.

Overall, as the tables make very clear, there was little evidence that either medium of communication or mode of observation had any important effects on our measures. All three predictions received occasional support from one or other of the dependent variables, but the effects were generally weak and there was no consistent pattern. What mattered more than anything was again the subjects' task, and often the most salient information was what the target said. Sometimes visual signals affect impressions, it seems, but typically they do not, and the factor which decides is task.

Content

As shown at the start of the chapter, some of the earliest systematic research on outcome was conducted by Morley & Stephenson (1969, 1970a, b). They were interested in the role of visual communication in negotiations, and they found that when visual cues were absent the side with objectively the stronger case held a distinct advantage over the weaker side; face-to-face, the advantage

Main effects	P	O	df	F	Interaction effects	P	O	df	F
Quality					*Quality*				
(a) Sociopolitical	Factor 1, 2.	No significant effects			(a) Sociopolitical	Factor 1, 2.	No significant effects		
(b) Behaviour	Factor 1, 2, 3.	No significant effects			(b) Behaviour	Factor 1, 2, 3.	No significant effects		
(c) Personality	Factor 1, 2, 3.	No significant effects			(c) Personality	Factor 2			
					FF	0·05	0·88	1, 10	6·5*
					A	0·45	−0·84		
Accuracy					*Accuracy*				
(a) Biographical	Item scores	No significant effects			(a) Biographical	Item scores	No significant effects		
(b) Sociopolitical	Item scores	No significant effects			(b) Sociopolitical	Item scores	No significant effects		
	Overall score	No significant effects				Overall score	No significant effects		
Confidence					*Confidence*				
(a) Biographical	Item scores	No significant effects			(a) Biographical	Music			
	Overall score	No significant effects			FF	52·1	37·5	1, 10	6·6*
					A	29·1	47·9		
						Overall score	No significant effects		
(b) Sociopolitical	Item scores	No significant effects			(b) Sociopolitical	Television			
	Overall score	No significant effects			FF	54·1	50·0	1, 10	5·0*
					A	50·0	60·4		
						Overall score	No significant effects		
(c) Behaviour	Item scores:				(c) Behaviour	Item scores	No significant effects		
	talkative	81·2	73·9	1, 10	6·0*		Overall score	No significant effects		
	active	78·1	59·3	1, 10	8·3*					
	direct	80·2	64·5	1, 10	8·5*					
	uninfluential	76·0	62·5	1, 10	7·8*					
	cheerful	79·2	64·5	1, 10	5·4*					
	Overall score	77·1	66·2	1, 10	13·0**					
(d) Personality	Item scores	No significant effects			(d) Personality	Dominant-submissive			
	Overall score	No significant effects			FF	60·4	64·6	1, 10	10·9**
					A	52·1	66·7		
						Overall score	No significant effects		

* $P < 0·05$; ** $P < 0·01$.

Note: Participants (P); observers (O); face-to-face (FF); audio (A).

Table 4.4 Kemp *et al.* (in press): quality, accuracy and confidence for mode of observation

Main effects

		SV	V	S	df	F
Quality						
(a) Sociopolitical	Factor 1, 2	No significant effects				
(b) Behaviour	Factor 1, 2, 3	No significant effects				
(c) Personality	Factor 2	0·93	0·70	−2·12	2, 20	3·6*
Accuracy						
(a) Biographical	Item scores	No significant effects				
(b) Sociopolitical	Item scores	No significant effects				
	Overall score	1·09	1·21	1·05	2, 20	3·7*
Confidence						
(a) Biographical	Smoking	50·0	64·6	39·6	2, 20	5·9**
	Drinking	51·0	65·6	53·1	2, 20	3·8*
(b) Sociopolitical	Overall	No significant effects				
	Item score	No significant effects				
	Overall score	No significant effects				
(c) Behaviour	Uninfluential	62·5	53·1	71·9	2, 20	5·0*
	Overall score	No significant effects				
(d) Personality	Item score	No significant effects				
	Overall score	No significant effects				

Interaction effects

		SV	V	S	df	F
Quality						
(a) Sociopolitical	Factor 1, 2	No significant effects				
(b) Behaviour	Factor 1, 2, 3	No significant effects				
(c) Personality	Factor 1, 2, 3	No significant effects				
Accuracy						
(a) Biographical	Item scores	No significant effects				
(b) Sociopolitical	Pornography					
	FF	1·09	0·67	0·75	2, 20	4·9*
	A	0·58	1·25	1·08		
	Overall score	No significant effects				
Confidence						
(a) Biographical	Drinking					
	FF	45·8	75·0	50·0	2, 20	3·8*
	A	56·2	56·2	56·2		
	Overall	No significant effects				
(b) Sociopolitical	Bloodsports					
	FF	50·0	67·7	60·4	2, 20	4·6*
	A	67·7	50·0	56·2		
	Church					
	FF	33·3	62·5	47·9	2, 20	4·3*
	A	62·5	52·1	56·2		
	Overall					
	FF	49·4	58·3	57·4	2, 20	3·6*
	A	63·7	51·2	61·3		
(c) Behaviour	Item scores	No significant effects				
	Overall score	No significant effects				
(d) Personality	Anxious					
	FF	66·1	75·0	58·4	2, 20	5·1*
	A	70·8	54·1	60·4		
	Overall score	No significant effects				

$* P < 0.05;\ ** P < 0.01$

Note: Sound and vision observers (SV); vision only (V); sound only (S); face-to-face (FF); audio (A).

disappeared. The likely interpretation, they argued, was that the removal of visual information disturbed the normal balance between interpersonal and interparty dimensions, and the latter predominated. Without the distraction of personal considerations, negotiators were free to concentrate on the issues and arguments, and the objective merits of the case prevailed.

Although the interpretation was most attractive it nevertheless lacked any direct evidence that audio negotiations really were task-oriented and depersonalized. For that, a content analysis of what the participants said would be necessary, but Morley & Stephenson had restricted themselves to outcome. In 1976, however, the gap was bridged, by a paper from Stephenson, Ayling & Rutter. Randomly selected students were asked to complete a questionnaire about union–management relations, and twelve male and twelve female pairs were formed, one member broadly pro-union, the other pro-management. Each pair held a 15-minute discussion, either face-to-face or over an audio link, and the task was to discuss one or two of the items which had revealed a disagreement. The disagreements were always in line with the subjects' overall persuasions, and it was made clear that the encounters were to be discussions and not negotiations. All the sessions were tape-recorded, and transcribed and typed verbatim, and then they were analysed by a new coding system, called Conference Process Analysis (CPA).

CPA was devised by Morley & Stephenson (1977), and Stephenson, Ayling & Rutter (1976) were the first to use it. The system is rooted in exchange theory and, although it was first intended only for 'industrial' material, it has since been adapted for many other types of setting also. First, the transcript is divided into 'acts', each act conveying one point, and every act is then coded on three dimensions: Mode; Resource; and Referent. The Mode dimension indicates whether participants are *offering, accepting, seeking* or *rejecting* a resource. The Resource dimension allocates to each act one of five categories: *outcome* (settlement point), *procedure* (way of conducting the interaction), *praise, blame* or *information*. The Referent dimension indicates whether any person or party directly involved in the encounter is mentioned in the act: *self, opponent, own party, opponent's party, both persons,* or *both parties*. Individual categories from any one dimension may be inspected in isolation, or interactions among them may be examined in combination. Figure 4.2 reproduces the system in detail, and Figure 4.3 gives coded examples from the present experiment.

Two sets of specific predictions were made: the first that audio discussions would be depersonalized in comparison with face-to-face discussions; the second that they would be more task-oriented. Depersonalization, it was expected, would result in, at least, increased blame and decreased praise for opponent, fewer self-references, more party references, and increased disagreement; while task-orientation would result in greater discussion of information and outcomes. In the event, both predictions received a degree of support, but the results were not dramatic (Table 4.5). Two of the five indices of depersonalization revealed significant differences between face-to-face and

Mode	Resource		Referent
1 Offer	*Structuring Activity*	0	No Referent
2 Accept	1 Procedure	1	Self
3 Reject	*Outcome Activity*	2	Person
4 Seek	2 Settlement point (a) initial (b) new	3	Other
	3 Limits	4	Party
	4 Positive consequences	5	Opponent
	of proposed outcomes	6	Both persons
	5 Negative consequences	7	Both parties
	of proposed outcomes		
	6 Other statements		
	about outcomes		
	Acknowledgement		
	7 Acknowledgement + (a) own and both sides, (b) other side		
	8 Acknowledgement − (a) own and both sides, (b) other side		
	Other information		
	9 Information		

Figure 4.2   Stephenson, Ayling & Rutter (1976): CPA categories

audio, and the remaining three showed trends in the expected direction. While task-relevant information did not discriminate between the conditions, discussion of outcomes did.

Several other findings also emerged, and the most important was that medium of communication interacted with union–management status. Each time a significant interaction was revealed, the 'union' subjects were more task-oriented in the audio condition than face-to-face, while the 'management' subjects tended in the opposite direction. At the time the experiment was conducted, the climate of industrial relations in Britain was such that unions were widely believed to be stronger than managements. Not unnaturally, therefore, most of the experimental sessions concentrated on union affairs and,

Speaker	Act
Union	'I've always been a keen trade unionist' (offers information about self)
Management	'I think the unions should have a 40–60 say in running a firm' (offers outcome for opponent's party)
Management	'I think on the whole union officials are honest men' (offers praise for opponent's party)
Management	'Union members don't listen to their leaders any more' (offers criticism of opponent's party)
Union	'I would agree that you're doing your best' (accepts information about opponent)
Union	'I don't think that's true' (rejects information)
Union	'Shall we discuss this one first?' (seeks procedure for both persons)
Union	'Is he in a power union?' (seeks information about own party)

Figure 4.3   Stephenson, Ayling & Rutter (1976): CPA coded examples

Table 4.5   Stephenson, Ayling & Rutter (1976): depersonalization and task-
orientation

	Means	
	Face-to-face	Telephone
(a) Depersonalization		
Blame for opponent	2·00	2·17
Praise for opponent	0·92	0·25*
'Self' references	7·58	7·25
'Party' references	7·67	11·17*
'Rejects' (disagreement)	0·67	1·08
(b) Task orientation		
Outcome	1·75	1·25
Offers of information	48·56	55·53*
'Union' offers of information about		
opponent's party	1·60	3·10*

F value for Face-to-face versus Telephone with df = 1,20* $P<0.·05$

since 'union' subjects came armed with the 'stronger' case, their behaviour in the audio condition was exactly what Morley & Stephenson would have predicted – concentration on interparty issues and disregard for interpersonal considerations.

A year later, Morley & Stephenson went on to conduct an analysis of their own data, applying CPA to their 1970a material (Morley & Stephenson, 1977). Students, it will be recalled, had role-played union–management negotiations, and the union side had been given the stronger case and had done particularly well in the audio condition. The outcome findings had thus been very impressive, but the content analysis proved to be disappointing, for only one significant effect was revealed, and even the non-significant trends were not all in the predicted direction. There was, however, a straightforward explanation, and it is one which may well apply more generally throughout the area – a ceiling effect had operated. In Morley & Stephenson's words:

Apparently, C.P.A. can detect differences in behaviour of the predicted sort [Stephenson, Ayling & Rutter, 1976], and the failure to find face-to-face/audio differences [in Morley & Stephenson, 1970a] cannot be attributed to the inadequacy of the category system *per se*. Rather, we are inclined to suggest that differences between the two situations were due to the differences in the tasks used. We used a formal negotiation task . . . whereas Stephenson, Ayling & Rutter did not. Furthermore, the latter authors gave subjects greater freedom to control the content of the 'agenda' than did the former. The implication is that in Morley & Stephenson (1970a) the task was so highly structured that the expected behavioural differences could not emerge (Morley & Stephenson, 1977, pp. 223–4).

Despite the ceiling effect, Morley & Stephenson did succeed in finding one important difference between face-to-face and audio discussions. In their subsidiary results, Stephenson, Ayling & Rutter (1976) had reported that the two conditions differed in 'responsiveness'. In the audio condition one subject would generally take the lead, and the other would make the responses, so that a strong negative correlation in 'responsiveness' emerged between them. In the face-to-face condition the correlation was still negative, but this time it was weak and non-significant. In other words the audio condition encouraged a clear differentiation of roles – with an obvious leader and an obvious follower – but the face-to-face condition did not. This being so, argued Morley & Stephenson (1977), the two speakers should also be more 'identifiable' in the audio condition. That is, if randomly selected passages from the transcripts were given to 'blind' observers, it ought to be easy for them to tell who was the 'union' subject and who was the 'management' subject in the audio condition, but hard for them to tell in the face-to-face condition. The prediction was confirmed, for material from both Morley & Stephenson (1970a) and Stephenson, Ayling & Rutter (1976). Thus, even when the removal of visual communication failed to affect content directly – or, perhaps more accurately, when the effects were too small to be detected – there were nevertheless clear effects upon role differentiation. Similar conclusions were later reached by Strickland et al. (1978).

In contrast to Morley & Stephenson, Tysoe (in press) was able to find strong differences between face-to-face and audio encounters. She too examined simulated union–management negotiations, but this time subjects argued in line with their own views and were not assigned to their roles at random. The sessions were analysed by CPA as before and although there was no evidence of depersonalization in the absence of visual communication, the audio encounters were noticeably more task-oriented than the face-to-face encounters, with much greater emphasis on specific outcomes. What is more, Tysoe went on to demonstrate that content and outcome were related – an important point which I have raised before and to which I shall return at length in Chapter 5. Face-to-face, the discussions were wide-ranging while in the audio condition they kept to the specifics of the immediate task, negotiating a settlement to the dispute. In consequence, the sessions were generally shorter in the audio condition than face-to-face. Moreover, audio subjects were less likely than face-to-face subjects to change their attitudes to union–management issues generally (because they had not discussed them), but more likely to leave the experiment with a low opinion of themselves (because the discussions had been short and task-specific, and there had been little opportunity to make a full contribution).

Apart from the research on industrial material using CPA, only two other studies of content have been published, as far as I know. The first was by Vitz & Kite (1970), and made use of an experimental game. Subjects were assigned to pairs, and each individual represented a different nation. One nation had more resources than the other, but the two had to form an alliance because both were threatened by a third party. The task was to negotiate how much each nation should contribute, and how large the defence fund should be altogether. The closer the resources of the two sides, it was predicted, the greater the conflict between the subjects. Conflict was measured from tape-recordings of the content of the negotiations, and the prediction was confirmed. There was, however, a second independent variable, for subjects communicated either by telephone or by written messages (which were dictated to a typist). The written messages, it was found, were more formal than the audio messages, and took longer; and they were generally more forceful, and referred more frequently to the contents of previous exchanges. Unfortunately, though, interpretation was very difficult, because there was no face-to-face condition, and the comparison between the audio and written messages was little more than anecdotal.

The second study was quite different from all the others. It was conducted by Wilson & Williams (1977), and consisted of an analysis of the Watergate Tapes, from the transcripts published by the *New York Times* in 1974. As far as possible the design was balanced so that, for each face-to-face conversation involving Nixon and one of his staff, a telephone conversation with the same individual was also included. Nixon, himself, of course, was present in all the recordings, and we do have to remember that he was able to assume rather more control over the enterprise than is usual for experimental subjects – what medium to use, what to discuss, what to record and, alas, what to erase.

Most of the analyses which Wilson & Williams undertook were concerned with style, but content too was examined, by means of a coding scheme they developed from Bales (1970) and Coulthard (1973). The transcripts were first divided into 'acts', and each act was then coded on two dimensions, 'Focus', and 'Activity', corresponding to 'Resource' and 'Mode' in CPA. There were two main findings: the telephone conversations included proportionately more disagreement than the face-to-face conversations, but proportionately fewer greetings and ritualized sequences. They also lasted a shorter time, and Wilson & Williams concluded that they were less 'pleasant' and less 'intimate'. Thus, just as we might have predicted, the absence of cues had depersonalized the conversations and made them more task-oriented. Not even American presidents, it seems, are immune.

Style

One of the earliest papers on style, as described at the start of the chapter, was published by Argyle, Lalljee & Cook (1968). Subjects were observed under a variety of unusual experimental conditions and, although no clear pattern was detected, visual communication appeared to be an important source of variance. Four years later, Cook & Lalljee (1972) went on to publish a follow-up study, and this time they restricted themselves to a straightforward comparison between face-to-face and audio encounters. Twelve pairs of unacquainted male students took part, and six were assigned to a face-to-face condition, in which subjects sat across a table placed in an open doorway, and the remainder were assigned to an audio condition, in which the door was closed and communication was by means of an intercom. The task was to 'make each other's acquaintance', and 10 minutes of conversation were tape-recorded and subsequently transcribed.

Three sets of predictions were made, and the first was that, when subjects were deprived of visual signals, verbal substitutes would take over. In particular it was predicted that: there would be more filled pauses in the audio condition than face-to-face, as Kasl and Mahl (1965) had found, since filled pauses are said to be a means of signalling that one has not yet finished (Maclay & Osgood, 1959); there should be more questions, because questions allow one deliberately to offer the floor; and there should be more attention signals from the listener, to say 'I am still here and listening, but I do not want to take over'. The second prediction was that the flow of conversation would break down without visual signals since, even if verbal substitutes were used, they would be less effective than visual cues for turn-taking. The result would be either more pausing between turns or more interrupting, but which was the more likely the authors chose not to speculate. The final prediction was that the structure of the encounters would differ. Because synchronization was expected to be harder to achieve in the audio condition than face-to-face there would be fewer changes of speaker and, correspondingly, the utterances would be longer; fewer words would be spoken overall because of the time wasted on interruptions and pauses; and speech disturbance would be greater because subjects would become anxious, and speech disturbance is known to increase when anxiety increases (Harper, Wiens & Matarazzo, 1978).

In the event the results were disappointing, for there were only two significant effects: more very short utterances in the audio condition than face-to-face (a finding which had not been predicted but which was at least consistent with expectations); and more frequent interruptions face-to-face (the opposite of what had been predicted). There was no evidence that verbal substitutes had taken over in the absence of visual signals; meshing had apparently not broken down; and the structure of the conversations had remained stable.

The findings were difficult to interpret. It was unlikely that the small sample size was responsible for the lack of effects, because the data did not even indicate trends, and the authors could offer very few suggestions. One was that verbal signals do substitute for visual cues, but the experiment had concentrated on the wrong ones. Another was that communication is so rich and redundant that the removal of just one set of cues has little effect. A third was that the result for interruptions, although not as predicted, did still point to a problem of meshing in the audio condition. Interruptions are both a means of 'stealing' the floor and a potential source of disruption and, because it is difficult to decide precisely when to interrupt in the absence of visual cues, people are reluctant to take the risk at all. Why there were so many short utterances in the audio condition remained a mystery, but they may have resulted from the slightly raised incidence of questions.

By the mid-1970s the literature had still made little progress, and we therefore set up an experiment of our own. The findings were reported by Rutter & Stephenson (1977), and the material we examined was the sessions which

Stephenson, Ayling & Rutter (1976) had used for the content analysis discussed in the last section. Subjects first completed a sociopolitical questionnaire about union–management relations, and they were then assigned to same-sex pairs to spend 15 minutes discussing one or two items which had revealed a difference of opinion. There were twelve male and twelve female pairs, and half sat face-to-face on adjacent sides of a table, while the remainder communicated from separate rooms over a microphone–headphone intercom. Like Cook & Lalljee (1972), we expected synchronization to be poorer in the audio condition than face-to-face, and we made two predictions: there would be more silence and simultaneous speech in the audio condition; and the structure of the conversations would differ, as the audio subjects compensated for the lack of visual communication. Compensation, we expected, would appear as a slower rate of speech and longer utterances, a grammatically more formal structure, more questions, more acknowledgement and attention signals, and more filled pauses and speech disturbance.

The results are given in Table 4.6. The first hypothesis received no support. There was no difference in silence and, just as in Cook & Lalljee (1972), simultaneous speech was significantly greater not in the audio condition but face-to-face. Simultaneous speech generally denoted interruptions, and both frequency and duration revealed significant differences. In contrast, the second hypothesis did receive support, though very little: utterances were longer on average in the audio condition; and their overall distribution also differed, with the majority of very short utterances in the face-to-face condition (the opposite of what Cook & Lalljee had found), and the majority of very long utterances in the audio condition.

Sex and time were also examined, and there were several main effects, though no interactions with communication condition itself. Men used more filled pauses than women, as Feldstein, Brenner & Jaffé (1963) and Lalljee & Cook (1973) had reported; and they produced more speech disturbance but fewer acknowledgement and attention signals. For men and women alike, filled pauses fell steadily over time, from the first to the second to the third 5-minute periods – as subjects became less attentive, perhaps, and felt less need to plan carefully what to say – but speech disturbance, which we measured according to the system of Mahl (1956), fluctuated from period to period.

Despite the lack of support for our predictions, we nevertheless argued at the time that visual communication did play an important role in synchronizing conversation – albeit a rather different role from the one we had anticipated. The key to our interpretation was interruptions.

> Face-to-face, interruption can occur freely because the visual channel allows the communication of nonverbal signals which maintain the interaction and prevent the breakdown which interruption might otherwise produce. Without the visual channel, such nonverbal signals cannot be communicated, and speech assumes greater importance in regulating the interaction. Accordingly, since interruptions may threaten the continuity of the encounter, they are made less frequently, with the consequence that utterances are longer in the audio condition simply because

Table 4.6   Rutter & Stephenson (1977): style. (Reproduced by permission of John Wiley & Sons Ltd.)

	Face-to-face		Audio		d.f.	F
	Mean	SD	Mean	SD		
No. occurrences simultaneous speech	14·7	4·6	9·0	3·9	1, 20	12·1**
Duration simultaneous speech (seconds)	18·7	4·7	9·4	3·0	1, 20	40·8***
Duration mutual silence (seconds)	18·9	9·3	14·4	7·0	1, 20	1·8
Length utterances (words)	25·7	7·4	34·3	11·5	1, 20	4·7*
No. utterances	18·2	4·7	15·3	3·5	1, 20	3·0
No. floor changes	28·7	8·4	25·3	6·5	1, 20	1·2
Duration speech (seconds)	145·0	4·8	142·3	4·3	1, 20	1·8
Total no. words	431·3	4·5	455·4	54·7	1, 20	1·3
Noun-verb ratio	1·5	0·1	1·5	0·1	1, 20	<1
Speech rate (words/second)	3·0	0·3	3·2	0·3	1, 20	2·6
No. questions†	5·3	1·3	4·9	2·0	1, 20	<1
No. utterances ending as question	2·5	1·0	2·5	1·6	1, 20	<1
% utterances ending as question	13·6	3·0	15·4	7·4	1, 20	<1
% floor changes preceded by question	20·4	4·5	21·1	8·3	1, 20	<1
No. attention signals††	6·1	2·2	4·3	3·3	1, 20	2·9
Filled pause ratio (per 100 words)	2·4	2·0	3·3	2·1	1, 20	2·0
Speech disturbance ratio (per 100 words)	6·3	2·3	8·2	2·6	1, 20	4·6*

† The number of questions includes questions which occur in mid-utterance.
†† Attention signals contribute to the word count but not to the utterance count or number of occurrences of simultaneous speech.
* $P<0.05$ ** $P<0.01$ *** $P<0.001$

they are less often broken by interruption. The raised incidence of speech disturbance probably stems from anxiety (Cook, 1969) the result either of the novelty of the situation or of the increased concern with speech. In summary, the role of visual communication seems to be to enable participants to converse spontaneously and interrupt freely without threatening the continuity of the interaction (Rutter & Stephenson, 1977, p. 35).

Despite our conclusion, we were well aware that caution was necessary. Earlier in the chapter, in the section on opinion change measures of outcome, I made the point that face-to-face and audio differ in not one respect but two. Face-to-face, subjects are in visual communication and they sit physically together in the same room; in the audio condition they lack both visual communication and physical presence, for they are hidden from each other in separate rooms. Traditionally in the literature, the crucial variable has been assumed to be visual communication but, conceivably, physical presence might be more important, or the two variables might even interact. What was needed, we made clear at the time, was some means of disentangling the variables – and, in fact, there already existed two pieces of published work.

The first was by Jaffé & Feldstein (1970). Sixty-four subjects were recruited, and each took part in three 40-minute conversations designed to resolve differences in racial attitudes. Half of each conversation took place face-to-face and, for the other half, the two subjects were separated by an opaque screen, with the result that visual communication was precluded but physical presence was retained. There was little evidence of consistency in the results from conversation to conversation but, in one of the three, simultaneous speech was longer face-to-face than in the screen condition; for two of the three, so were pauses between speakers; and for one of the three, so too were pauses overall. There was no difference between conditions in how much people said. The findings were thus relatively weak and, once again, the lack of visual cues had little effect upon meshing.

The second paper was by Siegman & Pope (1972), and it reported two experiments of interest. At the start of the chapter, I discussed the work of Moscovici and his colleagues (Moscovici, 1967), and it was shown that they put forward a very important argument. If variations in the physical setting do influence conversations, they said, then the effects are indirect and are mediated by the changes the physical conditions induce in the relationship between the speakers. Siegman & Pope agreed and, in different words, they made the same point. When visual feedback is unavailable, subjects become uncertain about how their partner is responding, and they experience 'relationship ambiguity'.

For the first of their experiments Siegman & Pope recruited thirty-two nursing students, and each took part in two interviews, one face-to-face, the other from behind an opaque screen. In the screen condition, utterances were shorter, speech rate was lower, and the incidence of filled pauses was higher, while speech disturbance, latency of response to questions, and duration of silences overall were unaffected. The second experiment examined subject and interviewer sitting back-to-back, and the results were similar to those of the screen condition. Both manipulations, the authors argued, had led to uncertainty about how the interviewer was responding – and 'relationship ambiguity', and hence changes in the style of speech, were the result.

Since the paper by Rutter & Stephenson (1977), only two laboratory studies have been published, as far as I know, apart from our own later work. The first was by Butterworth, Hine & Brady (1977), and its principal concern was hesitations and pauses. Subjects conversed over an audio link, through an opaque screen, or through a transparent screen, and, although there were several significant effects, there was no clear pattern.

The other study was by Williams (1978), and it consisted of a stylistic analysis of the conversations which Williams (1975c) had used to explore the formation of coalitions. From face-to-face, audio, and CCTV brainstorming sessions, three dependent measures were taken – the duration of interruptions (actually simultaneous speech); the duration of mutual silence; and the length of utterances lasting four-tenths of a second or more – and the first two revealed significant effects. Face-to-face, simultaneous speech was longer than in either of the other conditions, while audio and CCTV were equivalent; and the same pattern was found for silences. Thus, once again, simultaneous speech was most common face-to-face, but this time it was clear that visual communication could not be responsible, for the CCTV and audio conditions were very close together.

Apart from the laboratory research on style, there are only two other published studies, as far as I know, and both of them explored naturalistic telephone calls. The first, by Wilson & Williams (1977), was the Watergate study. As described in the section on content, the design was balanced as far as possible so that, for every face-to-face meeting between Nixon and a particular individual, a telephone conversation with that same person was also included. Unfortunately, the *New York Times* transcripts did not allow simultaneous speech to be examined, but the authors were able to take four other measures and, in each case, the values for telephone conversations were lower than those for the face-to-face encounters: the duration of the meeting; the mean word length of utterances; the mean word length of acts (where 'acts' were derived from the content analysis and corresponded approximately to Bales' (1970) definition); and the mean number of acts an utterance. The telephone conversations were shorter, the authors suggested, because they were less pleasant; and telephone acts and utterances were shorter because speakers were uncertain how they were being received because feedback was impaired. No evidence of verbal substitution was detected.

The second naturalistic study was by Beattie & Barnard (1979), and was based on Directory Enquiry calls. Over 700 calls were tape-recorded originally, but a so-called 'representative sample' of 18 was selected finally, ranging in length from 28 to 492 words. For comparison purposes the authors made use of material from university tutorials, on which they had first reported in Beattie (1977). The only significant effects concerned filled pauses, for subscribers were more likely than operators to begin their utterances with an 'er' or an 'um', and filled pauses were more frequent in the telephone calls overall. There were no differences in simultaneous speech or speaker-switch latencies, either between telephone and face-to-face or between subscribers and operators, and once again there was nothing to suggest that meshing broke down in the absence of visual communication. There was, however, some evidence that filled pauses were used as a means of retaining the floor and fending off interruption, but there were no other signs of verbal substitution for visual signals. Furthermore, the overall similarity between operators and subscribers suggested, against Butterworth, Hine & Brady (1977), that skill and experience were relatively unimportant – but more than that it was difficult to conclude, given the very small sample, the restricted and structured nature of the encounters, and the very different characteristics of the comparison material.

The most common finding to emerge from the literature on style is that interruptions occur more frequently face-to-face than in encounters which lack visual communication, and they last for longer at a time. The only other measure to stand out is filled pausing, which has generally been found to occur less frequently face-to-face than in audio-only encounters. While the latter finding suggests a degree of 'verbal' substitution for visual cues – filled pauses allow people to signal that they have not finished, as well as to plan their utterances – there is no evidence that meshing breaks down when visual cues are absent. The overall effect of removing visual information is that conversation loses its spontaneity, and speakers have to plan what to say more carefully, so that the content of their utterances is clear, and the possibility of ambiguity at potential speaker-switches is minimized.

Conclusion

From the literature on *looking*, I have turned in Chapter 4 to *seeing*, and three main areas have been examined: outcome, content, and style. A variety of questions have been explored, and some have been answered, but there remain a number of unresolved issues to which I shall return in Chapter 5. The first is whether the effects we have observed can truly be attributed to the absence of visual cues or whether some other variable may be responsible. Physical separation, and the interaction between visual communication and physical presence, are possible candidates and, as will be seen, it may well be that the critical factor is the aggregate number of social cues which people have available from whatever source – visual communication, physical presence, or elsewhere.

The second question concerns the role of verbal content. Earlier in the chapter, I argued that some of the effects which the removal of visual cues appears to have on outcomes may be mediated by content, and may not be direct. Exactly the same, I should now like to suggest, is true of style. The absence of cues makes people task-oriented and depersonalized in the content of what they say, and it is content which determines both outcome and style: outcomes favour the side with the stronger case; and style loses its spontaneity. In general, the literature has assumed that content, style, and outcome are independent – but, as will be seen, they are not.

The third and final question concerns an issue which I first discussed at the very start of the chapter in the context of Moscovici's work – whether the relationship between visual information and content, style, and outcome is itself mediated by something else. Traditionally, the literature has assumed a direct effect, but Moscovici argued otherwise. What mattered, according to him, was not the physical conditions themselves but the relationship between the participants which those conditions create – and, as will be seen, he was almost certainly right.

CHAPTER 5.

CUELESSNESS

By the late 1970s the literature on SEEING was well advanced. At first, attention had focused on outcomes – negotiation and conflict, attitude and opinion change, transmission of information and problem-solving, and person perception, – but soon it widened to include style, and content too. In all three cases, it appeared, visual communication was a significant source of variance, for when it was removed, encounters became more task-oriented and less personal in content, they lost their spontaneity of style and, sometimes at least, their outcomes changed too.

There was, however, an important limitation in much of the literature, and it is one discussed several times already: in most of the studies visual communication was confounded with a second variable, namely physical presence. Face-to-face, subjects were physically as well as visually *together*; in the audio condition they were physically as well as visually *apart*. Physical presence makes available a number of social cues which may be inaccessible or distorted in the audio condition – auditory cues from the voice, for example, drawing of breath, and shuffling – and it can also influence the way visual cues themselves are interpreted. Before we could be confident that visual communication really was the critical factor, some means of separating the two variables had to be found.

As shown in Chapter 4, several writers had already tackled the problem before we began our work. There were two groups: the first held physical presence constant and varied visual communication by means of screens (Jaffé & Feldstein, 1970; Siegman & Pope, 1972; Butterworth, Hine & Brady, 1977); and the second did the reverse, by means of closed-circuit television (Short, 1974; Morley & Stephenson, 1977; Williams, 1978). Taken separately the results were promising but, together, they were disappointing. For one thing, none of the studies had examined content and, for another, the findings were quite inconsistent. Short (1974) and Morley & Stephenson (1977) favoured visual communication, Williams (1978) favoured physical presence, and Butterworth, Hine & Brady (1977) favoured neither, with the remainder undecided. What was needed, we believed, was a more structured, systematic approach, and we therefore set up a test of our own.

Cuelessness

Our first experiment was published by Rutter, Stephenson & Dewey (1981), and it examined blind people. There were two main reasons for our choice. First, as well as trying to separate visual communication from physical presence, we were anxious to go beyond traditional laboratory research and examine people who lacked visual communication for reasons which had occurred *naturally*. Second, our previous work had concentrated exclusively on the short-term consequences of removing visual communication, and we knew nothing about *longer-term* effects. If physical presence and not visual communication were the critical variable, we argued, the differences between face-to-face and audio for blind pairs should be the same as for sighted pairs: while the physical arrangements were varied, visual communication was absent in both conditions. In comparison with face-to-face conversations, therefore, audio conversations should be more task-oriented and depersonalized in content, and less spontaneous in style.

In our previous research, 'task-orientation' and 'depersonalization' had been defined somewhat loosely, and now we tried to be more precise. Task-orientation, we suggested, should appear as high levels of exchange of information and perhaps discussion of outcomes and procedures, but low levels of information irrelevant to the task. Depersonalization we regarded as a more complex concept, with two principal meanings. The first was 'impersonal', and conversations which were depersonalized in this sense should contain very few references to oneself or other people present, and instead should refer mainly to third parties or even to nobody at all. The second meaning was 'antagonistic', and depersonalization in this sense should be evident in the speaker's rejection of his partner's contributions and unwillingness to accept them, and in criticism and lack of praise. Spontaneity of style would be marked by frequent and lengthy interruptions.

The experiment took place at a residential College of Further Education for the Blind, and pairs of students were allocated to face-to-face or audio to discuss a series of topical issues. All the conversations were sound-recorded as usual in stereo and, because we planned to analyse nonverbal signalling as well as speech in a sample of the subjects, the face-to-face encounters were also video-taped. Each of the sessions was subsequently transcribed as in our previous research, and the first, middle, and final 3-minute periods were coded. Content was examined by Conference Process Analysis, and style was analysed by the system we had used in Rutter & Stephenson (1977).

The results are given in Table 5.1 and at first they were very difficult to interpret. For content, there were no significant differences between conditions but for style there were, though the pattern they formed was quite unexpected. Speech disturbance was greater face-to-face than in the audio condition (the reverse of what we had found in Rutter & Stephenson, 1977), while speech rate was lower, floor changes were fewer, and simultaneous speech was longer in duration overall.

Table 5.1   Rutter, Stephenson & Dewey (1981): blind subjects

	Face-to-face	Audio
Offer	65·3	60·5
Accept	24·9	33·5
Reject	1·6	1·4
Seek	7·6	9·2
Procedure	1·3	2·9
Information	38·2	32·3
Irrelevant information	17·6	23·5
Positive acknowledgement	0·2	0·3
Negative acknowledgement	0·4	0·9
Outcomes	29·7	28·2
Self	13·4	15·4
Others excluding speaker	2·6	4·5
Persons present including speaker	1·1	0·7
Third parties	21·0	15·9
No referent	61·9	63·6
No. simultaneous speech	5·6	4·6
Duration sim. speech (seconds)	8·5	5·6*
Duration mutual silence (seconds)	21·9	36·7
No. utterances	8·9	13·4
Mean word-length utterances	32·8	24·2
No. floor changes	13·8	22·1*
Duration speech (seconds)	83·3	74·5
Total no. words	232·0	236·8
Noun–verb ratio	35·5	35·7
Speech rate (words/second)	2·8	3·3*
Percentage utterances ending as question	15·8	19·6
Percentage floor changes preceded by question	18·7	22·5
No. attention and acknowledgement signals	4·7	4·9
Filled pause ratio (per 100 words)	1·6	1·7
Speech disturbance ratio (per 100 words)	8·9	5·5**

F values for Face-to-face views Audio with df = h18   *$P<0·05$; **$P<0·01$

Speech disturbance – stutters, truncated sentences, slips of the tongue, and so on – is generally considered to be an index of situational anxiety (Harper, Wiens & Matarazzo, 1978) and it was the raised incidence face-to-face which eventually suggested a possible explanation. Face-to-face there were cameras – which may well have made the subjects anxious and apprehensive that they were to be evaluated in some way – but in the audio condition there were not. In an attempt to present themselves favourably, the face-to-face subjects spoke slowly to ensure that their arguments were clear, and floor changes therefore occurred less frequently than in the audio condition. Since speakers who were interrupted would be concerned to finish what they were saying, simultaneous speech was longer face-to-face because the remaining words took longer to articulate because of the slower speech rate. All four differences between conditions could thus be attributed to the effects of the cameras, we argued, and there was no evidence that physical presence had been responsible.

In summary, neither content nor style had been affected by physical presence, and visual communication continued to offer the more likely interpretation for our previous findings. Blind people had provided us with an interesting and special means of exploring the effects of physical presence, since the possibility of visual communication was denied by natural causes rather than experimental manipulation, and it had often been absent for many years. However, for exactly those reasons, of course, the study was not directly comparable with our earlier work. To be confident that the original findings could not be explained by physical presence, we needed to return to sighted subjects and devise some means of separating visual communication from physical presence experimentally. We therefore designed a second experiment.

The second experiment was published alongside the first in Rutter, Stephenson & Dewey (1981), and it proved to be an important turning-point. Its purpose was to re-examine the face-to-face and audio conditions, and to introduce two new manipulations. In the first, subjects conversed from separate rooms over a closed-circuit television link. Each sat in front of a camera which relayed his head-and-shoulders image to a monitor placed in front of his partner in the next room. Thus, while subjects were physically separated, a degree of visual communication was retained, albeit more limited than face-to-face in that looking and eye-contact could not occur. Sound was conveyed through the monitors. In the second condition a curtain was pulled part-way across the room between the subjects so that they were physically in the same room but visual communication was precluded. The face-to-face and audio conditions were identical to those in the original experiment, and the four conditions formed a two-by-two design – physically together/physically separate, and visual communication/no visual communication.

Our hypotheses were as follows. If the critical variable in the original experiment was physical presence, face-to-face and curtain together should differ from video and audio together. If the critical variable was visual communication, however, the main effects should be between face-to-face and video together and curtain and audio together. Either way, the original differences between face-to-face and audio ought to be confirmed. Thus, three sets of predictions were possible: (a) conversations in which subjects sat in separate rooms would be more task-oriented, more depersonalized, and less spontaneous than those in which they sat together in the same room; (b) conversations in which visual communication was precluded would be more task-oriented, more depersonalized, and less spontaneous than those in which visual communication was free to occur; (c) audio conversations would be more task-oriented, more depersonalized, and less spontaneous than face-to-face conversations.

Forty-eight subjects took part in the experiment, and they were selected randomly from the hundred or so people who responded to a newspaper advertisement inviting participation in 'an experiment on conversations'. A wide range of ages, educational attainments, and occupations was represented. Twenty-four same-sex pairs were formed, some male and some female, and six pairs were allocated at random to each of the four conditions. Subjects were first briefed individually by the experimenter, who explained that we were interested in 'tape-recording conversations'. They then completed a question-naire about the topics which had been used in the previous experiment, and the experimenter selected two or three items on which the views of the two people differed. The subjects were then introduced to each other and taken to the laboratory, and they were asked to spend 20 minutes discussing any or all of the divisive items, and trying to persuade each other to their own points of view. The conversations were sound-recorded and scored in our usual way, and the analyses were based on the first, middle, and final 3-minute segments of each conversation.

Table 5.2   Rutter, Stephenson & Dewey (1981): sighted subjects

	Face-to-face	Video	Curtain	Audio
Offer	60·3	61·7	64·2	64·7
Accept	26·8	23·6	24·2	20·7
Reject	2·0	2·3	0·9	1·3
Seek	8·8	10·8	9·3	12·1
Procedure	2·9	2·4	2·2	7·1**
Information	30·4	38·0	37·6	31·0
Irrelevant information	27·7	14·0	21·9	19·6
Positive acknowledgement	0·1	0·1	0·5	0·1
Negative acknowledgement	0·9	0·5	0·3	0·3
Outcomes	21·6	31·9	24·7	27·9
Self	18·5	18·2	19·3	21·2
Others excluding speaker	6·4	7·1	6·0	8·3
Persons present including speaker	0·4	1·4	1·1	1·6**
Third parties	8·2	12·2	8·8	7·6
No referent	66·5	61·0	64·8	61·2
No. simultaneous speech	8·3	8·9	8·1	5·8
Duration sim. speech (seconds)	12·7	9·9	11·7	7·6*
Duration mutual silence (seconds)	11·5	12·8	11·4	20·2
No. utterances	9·7	12·4	9·4	10·7
Mean word-length utterances	32·7	27·3	38·3	31·5
No. floor changes	15·9	21·7	14·4	18·3
Duration speech (seconds)	90·6	88·5	90·2	83·7
Total no. words	280·6	297·3	289·2	260·8
Noun–verb ratio	37·9	36·9	36·8	38·8
Speech rate (words/second)	3·2	3·4	3·3	3·2
Percentage utterances ending as question	14·4	21·5	17·9	22·9*
Percentage floor changes preceded by question	16·7	23·9	22·0	27·4*
No. attention and acknowledgement signals	7·2	4·7	5·8	3·6*
Filled pause ratio (per 100 words)	2·5	2·8	3·6	2·8
Speech disturbance ratio (per 100 words)	7·4	8·4	9·3	9·6*

t values for Face-to-face versus Audio with df $= 20$ *$P<0·05$; **$P<0·01$

Mean values are given in Table 5.2, for each of the four conditions separately. The data were first examined by analysis of variance, with physical presence and visual communication the two independent variables, and planned comparisons were then made between means by *t*-test.

The first prediction, that conversations in which subjects sat apart would be more task-oriented, more depersonalized, and less spontaneous than those in which they sat together, received no support. There were no differences in exchange of information or in discussion of outcomes, procedures, and irrelevant information; there were no differences in how impersonal or antagonistic the conversations appeared; and there were no differences in spontaneity. The second prediction, that conversations in which visual communication was precluded would be more task-oriented, more depersonalized, and less spontaneous than those in which it was free to occur, likewise received no support.

In contrast to the first two predictions, the third received good support. The prediction stated that the findings of our original experiment would be confirmed, so that audio conversations would be more task-oriented, more depersonalized, and less spontaneous than face-to-face conversations. What emerged first of all was that the audio conversations included significantly more discussion of procedures than the face-to-face conversations, as well as more frequent references to those present, presumably about the procedures they should follow. There was also rather more discussion about outcomes and less introduction of irrelevant material, but in both cases the trends were non-significant.

The second finding to emerge was that the audio conversations were less spontaneous than the face-to-face conversations. Simultaneous speech, which generally resulted from interruptions, was shorter in duration in the audio condition than face-to-face, just as Rutter & Stephenson (1977) had found. In addition, there were several differences in style which had not been predicted. There was more speech disturbance in the audio condition than face-to-face, as Rutter & Stephenson had found; the proportion of utterances which ended as a question was greater in the audio condition, as was the proportion of floor changes which immediately followed a question; and there were fewer acknowledgement signals than face-to-face. For all the last three results, the findings of Rutter & Stephenson (1977) had tended in the same direction, though non-significantly, so that the present findings both confirmed and extended the originals.

The third and final result of the comparison between face-to-face and audio conversations concerned depersonalization. At first there appeared to be no difference between the face-to-face and audio conditions, for the content analysis revealed no effects for either the 'impersonal' dimension or the 'antagonistic' dimension. But then we remembered the stylistic analysis, and we recalled particularly the finding that acknowledgement signals had occurred less frequently in the audio condition than face-to-face. In a way we had not appreciated, acknowledgement signals provide an index of 'person orientation', for they denote interest in what the other person is saying and an inclination to give feedback and to ease the flow of the interaction. Despite the lack of evidence from the content analysis, therefore, audio conversations did appear to be depersonalized to some extent, and so we were able to conclude in favour of our prediction: audio conversations were more task-oriented than face-to-face, more depersonalized, and less spontaneous.

It was now that we came to the most important point in our results. While face-to-face and audio had differed in some of the ways we had predicted, the differences could be attributed to neither visual communication nor physical presence, and we had failed, apparently, to identify the crucial variable. But then, eventually, we realized that the key to our problem lay in the other two conditions, video and curtain, for whenever there was a significant difference between face-to-face and audio, whether in task-orientation, depersonalization, or style, video and curtain lay somewhere *between* them. There was only one exception in the seven significant results, and it soon became clear that we had stumbled upon an important finding. Indeed, it was so important that at last it gave us a means of integrating the literature, in a way which had not been possible before.

In our 1976 and 1977 papers, and in common with most previous writers, we had argued as if the nonverbal cues which visual communication makes available had some special significance, and we had ignored the possible importance of cues which were conveyed by other channels, including those from physical presence. If, instead, we now consider visual communication and physical presence together, our four conditions can be placed on a continuum, according to the aggregate number of social cues they make available. Face-to-face, cues are available from both visual communication and physical presence; in the video and curtain conditions one set each is available, and in the audio condition neither is available. In other words, as we move from face-to-face, to video and curtain, to audio – exactly the rank-order we found for our dependent measures – the conditions become increasingly *cueless*. Thus, CUELESSNESS, we believe, is the crucial variable which had eluded us for so long, and it is the one concept which allows us to integrate all our previous findings. The smaller the aggregate number of available social cues from whatever source – visual communication, physical presence, or, indeed, any other – the more task-oriented and depersonalized the content, the less spontaneous the style and, in negotiations, the more likely the side with the stronger case to win a favourable outcome.

The question which now confronted us was how did cuelessness operate? How did it produce its effects on content, style, and outcome, and how were the dependent measures themselves related to one another? As shown in Chapter 4, one of the earliest suggestions in the literature on SEEING was that *outcome* differences between conditions might be explained by content differences. That is, cuelessness leads subjects to be task-oriented and depersonalized in the content of their discussion, and it is content which, in turn, produces the different outcomes. What we now suggest is that style too is mediated by content, so that task-oriented, depersonalized content produces a deliberate, unspontaneous style, as well as particular outcomes. Outcome and style, we believe, are independent of each other, but both are related to cuelessness through the mediation of content (Figure 5.1). As will be shown in the final section of the chapter, when discussing the relationships in more detail, the model has received good support.

Figure 5.1   Effects of cuelessness

After our 1981 paper, the most pressing question was how well the findings would stand up, and we therefore designed two further tests. The first was by Kemp & Rutter (1982), and its main purpose was to find another 'intermediate' condition which would preclude visual communication whilst retaining physical presence. The solution we chose was to place a small wooden screen on the table between the subjects (see also Rimé, 1982).

The experiment was conducted at the University of Warwick. Randomly selected students were first asked to complete a questionnaire about union–management relations, and fifteen male and fifteen female pairs were then formed on the basis of the scores, so that one subject was broadly pro-union and the other pro-management. The members of each pair were strangers, and pairs were assigned to meet either face-to-face, in the wooden screen condition, or over an audio link. Face-to-face and audio were the same as before, and the wooden screen condition was identical to face-to-face except that a screen measuring approximately 1 metre square was placed between the subjects. The screen was sufficiently large to preclude visual communication, but sound passed through unimpeded because the construction included vertical angled slits. Each pair was allocated two questionnaire items which had revealed a disagreement between the two subjects, and the task was to spend 15 minutes discussing either or both of the issues. The sessions were recorded and transcribed in our usual way, and the first, middle, and final 3-minute segments were extracted for analysis.

Two main hypotheses were tested, and the first was that audio conversations would be more task-oriented, more depersonalized and less spontaneous than face-to-face conversations, with the wooden screen condition in between because it was intermediate in cuelessness. The second hypothesis concerned the possibility that subjects would adapt to cuelessness over time. Previous studies had generally disregarded time, and the evidence which did exist suggested merely that subjects became more relaxed as time went on and their style became more spontaneous (Rutter & Stephenson, 1977; Rutter, Stephenson & Dewey, 1981). Content had never been examined, so far as we knew, and since there had been little interest in whether time and experimental conditions interacted, it remained an open question whether adaptation to cuelessness would be found. Our belief was that it would, and we therefore predicted that, for both content and style, the wooden screen and audio values would converge upon the face-to-face values as the discussions progressed.

The data were coded and analysed in the same ways as before, and the first prediction received a good measure of support. For content, there were no main effects of communication condition for any of the CPA categories, but planned comparisons revealed one significant difference, namely more 'acceptance' face-to-face than in the audio condition, with the wooden screen condition in between, as predicted. Unfortunately, though, since some thirty comparisons were made, the difference may well have occurred by chance. For style, there were rather more effects. For the duration of simultaneous speech, but especially the frequency, the values were greater face-to-face than in the audio condition and, again, the wooden screen condition lay in between. Filled pauses produced a main effect of conditions and, here too, face-to-face and audio were significantly different, with the wooden screen condition in between. Thus, in all four cases for which a difference between face-to-face and audio had been revealed, the wooden screen results lay between them, just as our model predicted.

In contrast to the first hypothesis, the second received no support. Several main effects of time emerged for both content and style (Table 5.3) and in general they suggested that the conversations became less task–oriented as time went on, but more depersonalized and more spontaneous. However, only one measure produced a significant interaction between time and communication condition, namely the frequency of interruptions and even though it behaved exactly as our hypothesis had predicted, the assumption must be that chance was responsible.

In summary, while there was no evidence that cuelessness produced task-oriented and depersonalized content, it did lead to a deliberate, unspontaneous style. What is more, the effects were genuinely attributable to cuelessness, because whenever a difference was revealed between face-to-face and audio, the wooden screen condition lay in between. There was no evidence that subjects adapted to cuelessness as time went on but, irrespective of experimental condition, their behaviour did change. In content they became less task-oriented and more depersonalized, and in style they became increasingly carefree about planning and phrasing and increasingly unlikely to ask questions.

Despite the apparent success of the cuelessness model, there remained some important questions and it was to them, or three in particular, that we turned in the second of our recent experiments (Rutter *et al.*, 1984). The first issue was that we still knew very little about outcomes, even though it was the outcome studies of Morley & Stephenson which had inspired much of the early research on SEEING. In part the problem was that most of the literature had focused on a very narrow range of encounters – often simulated negotiations or debates with

Table 5.3   Kemp & Rutter (1982): effects of time

	Time I Mean	Time II Mean	Time III Mean	F (d.f. = 2,48)
Content				
Mode				
Offer	58·1	59·8	59·3	< 1
Reject	25·5	26·2	26·2	< 1
Accept	2·0	2·0	1·6	< 1
Seek	10·3	7·2	10·0	3·4*
Resource				
Procedure	4·2	2·0	1·5	3·7*
Information	38·4	41·4	43·1	< 1
Irrelevant information	1·1	2·2	6·5	3·2*
Acknowledgement +	0·3	1·8	1·1	3·1
Acknowledgement −	2·6	6·9	5·1	3·2*
Outcome	40·9	30·6	30·7	5·1**
Overall task orientation	83·4	73·9	75·2	7·5**
Referent				
Self	9·2	6·9	7·7	2·3
Others excluding speaker	4·6	2·5	3·5	3·6*
Others including speaker	1·7	1·4	2·0	< 1
Third parties	28·6	28·1	29·0	< 1
No referent	56·0	61·1	57·8	4·7*
Overall depersonalization				
impersonal	84·5	89·2	86·8	4·2*
antagonistic	0·3	0·3	0·4	< 1
Style				
Simultaneous speech no.	5·1	5·2	5·5	< 1
Simultaneous speech duration (seconds)	8·2	8·8	9·6	1·5
Mutual silence duration (seconds)	14·4	17·4	20·2	1·8
Utterance length (words)	34·8	39·0	36·1	< 1
Utterance no.	9·8	8·3	8·6	2·9
Floor changes no.	16·1	13·8	14·0	1·7
Speech duration (seconds)	86·9	86·6	84·6	1·1
Words no.	267·6	270·6	265·5	< 1
Speech rate (words/second)	3·1	3·2	3·2	< 1
Percentage utterances = questions	21·1	14·5	16·5	5·6**
Attention signals no.	3·1	3·7	3·9	2·5
Filled pause ratio (per 100 words)	3·3	2·6	2·3	6·7**
Speech disturbance ratio (per 100 words)	3·4	4·2	4·6	8·1**

* $P < 0·05$; ** $P < 0·01$
Note. Simultaneous speech no.: communication condition × time: $F = 2·7$; d.f. = 4,48; $P < 0·05$.

strong task requirements – with a correspondingly narrow range of outcome measures. What was needed, we believed, was a different type of task, one which would encourage interpersonal considerations. The second issue was that almost all the previous research had restricted itself to dyads, and very little was known about the effects of cuelessness in larger groups. The final

issue was that, although we now knew something about the effects of cuelessness on content, style, and outcome separately, we still had relatively little
evidence about the relationships between them. All three issues were important to the development of the model, and we therefore set up the following
study. There were two experimental conditions: face-to-face and screen; two
sizes of group: two-person and four-person; and three sets of dependent
measures: content, style, and outcome.

The experiment was designed to test three hypotheses, and the first concerned outcome. When people hold discussions they sometimes change their
opinions and, as shown in Chapter 4, face-to-face and audio have occasionally
been reported to produce different amounts of change (Short, Williams &
Christie, 1976; Tysoe, in press). From our model it follows that cuelessness is
likely to be the critical variable, and that opinions will change only to the extent
that cuelessness leads to task-oriented, depersonalized arguments. Our prediction, therefore, was that in comparison with face-to-face discussions, screen
discussions would result in more task-oriented, depersonalized content, less
spontaneous style, and more opinion change.

Our second prediction concerned group size. When we meet people face-to-
face, the larger the group the fewer social cues we are able to monitor from
each individual and, so, the more cueless the encounter. Furthermore, if the
group meets not face-to-face but, say, over a medium which precludes visual
communication, cuelessness will be greater still. That is, medium and group
size will interact, so that a two-person face-to-face encounter will be high in
cues, a four-person screen encounter will be low in cues, and two-person screen
encounters and four-person face-to-face encounters will be intermediate. From
our model, therefore, we were able to predict that in comparison with two-
person encounters, four-person encounters would result in more task-oriented
and depersonalized content, less spontaneous style, and more opinion change.
Furthermore, medium and group size would interact, so that four-person
screen encounters would have the greatest task-orientation and depersonalization, the greatest lack of spontaneity, and the most opinion change, and
two-person face-to-face encounters would have the least.

The third prediction concerned the relationships between content, style, and
outcome. As we had suggested already in Rutter, Stephenson & Dewey (1981),
we believed that the effects of cuelessness on content, style, and outcome were
not independent. Instead, only content was influenced directly, and the effects
on style and outcome were produced indirectly, through the mediation of
content. So far, we had explored no further than content and style, but now we
were able for the first time to examine the relationships among all three
measures. The more task-oriented and depersonalized the content, we predicted, the less spontaneous the style and the greater the degree of opinion
change.

Ninety-six subjects took part in the experiment, and an outline of the
procedure was given in Chapter 4, in the section on outcome. Forty-eight of
the subjects were male and forty-eight were female and, while half were

university students, the remainder were people who responded to a newspaper advertisement. Within each sample, subjects were allocated to groups of two or four, giving eight groups of each size from the student sample and the same from the other sample. Two or three days before the experimental session, subjects were asked to complete a questionnaire about abortion and, during the session itself, the task for each group was to discuss the topic for 20 minutes, and to try to reach a consensus as to what the law in Britain should be. Half the groups held their discussion face-to-face, and half from behind cloth screens which precluded visual communication. At the end of the session each subject was asked to complete the questionnaire again.

For content and style, all our analyses examined the full transcripts, and coding was based on our usual systems. For opinion change, the measures we took were as follows: movement, which was the overall amount of change, in whatever direction; polarization, which was movement in the direction of one or other extreme; social progression, which was polarization in the direction of the extreme nearest which the subject had started; and agreement, which, unlike the other three, was a group measure, and represented the variability or lack of variability among the members of the group. All four measures were based on the individual subjects' final responses. Group consensus, which we had hoped originally to include as well, proved impossible to analyse because many of the discussions ended in deadlock.

Means and F ratios for the first two hypotheses are given in Table 5.4 and, in general, there was less support for our predictions than we might have hoped. The first hypothesis was that, in comparison with face-to-face discussions, screen discussions would be more task-oriented and depersonalized in content, less spontaneous in style, and more likely to produce opinion change. For content there were only two effects: more discussion of outcomes in the screen condition, apparently indicating greater task-orientation; but less discussion of relevant information, apparently indicating the opposite. In both cases, planned comparisons revealed that the effects held for two-person groups only and not four-person groups. There was no evidence that the screen discussions were depersonalized. For style, the results were rather stronger. Though there was no overall main effect for simultaneous speech, planned comparisons revealed that it did, as predicted, occur less frequently in four-person screen groups than four-person face-to-face groups, suggesting that subjects were trying to avoid interruption. There was also more filled pausing in the screen condition overall than face-to-face, indicating that speakers were planning and structuring their contributions. There were no effects for opinion change (see also de Alberdi, 1982).

The second hypothesis concerned group size, and we predicted that, in comparison with two-person groups, four-person groups would be more task-oriented and depersonalized in content, less spontaneous in style, and more likely to produce opinion change. Furthermore, group size and medium of communication were expected to interact, so that four-person screen discussions would show the greatest task-orientation and depersonalization, the

Table 5.4   Rutter *et al.* (1984): content, style and outcome

	Face-to-face		Screen				
	2	4	2	4	FF/S	2/4	Interaction
Offer	61·0	63·5	63·7	63·1	0·3	0·2	0·5
Accept	28·6	22·3	25·4	21·2	2·8	16·4***	0·7
Reject	1·0	2·8	1·3	3·1	0·2	5·8*	0·0
Seek	8·4	10·3	9·0	11·6	0·4	2·1	0·1
Procedure	0·9	1·4	1·1	1·1	0·0	0·2	0·2
Information	44·9	36·1	31·6	37·5	5·0*	0·3	7·7*
Irrelevant information	3·1	1·2	0·9	1·0	0·9	0·5	0·7
Praise	0·0	0·1	0·1	0·0	0·2	0·2	1·8
Blame	0·0	0·9	0·1	0·3	1·0	6·4*	2·2
Outcomes	36·6	41·8	49·5	43·9	13·4**	0·0	7·0*
Self	14·7	16·0	16·4	16·8	0·8	0·4	0·1
Others excluding speaker	3·3	5·9	3·9	3·4	0·8	0·8	1·9
Others including speaker	2·2	2·4	1·6	3·2	0·0	1·1	0·7
Third parties	10·8	9·1	11·2	8·1	0·1	2·4	0·2
No referent	68·9	66·6	67·0	68·6	0·0	0·1	1·6
No. simultaneous speech	2·5	3·3	2·3	1·6	3·4	0·0	2·3
No. utterances per person	3·5	2·5	3·3	1·8	1·7	16·2***	0·8
Word length of utterances	33·5	23·1	32·2	25·9	0·0	4·2	0·3
No. floor changes	5·2	6·8	5·2	6·5	0·1	3·5	0·1
No. words per person	88·0	50·2	95·2	42·4	0·0	219·7***	6·2*
Percentage utterances ending as question	13·7	15·5	19·1	17·4	2·2	0·0	0·5
No. attention signals	4·1	2·8	3·5	1·8	2·2	7·4*	0·1
Filled pause ratio	2·0	1·7	3·4	2·9	8·6**	0·9	0·1
Movement	8·1	8·1	9·6	8·1	0·4	0·9	0·5
Polarization	0·3	0·6	0·6	0·0	1·9	0·1	6·3*
Social progression	0·7	0·8	0·7	0·8	0·6	1·7	0·0
Agreement	0·6	0·7	0·4	0·8	0·0	4·1	1·0

* $P < 0.05$; ** $P < 0.01$; *** $P < 0.001$

greatest lack of spontaneity, and the greatest opinion change, and two-person face-to-face discussions would show the least.

The first set of predictions received some measure of support. Content was more depersonalized in the four-person groups than the dyads, with greater rejection and criticism and less acceptance, but there was no difference in task-orientation. For style, there was no evidence of reduced spontaneity in the four-person groups, but there were fewer acknowledgement signals than in the dyads. Moreover, each participant said less in total and made fewer contributions than in the dyads, but that was only to be expected since there were more potential speakers to share the floor. There were no effects for opinion change, and there was no evidence to support our second set of predictions.

While four measures produced significant interactions between group size and medium of communication, none of the effects followed the predicted pattern.

The third hypothesis concerned the relationships between content, style, and outcome, and we predicted that the more task-oriented and depersonalized the content, the less spontaneous the style, and the greater the degree of opinion change. For each group of subjects every CPA category was correlated with every measure of style and opinion change, and the correlations were examined separately for two-person groups and four-person groups. Since a full discussion of these and the corresponding analyses from our other experiments is to be included in the final section of the chapter, the results will not be presented here. In summary, though, once again the hypothesis received rather less support than we had hoped.

Our cuelessness model had now been examined in three separate papers – Rutter, Stephenson & Dewey (1981), Kemp & Rutter (1982), and Rutter *et al.* (1984) – and the differences between experimental conditions in the last of the three had proved the weakest of all and the least numerous. At first we were disappointed but, in fact, of course, the pattern was exactly what we should have predicted. The screen condition lies midway between face-to-face and audio in cuelessness, and our manipulation was therefore relatively weak and the subjects' behaviour was unaffected. The same is less likely to be true for our manipulation of group size – four-person groups have often been found to behave differently from dyads – nevertheless, it may still be that the manipulation was too weak for our particular measures. If so, content behaved in just the way the model predicts, and style and outcome simply followed suit.

As well as these main conclusions, three new issues emerged from the findings, and the first concerned the concept of task-orientation. Throughout our experiments we had argued that task-orientation is characterized by exchange of information, outcomes and procedures, and avoidance of irrelevant information. However, if the data are inspected closely, it becomes apparent that the two principal variables, information and outcome, are generally negatively related: $r = +0.05$ in the second experiment of Rutter, Stephenson & Dewey (1981); $r = -0.66$ in Kemp & Rutter (1982); and $r = -0.91$ for both two-person and four-person groups in Rutter *et al.* (1984). One explanation might be that, if speakers are using one particular category, they cannot be using another. More probably, though, the information category in fact tells us very little about task-orientation, since whether subjects are behaving in a task-oriented or interpersonal way, they always have relevant information to exchange. Indeed, the distinction between task-orientation and depersonalization, which is never easy to make, becomes especially fraught when the task requires one to be personal. That was precisely the case in the present experiment, where subjects were asked to talk about abortion, and it may well explain why exchange of information was greater face-to-face than in the screen condition, the reverse of what our definition of task-orientation had led us to predict. What we now suggest is that, since the goal for subjects in all our experiments, at least implicitly, is to debate a topic and to try to persuade others or reach some sort of agreement, task-orientation will be apparent in two principal measures: exchange of outcomes, and avoidance of information which is irrelevant to the task. Information is not a useful index, and procedures are seldom discussed.

The second issue is related to the first, and concerns the problem of ceiling effects. In Chapter 4, when discussing content, I made the point that experimental conversations are often so highly task-oriented whatever the setting or instructions that there is little opportunity for differences between conditions to emerge. Morley & Stephenson (1977) argued that that was why they had failed to detect differences in content between face-to-face and audio encounters, and Kemp & Rutter (1982) used the same explanation for their own data. What matters about the argument is that, if the cuelessness model is correct, and style and outcome do vary only to the extent that content varies, ceiling effects for content will mean that style and outcome will remain constant. Despite the change of task in Rutter et al. (1984) to something more interpersonal than before, still the ceiling effect remained, and the stability of style and outcome across conditions was therefore only to be expected.

The final issue concerns the nature of the social cues themselves. When we first developed the cuelessness model we took the critical variable to be the aggregate number of cues which were available to subjects. Since then, however, we have come to a different conclusion. Because people are limited in their capacity for processing information, they are seldom able to make use of all the cues which are available. The important variable, we now believe, is the number of *usable* cues, not *available* cues, and it is the former not the latter on which the model should be based.

Cuelessness and related concepts

Although cuelessness was a new term, there already existed in the literature a number of related concepts (Wilson, 1974; Guild, 1976; Short, Williams & Christie, 1976; Wish, 1977; Williams, 1977) and it is useful to divide them into two groups. The first assumes that behavioural differences between media are the result of differences in the levels and types of information available to subjects. Face-to-face, for example, is rich in information from nonverbal cues and elsewhere, while audio is not. The second approach argues that the objective characteristics of the setting are of only secondary importance, and what matters most is how subjects perceive the medium, and how close it makes them feel to one another, or how distant. Of the informational concepts, Mehrabian's 'immediacy' and Morley & Stephenson's 'formality' have been the most influential, while of the phenomenological group, much the most significant has been the Communications Studies Group's 'social presence'. While the various approaches may often appear superficially to be very similar, the discussion will make clear, I hope, that the assumptions which underpin them and the predictions they make are, in fact, very different.

Information: immediacy and formality

Immediacy. The concept of immediacy was introduced by Wiener & Mehrabian (1968), and the authors' concern was to offer an 'analysis of verbal forms which reflect changes in the degree of separation or non-identity of a speaker with the object of his communication, of a speaker with his addressee, or of a speaker and his communication' (Wiener & Mehrabian, 1968, p. 23). Although no single definition was given in the book, immediacy appeared to refer to directness of communication. Language, nonverbal signalling, and media of communication all had immediate and non-immediate forms for the communicator to choose, and what the choice offered was the opportunity to make oneself psychologically close to one's partner or psychologically distant.

Originally, the concept was used mainly to analyse speech, but soon it was extended to medium of communication as well (Mehrabian, 1972), and it was here that it had most to say about seeing. What became clear was that immediacy was now being used to describe the physical conditions of the setting, and that media which Mehrabian called 'non-immediate' were precisely those which we would describe as 'cueless'. The main difference between the two concepts was that while we were concerned to identify and quantify the physical properties of cueless media, as well as to examine their behavioural effects, Mehrabian was concerned only with the psychological consequences. The exact conditions which led to immediacy or non-immediacy were of little interest to him.

> The concept of immediacy can describe best the effects of a given space on the people who meet and/or interact there. Immediacy refers to the extent of mutual sensory stimulation between two persons and is measured in terms of spatio-temporal proximity or the number of 'communication channels' that are available. Communication channels are the means by which one conveys his thoughts and feelings to another . . . the closer two people are to one another, the more immediate their interaction. . . . The greater immediacy associated with more channels for communication is illustrated as follows: telegrams and letters are two of the least immediate ways of communicating, permitting the verbal channel alone. These are followed in order by telephone conversations (verbal and vocal channels), conversations on a picturephone (verbal, vocal and facial), and face-to-face meetings (Mehrabian, 1972, pp. 76–7).

Formality. The concept of formality was introduced by Morley & Stephenson (1969), in the first of their papers on the outcome of simulated negotiations, and it was defined 'in terms of the numbers of social cues available' (Morley & Stephenson, 1969, p. 543). The fewer the cues the more formal the setting, so that audio was more formal than face-to-face, for example, and a constrained discussion in which subjects were not allowed to interrupt one another was more formal than one in which they were. Formality and cuelessness thus appear to be identical – though the former, perhaps, allows for a wider definition of social cues, including information made available by interruption – and they make identical predictions about behaviour. Cuelessness, I have argued, leads to task-oriented, depersonalized content, an unspontaneous style, and a particular set of outcomes – and formality does exactly the same.

Phenomenology: social presence

The concept of social presence was introduced by the Communications Studies Group, and the most detailed of their accounts was published by Short, Williams & Christie (1976). Informational theories, they argued, were inadequate, because they failed to consider the encounter as a whole. Separate cues were taken in isolation, language was disregarded, and it was apparently of little concern that subjects might adapt their behaviour when cues were removed, that a particular set of cues might change its meaning from setting to setting, or that much of the system of communication might in any case be redundant. Small wonder that the empirical evidence was sometimes weak, for the most important variable had been ignored altogether, how subjects perceived and construed the medium. Social presence would have none of these shortcomings – but, unfortunately, it proved a most elusive concept to define. Here are the authors' own words.

> We regard Social Presence as being a quality of the communications medium. Although we would expect it to affect the way individuals perceive their discussions, and their relationships to the persons with whom they are communicating, it is important to emphasize that we are defining Social Presence as a quality of the medium itself. We hypothesize that communications media vary in their degree of Social Presence, and that these variations are important in determining the way individuals interact. We also hypothesize that the users of any given communications medium are in some sense aware of the degree of Social Presence of the medium and tend to avoid using the medium for certain types of interactions; specifically, interactions requiring a higher degree of Social Presence than they perceive the medium to have. Thus we believe that social presence is an important key to understanding person-to-person telecommunications. It varies between different media, it affects the nature of the interaction and it interacts with the purpose of the interaction to influence the medium chosen by the individual who wishes to communicate. . . . we conceive of the Social Presence of a medium as a perceptual or attitudinal dimension of the user, a 'mental set' towards the medium. Thus, when we said earlier that Social Presence is a quality of the medium we were not being strictly accurate. We wished then to distinguish between the medium itself and the communications for which the medium is used. Now we need to make a finer distinction. We conceive of Social Presence not as an objective quality of the medium, though it must surely be dependent upon the medium's objective qualities, but as a subjective quality of the medium. We believe that this is a more useful way of looking at Social Presence than trying to define it objectively. . . . in understanding the effects of telecommunications media, we believe that it is important to know how the user perceives the medium, what his feelings are and what his 'mental set' is (Short, Williams & Christie, 1976, pp. 65–6, Reproduced by permission of John Wiley & Sons, Ltd.).

What seems to be the case is that social presence is a perceptual measure, rather than an objective one, and that it denotes the extent to which a medium is perceived to allow psychologically close, interpersonal communication. What mattered now was how people would rate the various media, and the Communications Studies Group embarked on a series of studies. Some were laboratory experiments in which a variety of media were set up specially, and others were field studies of naturalistic encounters.

One of the earliest laboratory experiments was conducted by Champness (1972a), and many that followed used much the same approach (Champness, 1972c; Williams, 1972; Christie, 1973, 1974). Subjects met to discuss a variety of divisive issues, and each pair underwent three experimental conditions, face-to-face, closed-circuit television, and audio. After each encounter the participants rated the medium on twenty-four semantic differential scales, some of which were intended to tap social presence and some not, and a number of effects were noted, in particular that face-to-face ranked higher than audio, with closed-circuit television intermediate. Unfortunately, though, social presence merged with another factor, 'aesthetic appeal', and there was no clear evidence that social presence was what underpinned the rank-ordering. Exactly the same happened in Champness (1972c), but Christie (1973, 1974) was more successful, and managed both to isolate social presence as an independent factor and to include a variety of other experimental conditions. Face-to-face and the written medium were found to occupy opposite extremes, with closed-circuit television and a variety of audio conditions in between and, this time, social presence did appear to be responsible. The scales with the highest loadings were 'passive–active', 'insensitive–sensitive', and 'unsociable–sociable', with the second adjective in each case denoting social presence.

Of the field studies, one of the earliest was by Christie (1972), and its purpose was to ask a sample of businessmen to list the relative advantages and disadvantages of face-to-face and telephone meetings. One of the main factors to emerge was 'impersonality', and it loaded heavily on such comments as 'conceal identity if required', and 'allows for less stress in unpleasant tasks', both of which, it was assumed, would load on social presence. Short (1973b) used a similar 'free-response' design and, again, the users' comments were taken to indicate that social presence, or something very like it, was the crucial variable. The same was true when subjects were asked to complete 'closed' questionnaires (Champness, 1972b, 1973).

At first sight, the evidence for social presence may appear to be considerable, and it is certainly true that the Communications Studies Group have amassed an impressive volume of data. Unfortunately, though, closer inspection reveals a number of difficulties, and there are two in particular which deserve attention. The first concerns the methodology of the studies, and the second concerns the concept itself.

The main methodological problem with the research is that all subjects generally underwent all conditions. Although this meant that they acted as their own controls – the usual defence for such designs – the drawback was that they almost certainly rated the media in comparative terms, using the evaluation of one medium to colour their evaluation of the next. In some of the experiments, indeed, they were asked to rate all the media in one questionnaire at the end of the whole experiment. 'Carry-over' effects are always a hazard in 'repeated measures' designs and are likely to lead to contamination, but the experimenters apparently did nothing to combat them. Ratings from independent groups might well have produced quite different results.

Another methodological problem concerns the timing of measurement for, typically, subjects spent 15 minutes or so in their discussion and then rated the medium retrospectively. What this meant was that their perceptions reflected not just the medium itself but the proceedings also. The way in which the medium was evaluated was therefore confounded with whatever effects it had had on the discussion, and any attempt subsequently to use the ratings to account for what happened in the discussion was of little value because it was circular. Social presence could not be taken as a 'pure' index of the way in which people perceived the medium; nor could it be used to account for the medium's effects upon the process or outcome of an encounter. In both respects the result was disappointing.

The conceptual problems with social presence centre upon the definition. As shown already, Short, Williams & Christie (1976) were themselves not entirely clear about what they intended, but they appeared to mean that a medium's social presence denoted the extent to which it was perceived to allow psychologically close, interpersonal communication. The question this now raised was how subjects *arrived* at that perception, and it was here that the authors were least forthcoming. In rejecting informational concepts they had argued that there was more to media effects than the cues which subjects were permitted or denied; but, at the same time, they appeared to acknowledge that social cues were, nevertheless, what underpinned their concept.

> Social Presence depends upon not only the visual non-verbal cues transmitted, but also more subtle aspects such as the apparent distance of the other (influenced, perhaps, by voice, volume) and the 'realness' of the other (influenced, perhaps, by the fidelity of speech reproduction). Our prediction regarding differences in the Social Presence of various media is *not* simply that some media will be 'better' or more 'effective' than others. On the contrary, we hypothesize that the suitability of any given communications medium for a specified type of interaction will depend upon two things: the degree of Social Presence of the medium, and the degree of Social Presence required by the task. In particular, we would expect to observe the greatest distortions compared with face-to-face communication when a medium having a low degree of Social Presence is used for a type of person-to-person interaction requiring a high degree of Social Presence. . . . where the task does not require a high degree of Social Presence, we would not expect the Social Presence of the communications medium to be important. Thus, we would predict that in tasks where the emphasis is not on the people involved, and where the outcome does not reflect on the personal qualities of the individuals communicating, the outcome will be unaffected by the degree of Social Presence of the medium. Such tasks would include, for example, information transmission and simple problem-solving tasks (Short, Williams & Christie, 1976, pp. 74–5; authors' emphasis).

and

> We would suggest that non-verbal communication only has effects on the outcomes of mediated interactions to the extent that it determines feelings of Social Presence. Social Presence is a phenomenological variable more complex than the relatively simple variations in, say, amount of gaze. It is affected not simply by the transmission of single non-verbal cues, but by whole constellations of cues which affect the 'apparent distance' of the other. In turn, it is more useful than any simple knowledge of the functions of non-verbal cues in predicting which tasks would be affected by medium of communication, and which would be unaffected (Short, Williams & Christie, 1976, p. 157).

At the time when Short, Williams & Christie (1976) was published we had not yet devised our concept of cuelessness, and the authors therefore had no opportunity to comment on it. They did, however, discuss the relationship between social presence and two other concepts: intimacy and immediacy. With respect to intimacy, they suggested simply that the social presence of a medium should be included alongside gaze, smiling, and so on, as one of the independent variables. For example, just as high levels of eye-contact indicated an intimate relationship so too, they argued, did the decision to communicate face-to-face rather than over the telephone or in writing.

With respect to immediacy, the position was more complex. In some cases social presence and immediacy would covary. If, for example, two people had to choose to meet over a telephone or a videophone, and both media were available, social presence and immediacy would both be greater if they chose the latter. In other cases, however, the relationship would be different.

> For example, if a person uses his telephone to speak to someone in an adjacent office when it would be just as convenient to go and see him, an impression of 'distance' and non-immediacy is likely to be created, especially if the person making the call is the other's superior. However, the non-immediacy associated with the use of the telephone in this instance is less likely to be replicated when the two parties are separated by considerable physical distances. In these cases, where face-to-face communication is not practicable, the use of the telephone does not carry the same connotation. Although immediacy varies in these two kinds of situation, the Social Presence afforded by the telephone will be the same (unless, of course, the quality of the sound is affected by the distances involved; if so, Social Presence will be *greater*, not less, when the two parties are in adjacent offices) (Short, Williams & Christie, 1976, p. 73; authors' emphasis).

Cuelessness revisited: some refinements

The concept of cuelessness first appeared in a paper by Rutter & Stephenson (1979a) and at that time we were very clear about its status. It was an informational concept, not a phenomenological one, and it referred simply to the aggregate number of social cues which were available to subjects. Since then, however, our ideas have changed in certain respects, and we have introduced a number of refinements. Two main issues have preoccupied us – the definition of cuelessness and the mechanism by which cuelessness has its effects – and I should like to conclude this section of the chapter by discussing them both.

The first issue, how to define cuelessness, arose from the experiment by Rutter *et al.* (1984), in which for the first time we introduced groups of more than two people. The problem was, as shown earlier, that although there were now more cues available than in dyads, people seemed unable to make use of them. In social interaction, just as in any other task, our capacity to process information is limited, and the addition of extra participants meant that less and less information could be absorbed from each one. The important measure, we therefore concluded, was not *available* cues but *usable* cues, and it is the latter which we now take to underpin our concept. As the aggregate number of usable cues decreases, cuelessness increases.

Despite our new definition, many conceptual questions remain, and it is only fair to acknowledge that we have not yet managed to resolve them all. At present the concept of cuelessness still lacks precision, and we are able to do no more than rank-order our experimental conditions. For example, while we can say that closed-circuit television is more cueless than face-to-face and less so than audio, we cannot say with any precision which are the most important cues it makes available, or how they function together, or what happens when they are removed. Nor, as yet, can we properly quantify the distinction between 'available' and 'usable' – though we are confident that the distinction is important.

A related question is whether quantity of information is all that matters, or whether quality may be important too. Audio, for example, removes some cues altogether, but many others are merely degraded, and we do not yet know how significant the distinction between removal and degradation may be. Indeed, should not cues in any case be weighted, to acknowledge that some are more salient than others; and might not the salience of a particular cue change as the encounter develops – the stare or mutter which alters the whole course of the interaction? Moreover, if cues do vary in salience, perhaps people use selective attention and simply ignore all but the most important. If so, perhaps much of the information which the richest settings make available is redundant, and face-to-face does not necessarily produce the 'maximal' or 'optimal' performance which has often been assumed and regarded as the 'baseline' for comparison. Finally, if people do attend selectively, and if 'usable' rather than 'available' cues is the crucial variable, have we not changed the status of our concept? Have we not stepped back from an informational description of the physical properties of media and settings to a psychological, perhaps even phenomenological, description of the cognitions of people? In fact we have not, but, as will be shown below, we do now acknowledge that phenomenology has a significant role to play.

Apart from definition and conceptualization, our other main concern at present is the mechanism by which cuelessness has its effects. When we first developed our model we assumed that cuelessness had a direct effect upon behaviour, and the first thing it influenced was the content of what was said. If, for example, a wooden screen was placed between two people, visual cues were removed altogether and, apart from smell, heat, and touch, all that remained was auditory cues, themselves probably degraded to some extent. Together, the reduction and degradation of information meant that the setting was relatively cueless, and the nett result was a direct effect upon content.

The problem we faced was that it was very difficult to see how cues such as heat and smell could, in fact, influence speech directly, and we were therefore compelled to revise our model. What we now suggest is that the effect is indirect, and that cuelessness operates by inducing a certain 'psychological set', in rather the way that Moscovici first suggested. At the start of the encounter, subjects make use of whatever social cues they can to form an impression of psychological proximity or distance – the feeling that their partner is 'there' or 'not there' – and it is this which in turn determines the content of what is said, and so the style and outcome of the interaction. Cuelessness remains firmly an informational concept, but we now acknowledge that phenomenology does play a role, namely as the mediating link between cues and content. The revised version of the model is given in Figure 5.2.

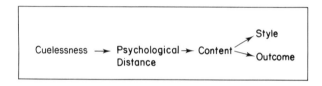

Figure 5.2   Revised model of cuelessness

Although the introduction of psychological set may appear to be a small change, there are a number of important implications, and two in particular deserve attention. The first is that a variety of factors quite apart from cuelessness may also influence set. The purpose of the encounter, for example, may well be one, and so too may the relationship between the subjects, and their degree of familiarity with the setting. Each is likely to have its own independent effects upon set, but there will also be interactions between them, and changes over time.

The second implication concerns the relationship of cuelessness to social presence, for it may appear that there is now very little difference between them. For practical purposes that may well be true but, conceptually, the two remain quite distinct, in at least three respects. First, while our model explicitly separates social cues from set, the concept of social presence does not. For us, cuelessness merely *influences* set; for the Communications Studies Group, social presence *is* that set. Second, while – at least, in principle – we can specify and quantify in advance what produces a particular set, the Communications Studies Group cannot, for the social presence of a medium is measured only at the end of an encounter, and there is no way of knowing how the judgement is reached or what underpins it. Finally, there is a difference too in the aims with which the models were developed. Social presence was intended to account for everyday practical issues in telecommunications, more than anything, while cuelessness was concerned with theoretical and empirical issues in social psychology. There were many questions which interested us and, not least, we hoped to be able to demonstrate that, within our one theoretical framework, all the disparate findings discussed in this and the previous chapter could be integrated together – content, style and outcome. It is to that issue that I now turn, in the final section of the chapter.

Relationships between content, style, and outcome

The cuelessness model makes two predictions: that content, style, and outcome will vary according to the aggregate number of usable cues available to subjects; and that content, style, and outcome are interrelated. The effect of cuelessness is to produce task-oriented, depersonalized content, an unspontaneous style, and a particular range of outcomes; and the relationship between the dependent measures is such that both style and outcome are the products of content. The main purpose of this final section of the chapter is to examine the second prediction in detail but, before that, we must briefly reconsider the first.

The first of our studies was concerned with content, and it was published by Stephenson, Ayling & Rutter (1976). Face-to-face and audio discussions about union–management relations were compared by means of Conference Process Analysis, and it was expected that task-orientation would appear as exchange of task-relevant information and discussion of outcomes, while the main indices of depersonalization would be criticism and lack of praise for one's opponent, a tendency towards frequent disagreements, and a lack of reference to oneself balanced against frequent references to the party one represented.

Very similar definitions were later used by Morley & Stephenson (1977) and Tysoe (in press) in their own research on union–management relations but in a paper by Rutter, Stephenson & Dewey (1981), as shown earlier, it was suggested that the concepts should be revised. Task-orientation, we argued, would appear as frequent exchange of task-relevant information, frequent discussion of outcomes and procedures, and a concern to avoid irrelevant information – a definition which was reasonably close to the original. 'Depersonalization', however, had confused two separate dimensions: 'impersonal' and 'antagonistic'. Impersonal discussions, we believed, would be marked by frequent references to third parties outside the encounter or to nobody at all, and only occasional references to oneself or the other people who were present; and antagonistic comments – or 'negative personal acts', as Bales (1950) called them – would appear as rejection and unwillingness to accept what one's partner contributed, and criticism and lack of praise. Similarly amended definitions were also adopted by Kemp & Rutter (1982) and Rutter et al. (1984).

All six studies, from Stephenson, Ayling & Rutter (1976) to Rutter et al. (1984), have already been presented in detail in this or the previous chapter but, for the sake of clarity, all the results for content are reproduced together in one table, Table 5.5. Only face-to-face and audio are shown (or screen where there was no audio condition), and the table gives means and significance levels

Table 5.5 Analyses of content

	Rutter, Stephenson & Dewey (1981) Exp. II		Kemp & Rutter (1982)		Rutter et al. (1984), two-person groups		Rutter et al. (1984), four-person groups		Stephenson, Ayling & Rutter (1976)		Morley & Stephenson (1977), 'Demy Ltd.'		Tysoe (in press)	
	FF	A	FF	A	FF	S	FF	S	FF	A	FF	A	FF	A
Task-orientation														
Information	30·4	31·0	44·6	40·8	44·9	31·6**	36·1	37·5	48·6	55·5*	15·9	13·9	33·2	27·3
Irrelevant information	27·7	19·6	2·1	3·9	3·1	0·9	1·2	1·0	Not recorded		Not recorded		Not recorded	
Outcomes	21·6	27·9	32·3	34·7	36·6	49·5***	41·8	43·9	1·8	1·3	17·8	18·4	41·1	49·3
Procedures	2·9	7·1**	1·7	2·9	0·9	1·1	1·4	1·1	Not known		1·3	1·1	3·6	5·5
Impersonal content														
Self	18·5	21·2	7·4	8·1	14·7	16·4	16·0	16·8	7·6	7·3	4·9	6·6	8·4	8·4
Others excluding speaker	6·4	8·3	3·3	3·2	3·3	3·9	5·9	3·4	Not known		Not recorded		Not recorded	
Others including speaker	0·4	1·6**	1·6	1·3	2·2	1·6	2·4	3·2	7·7	11·2*	7·9	11·5*	Not recorded	
Third parties	8·2	7·6	29·8	27·6	10·8	11·2	9·1	8·1	Not known		Not recorded		Not recorded	
No referent	66·5	61·2	57·9	59·9	68·9	67·0	66·6	68·6	Not known		14·1	15·2	61·0	64·9
Antagonistic content														
Reject	2·0	1·3	25·0	28·2	1·0	1·3	2·8	3·1	0·7	1·1	3·1	2·8	Not known	
Accept	26·8	20·7	2·6	0·9*	28·6	25·4	22·3	21·2	Not known		3·1	4·2	Not known	
Praise	0·1	0·1	0·9	0·4	0·0	0·1	0·1	0·0	0·9	0·3*	5·5	6·8*	0·2	0·3
Criticism	0·9	0·3	6·0	3·1	0·0	0·1	0·9	0·3	2·0	2·2	3·8	3·4	0·1	0·4

* $P < 0.05$; ** $P < 0.01$; *** $P < 0.001$

for every CPA category. In general, as we have seen already, the most consistent effects came from the 'outcomes' category of task-orientation and the 'accept' category of antagonism. For six of the seven sets of data there was more discussion of outcomes in the cueless condition than face-to-face, though significantly so only in Rutter, Stephenson & Dewey (1981); and in all but one of the recorded results, there was more acceptance face-to-face than in the cueless setting, though again significantly so in only one of the cases. Overall, the effects of cuelessness were less marked than we had hoped, and we therefore wondered whether further refinements to our concepts might be necessary before we could go on to a proper examination of the relationships between content, style and outcome.

The question which concerned us most was the 'internal validity' or 'construct validity' of CPA – whether the categories which we believed ought to hang together actually did. To find out, we proceeded as follows. For all four sets of data for which content and style had both been measured – Rutter, Stephenson & Dewey (1981), Kemp & Rutter (1982), Rutter et al. (1984) two-person groups, and Rutter et al. (1984) four-person groups – we took all three of our dimensions and calculated the correlation for every pair of indices within each one. The calculations were carried out across all subjects, irrespective of medium, and the results are presented in Table 5.6.

The first dimension we examined was 'task-orientation', and what we expected to find was that 'information', 'outcomes', and 'procedure' would all correlate positively. What we actually found was something very different, namely strong negative correlations between 'outcomes' and 'information', and 'outcomes' and 'irrelevant information', and little else. Throughout our experiments 'information' has almost always been the most frequently used category, and what the correlations suggest, despite our original belief, is that 'information' need not signal task-orientation. Whether subjects are behaving in a task-oriented way or an interpersonal way, they will always have relevant information to exchange, and 'information' will frequently correlate negatively with other categories simply because the more a subject uses relevant information the less the other categories can be used. Furthermore, the distinction between task-orientation and depersonalization is in any case particularly fraught when the task requires one to be personal, as was the case in Rutter et al. (1984). As shown in the discussion of that particular paper, what we now believe is that, since the goal for subjects in all our experiments, at least implicitly, is to debate a topic and to try to persuade others to one's point of view or reach some sort of agreement, task-orientation will be apparent in two principal measures – exchange of outcomes, and avoidance of information which is irrelevant to the task. 'Information' is not a useful index, and 'procedures' are seldom discussed.

A similar conclusion emerged also from the paper by Tysoe (in press). When face-to-face and audio were compared for 'information' overall, there was no significant difference but, when the category was broken down into seven types of information, three significant effects appeared – and in each case the value

Table 5.6 Relationships between content categories

	Rutter, Stephenson & Dewey (1981), Exp. II	Kemp & Rutter (1982)	Rutter et al. (1984), two-person groups	Rutter et al. (1984), four-person groups
Task-orientation				
(a) Information × Irrelevant				
information	− 71***	− 11	+ 28	+ 03
Outcome	+ 05	− 66***	− 91***	− 91***
Procedure	− 23	− 43*	+ 12	+ 03
(b) Irrelevant information ×				
Outcome	− 69***	− 46**	− 57*	+ 07
Procedure	− 10	+ 20	− 13	+ 24
(c) Outcome × Procedure	+ 17	+ 02	− 14	− 14
Impersonal content				
(a) Self × Others excluding				
speaker	− 14	+ 05	− 48	+ 19
Others including speaker	+ 18	+ 47**	− 15	− 24
Third parties	− 38	− 38*	− 44	− 27
No referent	− 63**	− 15	− 30	− 70*
(b) Others excluding speaker ×				
Others including speaker	+ 18	+ 02	− 20	− 23
Third parties	− 15	+ 09	+ 46	− 42
No referent	− 38	− 40*	− 25	− 51*
(c) Others including speaker ×				
Third parties	− 27	− 40*	− 32	− 24
No referent	− 24	− 01	+ 19	+ 07
(d) Third parties ×				
No referent	− 20	− 80**	− 64*	− 03
Antagonistic content				
(a) Reject × Accept	− 15	− 25	− 30	− 06
Praise	− 27	+ 01	+ 06	+ 35
Criticism	+ 32	+ 01	+ 56*	+ 26
(b) Accept × Praise	+ 26	+ 28	+ 12	− 26
Criticism	+ 07	+ 22	− 56*	− 44
(c) Praise × Criticism	+ 06	+ 14	− 06	+ 48

* $P < 0.05$; ** $P < 0.01$; *** $P < 0.001$

for face-to-face was larger than for audio. Similarly, it may sometimes be useful to examine *interactions* between Mode and Resource, rather than Modes and Resources separately, for the fact that one has chosen a particular resource may be less interesting than what one does with it.

The second dimension we examined was 'impersonal', and here the prediction was that, if subjects were avoiding reference to people present, they would tend to refer to third parties or to nobody at all. That is, 'self', 'others excluding the speaker', and 'others including the speaker' would each correlate negatively with 'third parties' and 'no referent'. In general our expectations were borne out, though few of the values were statistically reliable. All eight of the predicted correlations for 'self' were negative, two significantly so; and the corresponding figures were six out of eight for 'others excluding the speaker', with one significant result, and six out of eight for 'others including the speaker', again with one significant effect. Our definition of 'impersonal' thus received moderately good support, though it does have to be acknowledged that the internal correlations between 'self', 'others excluding the speaker', and 'others including the speaker' on the one hand, and 'third parties' and 'no referent' on the other, were not convincing – though perhaps only because the more subjects used one referent, the less they could use another.

The final dimension we examined was 'antagonism', and this time the prediction was that the more people accepted what was said, and the more they offered praise, the less rejection and criticism there would be. That is, 'accept' and 'praise' would correlate positively, as would 'reject' and 'criticism', but the relationship between the two clusters would be negative. As with 'impersonal', the results were in the main supportive when taken together, but few of the individual correlations were statistically reliable. 'Accept' and 'praise' correlated positively (in three out of four cases), and so did 'reject' and 'criticism' (in all four cases), but none of the former and only one of the latter was statistically significant. 'Accept' correlated negatively with 'reject', though non-significantly in all four cases; and none of the remaining correlations revealed any clear pattern. 'Accept' × 'criticism' produced only one significant negative correlation, and neither 'reject' × 'praise' nor 'criticism' × 'praise' yielded any significant effects. Thus, it was difficult to know quite what to conclude about the concept of 'antagonism'. The most important point to note, perhaps, is that all the categories apart from 'accept' were used only rarely and, for that reason, a clear pattern of correlations should, perhaps, not have been expected in the first place.

From an analysis of the 'internal validity' of our three concepts – task-orientation, depersonalization, and antagonism – we were now ready to turn to the main issue which concerned us, the relationships between content, style, and outcome. First we explored content and style, and our prediction was that the more task-oriented, impersonal, and antagonistic the content, the less spontaneous the style. Spontaneity, it will be recalled, was measured by the frequency and duration of simultaneous speech and, for the sake of clarity, the results from all five of our sets of data are reproduced in Table 5.7. All the other measures of style are also included, and as in the corresponding table for content, only the results for face-to-face and audio are shown, or screen where no audio condition was included. Generally, as the table makes clear, effects of cuelessness on simultaneous speech were easy to detect and, indeed, they were among the strongest and most consistent of all our findings. The question now was how well our measures of content and simultaneous speech would correlate together.

The results of our calculations are presented in Table 5.8. For all four sets of

160

Table 5.7 Analyses of style: mean values

	Rutter & Stephenson (1977)		Rutter, Stephenson & Dewey (1981) Exp. II		Kemp & Rutter (1982)		Rutter et al. (1984), two-person groups		Rutter et al. (1984), four-person groups	
	FF	A	FF	A	FF	A	FF	S	FF	S
Duration simultaneous speech (seconds)	18·7	9·4***	8·3	5·8*	12·5	6·5*	Not recorded		Not recorded	
No. simultaneous speech	14·7	9·0**	12·7	7·6	7·0	4·3	2·5	2·3	3·3	1·6*
Duration silence (seconds)	18·9	14·4	11·5	20·2	16·5	14·5	Not recorded		Not recorded	
No. utterances	18·2	15·3	9·7	10·7	9·4	7·7	3·5	3·3	2·5	1·8
Length utterances (seconds)	25·7	34·3*	32·7	31·5	34·3	40·0	33·5	32·2	23·1	25·9
No. floor changes	28·7	25·3	15·9	18·3	16·0	12·6	5·2	5·2	6·8	6·5
Duration speech (seconds)	145·0	142·3	90·6	83·7	88·0	87·1	Not recorded		Not recorded	
No. words	431·3	455·4	280·6	260·8	231·0	260·3	88·0	95·2	50·2	42·4
Noun–verb ratio	1·5	1·5	37·9	38·8	Not recorded		Not recorded		Not recorded	
Speech rate (words/second)	3·0	3·2	3·2	3·2	3·2	3·0	Not recorded		Not recorded	
Percentage utterances ending as question	13·6	15·4	14·4	22·9*	16·1	18·8	13·7	19·1	15·5	17·4
Percentage floor changes following question	20·4	21·1	16·7	27·4*	Not recorded		Not recorded		Not recorded	
No. acknowledgement signals	6·1	4·3	7·2	3·6*	3·5	3·6	4·1	3·5	2·8	1·8
Filled pause ratio	2·4	3·3	2·5	2·8	1·8	4·0**	2·0	3·4	1·7	2·9
Speech disturbance ratio	6·3	8·2*	7·4	9·6*	3·8	4·7	Not recorded		Not recorded	

* $P < 0·05$; ** $P < 0·01$; *** $P < 0·001$.

Table 5.8 Predicted relationships between content and style

	Simultaneous speech duration				Simultaneous speech number			
	Rutter, Stephenson & Dewey (1981) Exp. II	Kemp & Rutter (1982)	Rutter et al. (1984), two-person groups	Rutter et al. (1984), four-person groups	Rutter, Stephenson & Dewey (1981), Exp. II	Kemp & Rutter (1982)	Rutter et al. (1984), two-person groups	Rutter et al. (1984), four-person groups
Outcome	− 43*	− 38*	− 57*	—	− 28	− 18	− 67**	− 13
Irrelevant information	+ 39	+ 27	+ 18	—	+ 20	+ 10	+ 39	− 25
Self	+ 12	− 19	− 29	—	+ 10	− 16	− 29	− 34
Others excluding speaker	− 35	− 08	+ 02	—	− 11	+ 08	+ 27	+ 35
Others including speaker	− 28	− 12	+ 09	—	− 13	− 25	+ 07	− 15
Third parties	− 28	− 32	+ 12	—	− 33	− 16	+ 08	− 14
No referent	+ 32	+ 46**	+ 11	—	+ 21	+ 25	+ 09	+ 21
Reject	+ 01	+ 31	− 15	—	+ 27	+ 13	+ 22	+ 41
Accept	+ 54**	+ 49**	+ 35	—	+ 16	+ 65**	+ 17	+ 26
Praise	+ 45*	+ 05	− 29	—	+ 42*	+ 06	− 35	− 17
Criticism	+ 23	+ 07	− 09	—	+ 18	+ 10	+ 14	+ 33

* $P < 0.05$; ** $P < 0.01$.

data for which the appropriate information was available, we simply correlated all three groups of content categories with our two measures of simultaneous speech, duration and frequency. For 'task-orientation' the results were very clear and were exactly what we had predicted. For 'outcomes' all three correlations with the duration of simultaneous speech were negative and statistically reliable, and all four with frequency were likewise negative, though only one was statistically reliable this time. For 'irrelevant information' six of the correlations were positive, though none was significant. Thus, all the significant correlations favoured our prediction, and all but one of the remainder tended in the same direction.

For 'impersonal' the results were less clear, and only one of the thirty-five correlations was statistically reliable. What is more, the direction was often the opposite of what we had predicted. Thus, five out of seven correlations with 'self', and five out of seven with 'others including the speaker' were negative rather than positive, and so were three out of seven with 'others excluding the speaker'; and while five out of seven correlations with 'third parties' were negative as predicted, all seven with 'no referent' were positive – the opposite of prediction. The latter finding was particularly puzzling, since it was consistent across all our experiments and even reached significance in one case, but a possible explanation is that utterances which contained no referent were often brief questions or comments which people interpolated spontaneously. If so, we may have discovered an unexpected link between content and style but, be that as it may, there was little support for our original prediction.

The final variable was 'antagonism', and this time the findings were strong and reliable, and in general they were consistent with our prediction. The most convincing pattern was for 'accept', where all seven correlations were positive, as predicted, and three reached statistical significance. For 'praise', the trend was similar, with four out of seven correlations positive, and two of them significant; but for both 'reject' and 'criticism' the majority were negative rather than positive, though none was statistically reliable. Thus, all the significant correlations favoured our prediction, but the trends among the remainder were unclear.

For the sake of completeness we concluded our analysis of style by examining all the other correlations with 'task-orientation', 'impersonal', and 'antagonism'. The results are presented in Table 5.9 and, although there was no overall pattern, there were a number of consistencies. Task-orientation tended to correlate with conciseness and, while impersonal content produced no significant relationships, personal content was associated with silence and reticence. Antagonism revealed no relationships for 'praise' and 'criticism' – which in any case were very rare – but twice 'accept' correlated positively with acknowledgement signals and with frequency of utterances. Thus, the most encouraging feature of the supplementary findings was that they were less consistent than those for which our model had made predictions, as well as less widespread across our experiments.

From the relationships between content and style, we turned finally to

Table 5·9 Supplementary relationships between content and style

	Rutter, Stephenson & Dewey (1981) Exp. II.	Kemp & Rutter (1982)	Rutter et al. (1984), two-person groups	Rutter et al. (1984), four-person groups
Outcome	Word No. −44*	SD +39*	–	–
Irrelevant information	Word No. +49* Speech rate +48* AA +48*	Utterance length −35* Utterance No. +48* FC No. +49**	–	–
Self	–	–	–	No. utterances per person −51* No. FC −50*
Others excluding speaker	Duration of silence +53** Duration of speech −55**	AA −51** SD +42*	Percentage utterances = question +52*	Words per person +61*
Others including speaker	–	Duration of silence +39* Duration of speech −41*	No. FC +55* FP +50*	
Third parties	–	Speech rate +38*	–	–
No referent	Percentage utterances = question −44* Percentage FC →? −41*	AA +48**	–	–
Reject	Utterance No. +45* FC No. +47**	AA +57***	Percentage utterances = question +56*	Utterance length +60*
Accept	AA +75***	Utterance No. +63*** FC No. +53*** Word No. +43* Speech rate +45* FP−41*	AA +72**	Utterance No. +49* Utterance length −53*
Praise	–	–	–	–
Criticism	–	–	FP −51*	–

*P < 0·05; **P < 0·01; ***P < 0·001

164

content and outcome, and our prediction was that, the more task-oriented, impersonal, and antagonistic the content, the greater the degree of opinion change. This time there was only one experiment to examine, Rutter *et al.* (1984), and for two-person and four-person groups separately, we correlated all eleven measures of content with all four measures of outcome – movement, polarization, social progression, and agreement. The results are given in Table 5.10.

Table 5·10 Rutter *et al.* (1984): relationships between content and outcome

	Two-person groups				Four-person groups			
	M	P	SP	A	M	P	SP	A
Outcome	+10	+05	−07	+08	+13	+45	+32	−05
Irrelevant information	−06	+34	+12	+01	−38	+02	00	+48
Self	−61*	−05	+56*	−05	−41	−32	+08	−21
Others excluding speaker	+62*	+26	−54*	+02	−21	+12	+52*	−49*
Others including speaker	−04	+29	+13	+01	+35	+12	−19	+59*
Third parties	+25	−47	−43	−18	−22	+08	+05	+35
No referent	+15	+36	+03	+23	+51*	+05	−42	+02
Reject	+42	+19	−30	−14	−18	−09	+33	−43
Accept	−42	+18	+44	−01	+41	+41	−07	−04
Praise	+20	−04	−38	+30	−19	+13	+40	−36
Blame	+89**	+15	−75**	−11	−07	−11	+12	−46

*$P < 0.05$; **$P < 0.01$.
M = movement; P = polarization; SP = social progression; A = agreement.

For 'task-orientation' there were no significant effects for either two-person or four-person groups but, for 'impersonal', there were several for both. In two-person groups the more subjects referred to themselves, the less movement and the more social progression they showed, while the correlations for reference to others present excluding the speaker showed exactly the opposite pattern. In four-person groups, reference to others excluding the speaker was associated with more social progression but less group agreement, while reference to others including the speaker correlated positively with group agreement. The more subjects avoided referring to anyone at all, the more overall movement they showed. For 'antagonism', subjects in two-person groups showed a positive association between criticism and movement and a negative association between criticism and social progression, while subjects in four-person groups showed no associations at all.

Though there was good evidence that content and outcome did correlate, it is clear that the pattern was quite different from what we had predicted. For task-orientation there were no effects, and it may well be, as I suggested earlier, that because the task was to discuss abortion, an issue which is very

Table 5·11   Rutter *et al.* (1984): relationships between style and outcome

	Two-person groups				Four-person groups			
	M	P	SP	A	M	P	SP	A
No. simultaneous								
speech	+06	+29	+01	−28	+23	−05	−14	−34
No. utterances	−16	+51	+34	−18	+33	+32	−01	−11
Length utterances	+11	−52	−34	+33	−37	−22	+25	+10
No. floor changes	−13	+47	+31	−18	+54	+34	−21	+10
No. words	−14	+18	+18	−21	+26	00	+01	−39
Percentage utterances								
ending as question	+14	+14	−04	−39	+23	+15	−20	+43
Acknowledgement								
signals	−34	+20	+41	−12	+35	+07	−10	−22
Filled pause ratio	+15	+31	−14	−17	+31	+23	−10	+32

No significant effects.
Abbreviations as in Table 5·10.

personal, the concept of task-orientation is of little relevance, and quite different effects would be found if a different topic were used. For depersonalization, at least in two-person groups, concentrating the discussion on oneself seems to have been associated with moving towards the pole one already favoured, while reference to other people and antagonism towards them were associated with movement back from the pole towards the centre. There was no obvious interpretation for the four-person results and, just as for task-orientation, it would be interesting to repeat the experiment with a different topic.

To complete our analysis there was just one set of relationships left to examine, and that was the correlations between style and outcome. Data were available for only the last of our experiments, of course, Rutter *et al.* (1984), and the correlations for two-person and four-person groups separately are given in Table 5.11. The results were striking, for, although a total of sixty-four correlations was calculated, not one of them was statistically reliable. Thus, while content predicted both style and outcome, the latter were unrelated – just as we had argued – and it is tempting indeed to conclude that content is causal, as we believe. As yet, however, we cannot, for the evidence at present is no more than 'circumstantial' and before we can be sure, we shall need more sophisticated statistical analyses, direct experimental manipulations of content and, above all, applied research in the field. It is to that that I turn in Chapter 6.

CHAPTER 6.

APPLICATIONS

We come now to the final chapter of the book. In the first three chapters I examined the literature on LOOKING. First I discussed the everyday pattern and structure of gaze, then I moved on to its emotional significance, and finally I considered its role in offering and collecting information. An impressive body of research was included, but the closer we explored, the clearer it became that what mattered most to people was not LOOKING but SEEING – visual access to the whole person. In Chapter 4 I discussed SEEING in detail and, in Chapter 5, I proposed a model to try to bring the findings together in one theoretical framework.

At the heart of the model lay CUELESSNESS. Social cues, it was suggested, combine to form an aggregate, and they produce a psychological set. If cues are plentiful the partner will seem to be psychologically close, but if the setting is 'cueless' a feeling of psychological distance will predominate. Either way, the immediate effect will be to influence behaviour, first the content of what the participants say, and then the style they use and the outcomes they reach. The more cueless the setting, the more task-oriented and depersonalized the content, the less spontaneous the style and, in negotiations, the more likely the side with the stronger case to prevail.

The question to be asked now is how far our conclusions will extend to everyday life outside the laboratory. From time to time, it is true, occasional field experiments and naturalistic studies have been identified already, but very little of what has been discussed has concerned itself directly with applying the literature systematically. There are, however, two important areas in which applied research has been conducted – blindness and 'telephone conferencing' – and it is to these areas that the chapter is devoted. In each case the aims of the discussion will be both theoretical and practical. Theoretically, I shall examine how far our conclusions hold up, and how far one can make use of applied settings to improve and extend them; and, practically, I shall consider the implications of the literature for everyday social change.

Blindness

Definitions; prevalence; causes

Although it is generally agreed that total blindness should be defined as an inability to perceive light in either eye, only 10% of people who are registered blind have no sight at all, and there is little agreement about how to define the remainder. Two main approaches have been taken: one quantitative, the other functional. The quantitative approach measures the subject's visual acuity, and compares it with standardized norms. Normal vision is 20/20, and blindness is commonly taken to start at 20/200 in the better eye. That is, to read a display which someone of normal vision can read at 200 centimetres, the subject has to stand at 20 centimetres. People who are 'partially sighted' or 'visually impaired' are generally said to range from 20/70 to 20/200 (Ashcroft, 1963). The functional approach, in contrast, measures what the subject can do – travelling, climbing stairs, reading the newspaper, and so on – and the correlation with visual acuity is often very low.

The second question to ask about blindness is how prevalent it is and here, too, it is difficult to give a confident answer. While the USA includes items about blindness in its national census, Britain does not, and registration remains voluntary. Though some estimates suggest that as many as 0·5% of people in Britain are blind or visually handicapped (Cullinan, 1977), official figures are much lower. In 1980, for example, the DHSS register included only 108,000 blind people and 51,000 partially sighted, and around 25% also had other handicaps – making their detection more likely. Seventy-five per cent of the blind group were aged 65 or over, but only 2% were fifteen or under, and as few as 0·05% – a total of 254 children – were at or under 2 years of age. In all age groups from 0 to 59, males outnumbered females, but thereafter the balance was reversed, presumably because women have a longer life expectancy. Of people on the register aged 16–64, almost 35% were employed.

As to the causes of blindness, again the evidence is incomplete. Sorsby (1972), for example, in a DHSS report on blind people in England and Wales aged 0 to 65, found that over 40% of cases were due to either 'unknown aetiology' or 'myopic degeneration'. Under 25% were attributable to pre-natal effects and, of those that were, the majority lost their sight in later life, and very few were born blind – consistent with the 1980 figure that only 0·05% were 2 years of age or under. Of people who lost their sight adventitiously, the majority contracted some form of systemic disease, and much the most common was diabetes, accounting for over 15% of all the cases. Tumours, infectious diseases, and poisoning were together responsible for a little over 5%, while accidents accounted for under 1·5%.

Psychological development in childhood

The development of blind children and those who are visually impaired has been studied extensively but, unfortunately, conclusions are very difficult to draw. Much of the literature has relied on single-case studies or clinical observations, and there have been very few controlled investigations. What is more, the literature has been greatly influenced by psychoanalytic theory, and few systematic alternatives have been pursued. Nevertheless, there is some interesting material to review, and excellent accounts have been published by Lowenfield (1971), Warren (1977), and Kemp (1981b) – on whose paper much of this and the following section on adulthood are based.

The first area which has attracted attention is perceptual-motor and cognitive development and, as one would expect, many blind children show marked deficits. Perceptual-motor performance is often impaired, especially in 'higher order' skills such as form identification, spatial relations, and perceptual-motor co-ordination, and cognitive deficits are common too. The precise significance of visual impairment is seldom easy to establish, however, because many of the children also have other handicaps.

A second area of interest, but one which has received much less attention than the first, has been the development of communication skills, and much of the work has centred on language. Speech production and the acquisition of vocabulary and syntactic structure have generally been found to be quite normal, and the most common problems for blind children have been in their semantic development. Many words carry meaning only if we have a visual referent to which to tie them – colour words, for example – yet blind children will often try to make up their own verbal descriptions. The result is vague or even meaningless 'verbalisms', as they are sometimes called, and the problem is particularly acute for congenitally blind children. It has sometimes been claimed that serious intellectual impairment can follow.

Research on nonverbal communication has concentrated on expressiveness, and occasionally it has been suggested that blind children appear 'flattened' in their expression of emotions, and use relatively few signals to accompany what they say. Systematic research, however, has revealed little of significance and, indeed, so alike are blind and sighted children that the similarity has even been used as an argument that nonverbal signalling is innate (Eibl-Eibesfeldt, 1970; Ekman & Oster, 1979). The only abnormality which does appear to be well established is that blind children often develop inappropriate, stereotyped forms of behaviour known as 'blindisms' – rocking, rubbing the eyes, grimacing, and so on. Moreover, unless an attempt is made at remedial training, the abnormalities often become exaggerated over time, and the differences between blind and sighted children increase.

The third and final area of interest has been the development of personality and social behaviour. How to measure personality is, of course, a vexed issue even in the literature on sighted children, and blindness brings additional problems – in particular, how to administer a test which has been standardized on sighted children, and how to interpret the results in the absence of appropriate published norms. The most common response has been to move away from nomothetic tests altogether, and to pursue an idiographic approach, generally from a psychoanalytic viewpoint. Taken as a whole, the evidence suggests that blind children may be more passive, more dependent, more disturbed, and less aggressive than sighted children – but, as Warren (1977) cautions, 'there is relatively little known about either the determinants of, or the functional significance of, personality characteristics in blind children' (Warren, 1977, p. 246).

With respect to social behaviour, there is good evidence that blind children are often impaired – though sighted children with a blind parent do not appear to suffer (Collis & Bryant, 1981). Research on attachment and responsiveness, for example – smiling, separation anxiety, fear of strangers, and so on – has often suggested that blind children develop more slowly than sighted children, and that their problems are generally more marked. There is also evidence that the problems remain, and that the parents of blind children develop rather different attitudes towards socialization from those of the parents of sighted children, and perhaps treat their children rather differently. In the absence of properly controlled research, however, it is quite impossible to say what should be attributed to the initial disability and what should be attributed to other factors.

Social adjustment in adulthood

As has been shown already, the majority of blind or partially sighted people lose their sight adventitiously, most commonly as they approach old age. Whereas the literature on children has concentrated on the effects of blindness on psychological development, research on adults has focused on adaptation and adjustment. Once again, many authors have taken a psychoanalytic approach, and it is sometimes suggested that the immediate period of adjustment resembles grief and mourning. Other writers have explored personality and while there is no evidence that blind people as a group develop any special traits of their own, it is well established that many of them suffer from low self-esteem. How much should be attributed to the loss of vision, however, and how much to handicap in general, or to age and social isolation, for example, it is very difficult to say because proper controls have seldom, if ever, been used.

The most consistent finding on adjustment is that the greatest problem of all for blind people is often the reactions of sighted people. Stereotyped views of 'the blind' are commonplace – sometimes positive but frequently negative – and it is often argued that the eventual status of the blind person is defined much less by what he or she achieves than by the attitudes and behaviour of the population at large. Much the same is true for other handicaps.

The other main area of interest has been communication and social interaction and, although there have been very few experimental investigations, there are many reports of single-case studies and people's own experiences. The most obvious effects of losing one's sight are that reading and writing are made more difficult, and information is lost about one's physical and social environment, so that even sharing one's experiences with other people becomes a considerable task. Though technology can sometimes help – Braille, tape-recorders, and so on – for the majority the problems are hard to overcome.

What is less appreciated is that blind people often report great difficulty in the apparently commonplace activity of holding conversations. Visual communication plays a significant part in social encounters, as has been shown throughout the book, and the experience of blind people provides good support for many of our arguments. Unfortunately, though, it has to be stressed again that much of what has been written is unsystematic and poorly controlled: congenital and adventitious groups are treated as equivalent; totally blind and partially sighted people are grouped together; confounding variables are allowed to contaminate the conclusions. Nevertheless, there are some useful observations to consider.

One of the earliest papers was by Brieland (1950), and he began by noting that blind people are often described in the following ways: they speak more slowly than sighted people; their voices are louder, with less modulation, giving the impression of a 'broadcast' voice; they have less vocal variety; they use fewer facial expressions when they talk, and fewer gestures and movements of the body; and they move their lips less. Some at least of the descriptions were subsequently confirmed in Brieland's own experimental study, and Carroll (1961) went on to offer a first-hand interpretation in what is, perhaps, the most detailed and sensitive account to have been published of a blind person's own experience. Among the most important problems, he argued, were the lack of feedback and contextual information, the difficulty in locating and identifying speakers, and the difficulty in forming impressions of people. In each case, he believed, the underlying problem, and the most serious, was the loss of communication of affect.

Very similar conclusions were reached by Scott (1969), and his particular concerns were impression-formation and self-presentation. The most uncomfortable type of encounter, he suggested, was the first meeting between a blind person and a sighted person. The participants came with stereotyped beliefs about each other; the sighted person would often regard blindness as a stigma; the 'mechanics' of the encounter would be disturbed; and the relationship would be one of dependency, with the blind person subordinate. Where Carroll had regarded the loss of affective information as the crucial problem, Scott blamed the asymmetry of the relationship.

Experimental studies of social interaction

As has been shown in the two previous sections – psychological development in childhood, and social adjustment in adulthood – the most important limitation in the existing literature is that very little of the evidence has come from properly controlled, experimental studies. For both theoretical and practical reasons, what most concerned myself and my colleagues was social interaction in blind adults, and we therefore set up an investigation of our own. There were three experiments altogether. The first was by Rutter, Stephenson & Dewey

(1981) and was discussed in outline in Chapter 5, and the other two were by Kemp. One examined a series of two-person conversations – blind–blind, blind–sighted, and sighted–sighted – and the other made use of questionnaires. Both were designed to explore content, style, and outcome together, and both were reported in full in Kemp (1981a).

The first experiment in the series, by Rutter, Stephenson & Dewey (1981), was designed to test the cuelessness model, and it was not intended as a comparison between blind and sighted people or as an examination of the difficulties which blind people are said to experience in social interaction. All the subjects were blind students, as described in Chapter 5, and they were observed debating in pairs. Half met face-to-face and half over an audio link, and the object of the 15-minute discussion was to persuade one's partner to one's own point of view. Both congenital and adventitious subjects were included, and measures were taken of content and style.

The results revealed a number of differences between the face-to-face and audio conditions, all of them in style but, unfortunately, they were of little theoretical value. Face-to-face we had used cameras to record the proceedings but in the audio condition we had not, and all the significant effects were consistent with the view that the cameras had made subjects anxious and apprehensive. Moreover, informal comparisons between this and our earlier experiments suggested that blind and sighted people behaved very similarly for the most part, and the similarities far outweighed any observable differences.

The purpose of the second experiment, by Kemp (1981a), was to test this last suggestion in more detail, and there were two main objectives: to re-examine our model of cuelessness; and to offer a description of how blind people behave in conversations. Because of their handicap, blind people are limited in the social cues they can use, and their conversations can therefore be regarded as cueless, with blind–blind encounters the most cueless, sighted–sighted the richest in cues and blind–sighted in between – in much the way that video, curtain, and wooden screen were intermediate in our research with sighted people (Chapter 5). Furthermore, just as those experiments revealed that cuelessness affects not only outcome but also content and style, so it should be possible to detect similar effects here. The design of the experiment therefore included all three types of encounter and all three types of measure. Outcome was represented by subjects' impressions, particularly of the other person.

The predictions were as follows. First, it was expected that blind–blind conversations would be more task-oriented in content than sighted–sighted conversations, and also depersonalized. Second, they would lack spontaneity of style and, for both this and the first prediction, blind–sighted conversations would lie between the other two. Third, the evaluative quality of subjects' impressions would vary from condition to condition, and blind subjects would be less accurate than sighted subjects and also less confident. Finally, just as in our previous research, content and style would be related, and it would be found that the more task-oriented and depersonalized the content, the less spontaneous the style.

The experiment was begun at the University of Warwick and completed at the University of Kent at Canterbury, and sixty subjects took part – thirty blind and thirty sighted. The blind subjects were recruited through local federations, and through the DHSS and personal contacts, and there were three criteria for inclusion: blindness should be the only significant handicap; subjects should be self-supporting in the community and should not be living in an institution; and they should be registered blind. Twelve of the group were congenitally blind and eighteen were adventitious cases. Twenty-three had no sight at all, and the remaining seven were so badly impaired that they were unable to distinguish facial features. The congenital and adventitious groups were similar in age but, on average, the former had been blind for twice as long as the latter.

In contrast to the blind subjects, the sighted subjects were recruited through an advertisement in the local evening newspaper, and they were simply invited to take part in 'a study of conversations'. There were no criteria for inclusion. A wide variety of backgrounds was represented in both the blind and the sighted groups, and ages ranged from 19 to 74 years, with a mean of 46 for the blind subjects and 41 for the sighted subjects, a difference which was not significant.

From the pool of blind and sighted volunteers, we now made up thirty pairs, ten blind–blind, ten blind–sighted, and ten sighted–sighted. Half of each type were male and half were female and, as far as possible, the ages of the two subjects were similar. Each pair was then brought to the laboratory, and there the sessions began.

The proceedings fell into three parts. In the first, the subjects were introduced to each other and to the experimental layout and procedures, and were then taken to separate rooms to be interviewed. The interviews were conducted by the experimenters, and were designed to cover a brief inventory of biographical information – age, marital status, occupation, education, and so on. There then followed a seven-item questionnaire about a variety of socio-political opinions similar to those we had included in our earlier experiments – blood sports, national service, corporal punishment, and so on. The statements were presented by tape-recorder, and subjects were asked to say aloud whether they 'agreed' or 'disagreed' with each one. The responses were tape-recorded.

For the second stage of the procedure the subjects were reunited, and now they were asked to spend 15 minutes discussing one or more of the opinion statements to which they had just responded. Items which revealed a disagreement were chosen as far as possible, and the discussions were recorded on video-tape in split screen, and on audio-tape in stereo. A short coffee break followed.

The final stage of the experiment consisted of five questionnaires, each of which was an abbreviated and simplified version of the material first used by Kemp et al. (in press). The participants were separated again, and the items were presented by tape-recorder. The first questionnaire asked subjects to complete twelve bipolar items about their own behaviour during the discussion, and the structure was such that they had to choose one of two adjectives each time – 'co-operative'/'competitive', 'talkative'/'quiet', 'tense'/'relaxed', and so on. All the responses were tape-recorded and, after every item on both

Table 6·1   Kemp (1981a): content

Category	Blind–blind Mean	Blind–sighted Mean	Sighted–sighted Mean	d.f.	F
Mode 0	3·9	3·6	4·1	2,24	<1
Offer	54·0	58·6	63·7	2,24	5·5**
Reject	1·0	1·0	0·9	2,24	<1
Accept	32·3	29·5	24·5	2,24	3·2*
Seek	8·9	7·1	6·5	2,24	1·7
Resource 0	12·6	15·9	18·1	2,24	6·6**
Procedure	2·0	1·5	0·5	2,24	3·9*
Information	36·4	33·9	44·7	2,24	1·6
Irrelevant information	18·7	18·6	2·4	2,24	3·5*
Acknowledgement +	0·8	0·1	0·2	2,24	1·9
Acknowledgement −	1·5	1·1	0·7	2,24	<1
Outcome	28·1	28·8	33·5	2,24	<1
Referent 0	69·4	65·6	69·8	2,24	2·0
Self	13·8	15·3	14·5	2,24	<1
Others excluding speaker	4·0	3·9	3·2	2,24	<1
Others including speaker	1·2	0·7	0·7	2,24	2·0
Third parties	11·3	14·6	11·8	2,24	1·6

$*P<0.05; **P<0.01$

this and the remaining questionnaires, subjects were asked to say how confident they felt about the judgement they had just made, from 0% to 100%. The second set of questions asked subjects to respond to the biographical questionnaire again, but this time as if they were their partner, and the third did the same for the sociopolitical questionnaire. The fourth presented the twelve items from the first questionnaire again, but this time asking subjects to describe the other person's behaviour rather than their own, and the fifth consisted of fifteen adjective pairs to describe the other person's personality. With that, the procedure was complete, and the subjects were reunited for a thorough debriefing. On average, the experiment took 2 hours.

To test our hypotheses a variety of analyses were conducted, and the first examined the content of the discussions. Detailed verbatim transcripts were made according to our usual system, and the sessions were coded by Conference Process Analysis. Mean values for each dimension were calculated for every pair, and the differences between the three types of conversation were examined by analysis of variance. Significant effects were inspected by multiple comparisons.

The results are given in Table 6.1. The first prediction concerned task-orientation, and it was expected that, the more cueless the encounter, the more the discussion would focus on outcomes, and the less on information which was irrelevant to the task. In the event, the findings were exactly the opposite, for there was more not less irrelevant information in the blind–blind condition than the sighted–sighted condition, and less not more consideration of outcomes, though the latter effect was no more than a trend. The one prediction which did receive support was that, for both measures, the blind–sighted condition lay between the other two. Other findings revealed that there was more discussion of procedures in blind–blind conversations than sighted–sighted conversations, but less offering, and fewer incomplete utterances. In each case the blind–sighted condition again lay between the other two. Furthermore, there was less and less discussion of outcomes as time progressed, and the decrease was especially marked in the blind–blind condition.

The second prediction for content concerned depersonalization, and here we expected that blind–blind conversations would be less personal and more antagonistic than sighted–sighted conversations. Again, the prediction was rejected. There were no effects for any of the 'impersonal' indices, and the only effect for 'antagonism', 'accept', once more showed the opposite of what we had expected, with more acceptance in the blind–blind conversations, not less. Again, though, the blind–sighted condition was intermediate.

At first the findings were very difficult to understand because whenever a significant difference was revealed between blind–blind and sighted–sighted conversations, it was exactly the opposite of what we had expected. The one prediction which did receive support, however, was that the blind–sighted condition lay between the other two – and it was this that eventually led us to a possible interpretation.

What had happened, we suggested, was something very simple. Because the blind–blind conversations were lacking in social cues, subjects found them-selves without the information they needed about their partners, and they therefore asked for it in words. More time was spent on personal information, which was supposedly irrelevant to the task, and less time on the task itself, and it was precisely because of cuelessness that that was how subjects behaved. Sighted people faced with cuelessness – over an audio link, for example – have little relevant experience, and their way of coping is to avoid and ignore personal information. Blind people, however, do have that experience and, far from avoiding the personal dimension, they confront it directly and ask for the missing information in words. When only one member of a conversation is blind, the encounter lies somewhere between the other two. What we had done was simply to make the wrong predictions. Cuelessness remained the most parsimonious account.

From content we turned to style. A variety of measures were taken, as in our previous experiments, and this time the analysis was based on values for the individual rather than the pair. For the first time, therefore, we were able to make direct comparisons between the blind and sighted subjects in the blind–sighted condition – though, in the event, no significant differences emerged. As with content, the data were examined by analysis of variance, and significant effects were inspected by multiple comparisons.

The results are given in Table 6.2, and the prediction was that the more cueless the encounter, the less spontaneous the style, where spontaneity was measured by interruptions. For the frequency of interruptions, which was indicated by the number of times simultaneous speech occurred, there was a strong effect but, just as in our content analyses, it was the reverse of what we had predicted, with blind–blind conversations more spontaneous than sighted–sighted conversations. Though non-significant, the results for frequency showed just the same trend and in both cases the blind-sighted condition lay in between, as we had expected. The only other effect was that the blind–blind conversations included more utterances than the sighted–sighted conver-sations, presumably because they were interrupted more frequently, and again the blind–sighted condition was intermediate. There was no evidence that blind people spoke more slowly than sighted people, despite the claims of the previous literature (Brieland, 1950; Cutsforth, 1951; Carroll, 1961), and there were no effects of time.

Although the results were once again the opposite of what we had predicted initially, this time they were easy to interpret because we already knew the findings for content. According to our model, style is the product of content and the more task-oriented and depersonalized the latter, the less spontaneous the former. Blind–blind conversations, we found, were less task-oriented than the others, and to some extent more personal, and style simply followed suit.

From content and style we moved thirdly to outcome, and here we were concerned with subjects' impressions of each other and of their own behaviour during the discussion. Three sets of measures were taken – the evaluative quality of the impressions, their accuracy, and the confidence with which they

Table 6.2 Kemp (1981a): style

	Blind–blind		Blind–sighted		Sighted–sighted		d.f.	F
	Mean	SD	Mean	SD	Mean	SD		
No. occurrences of simultaneous speech	8·0	6·5	7·2	7·2	4·8	5·0	2,24	1·2
Duration of simultaneous speech (seconds)	34·8	12·4	27·6	18·0	18·6	6·9	2,24	4·1*
Duration of mutual silence (seconds)	15·3	9·8	11·0	9·3	15·4	17·3	2,24	<1
Length utterances (words)	27·5	14·6	43·6	25·5	48·1	35·9	2,24	3·0
No. utterances	20·6	7·2	14·6	7·5	13·3	6·3	2,24	4·1*
No. floor changes	13·2	6·6	8·7	4·3	9·7	5·7	2,24	2·7
Duration of speech (seconds)	159·6	46·3	158·3	45·4	151·7	36·6	2,24	2·9
Total no. words	443·3	145·4	459·7	126·7	441·3	112·9	2,24	<1
Speech rate (words per second)	2·8	0·5	3·0	0·5	2·9	0·5	2,24	<1
Percentage utterances ending as question	13·0	12·1	15·6	13·6	13·4	13·1	2,24	<1
No. attention signals	12·8	9·8	15·0	11·2	10·3	8·6	2,24	1·4
Filled pause ratio (per 100 words)	2·7	1·6	3·6	2·0	2·7	1·5	2,24	1·2
Speech disturbance ratio (per 100 words)	3·7	2·1	3·5	1·7	4·0	1·9	2,24	<1

*$P<0.05$

were held – and we predicted that, as cuelessness varied, so the evaluative quality would vary, and the greater the cuelessness, the less accurate the impressions would become and the less confidently they would be held.

To examine evaluative quality, we first factor-analysed each of the four questionnaires separately, taking the responses of all sixty subjects together – own behaviour, other's sociopolitical opinions, other's behaviour, and other's personality – and, in general, the factor structure which emerged was very similar to that which Kemp *et al.* (in press) had reported. For each question-naire in turn we then went on to examine the factors separately, by analysis of variance across the three types of conversation. The first questionnaire produced four factors, the second three, and the third four, but not one of the analyses revealed a significant effect of conditions. The final questionnaire, 'other's personality', produced three factors and this time there was one significant effect. The factor in question was 'sociable and balanced', and while people in the blind–blind condition formed positive impressions of each other, sighted–sighted perceptions were somewhat critical, and those in the blind–sighted condition were neutral.

To examine accuracy, a rather different approach was necessary. When we form impressions of people it is difficult to know whether they are accurate unless there is some tangible criterion against which to test them. In the case of two of our questionnaires, the biographical and sociopolitical inventories, we had such a criterion – the subject's own responses – and we were therefore able to compare the partner's impressions with the information the subject had already given us. Our analyses were based on chi-square tests and, because some of the expected frequencies would have been very small if the three experimental conditions had been taken separately, we chose simply to compare the thirty blind people with the thirty sighted people. In retrospect, since all the information a subject needed to form an accurate impression was likely to be contained in what was said in the discussion rather than what was conveyed nonverbally, we ought not, perhaps, to have expected any significant effects – and, indeed, none emerged. There was nothing to choose between the groups and, for the most part, there were very few errors.

Our final analysis concerned confidence, and here we were able to use all five questionnaires. After every item, subjects had been asked to note how confi-dent they felt in the judgement they had just made, and now the ratings were examined one by one, by analysis of variance across the three conditions. Of the fifty-five analyses only three produced a significant effect, scarcely more than chance would predict. In general, subjects were very confident indeed, from an average of 73% overall for the biographical questionnaire to 86% for the ratings of the other's behaviour, and there was no evidence that cuelessness had had any effect.

In summary, the findings for impression formation revealed very little. There were few significant effects, and those which did occur were probably due to chance. Like Kemp *et al.* (in press), we concluded, therefore, that visual communication played little part in the process, and was much less important than earlier writers had suggested. Furthermore, it also became clear from our supplementary analyses that congenital and adventitious subjects behaved very similarly, and so too did the blind and sighted members of the blind–sighted pairs, despite the 'asymmetry' to which previous writers had drawn attention (Scott, 1969).

From the outcome of the conversations we turned finally to the relationship between content and style, and we predicted that the more task-oriented and depersonalized the former, the less spontaneous the latter. Spontaneity was measured by the frequency and duration of interruptions, and our analysis consisted of correlations across all thirty pairs of subjects, irrespective of experimental condition. The measures were based on the pair.

The results are given in Table 6.3. First, we examined task-orientation, measured by concentration on outcomes and avoidance of irrelevant information, and the prediction received good support. All four correlations followed the expected pattern, and all but one reached statistical significance. The second set of measures, however – those concerned with impersonal content – was less clear. Five indices were examined altogether, and while all five followed the predicted pattern for the duration of interruptions, only one did so significantly and there was no detectable trend for frequency. The final set of correlations concerned 'antagonism', and here again the results were uncertain. For 'accept' and 'praise', all four values followed the predicted pattern, though only two reached statistical significance, while for 'reject', the correlations were practically zero, and for 'criticism' they were significantly positive, the reverse of what we had predicted. The latter finding was especially intriguing – though there is no obvious interpretation – because a subsequent analysis revealed that 'criticism' and 'praise' correlated positively together, something which we certainly did not expect.

Our experiment had begun with two main objectives – to re-examine the model of cuelessness, and to offer a description of how blind people behave in conversations – and, in summary, both had been achieved. First we examined the content and style of the discussions, and to our surprise, the behaviour we observed was exactly the opposite of what we had predicted, with blind–blind pairs significantly less task-oriented than sighted–sighted pairs and significantly more personal and spontaneous. There was, however, a straightforward explanation. Precisely because the blind–blind conversations were lacking in social cues, subjects found themselves without the personal information they needed about their partners, and they therefore asked for it in words. The consequence – which was reminiscent of the reversal between 'face-to-face' and 'screen' in the discussions of abortion in Rutter et al. (1984) – was an unexpectedly high level of personal exchange in the blind–blind condition, and a correspondingly low level of task-orientation. The blind–sighted condition lay between the other two, as we had expected, and content was once again a good predictor of style. Just as we had found for sighted subjects in our earlier work (Kemp et al., in press), cuelessness had little effect on impression formation.

As to our description of the behaviour of blind people, there was little if any

Table 6·3   Kemp (1981a): Relationships between content and style

Two-tailed

d.f. 29; $P < 0.05$; $r = 0·306$
$P < 0.01$; $r = 0·423$

		1	2	3	4	5	6	7	8	9	10	11	12	13	14	15	16	17	18	19	20	21	22	23	24	25	26	27	28	29	30
1	No. occurrences of simultaneous speech																														
2	Duration of simultaneous speech	67																													
3	Duration mutual silence	-15	03																												
4	Utterance length	-49	-53	-10																											
5	No. utterances	74	77	21	-82																										
6	No. floor changes	21	52	44	-77	80																									
7	Duration of speech	65	84	-52	-39	54	20																								
8	Total no. words	74	57	-11	-35	64	31	55																							
9	Speech rate	57	29	05	-21	48	24	22	93																						
10	Percentage utterances as questions	-23	03	28	-13	06	29	-12	-11	-08																					
11	No. of attention signals	61	64	-19	03	29	-13	65	54	35	-10																				
12	Filled pause ratio	-28	-34	-07	30	-47	-25	-50	-47	-11	-01	-01																			
13	Speech disturbance ratio	10	-24	-18	17	-18	-34	-11	-02	01	-07	-01	31																		
14	Mode 0 unclassified	51	10	-05	-45	42	19	16	30	27	-25	04	03	31																	
15	1 Offer	-32	-71	-11	46	-50	-43	-54	-18	05	-19	-54	08	19	05																
16	2 Reject	-12	01	34	01	02	14	-17	-19	-17	43	66	01	-29	-24	-87															
17	3 Accept	26	62	-02	-17	25	12	52	10	-12	-03	-12	18	35	-11	-16	-06														
18	4 Seek	-05	31	25	-47	41	61	13	09	02	57	-13	-23	-03	-11	-49	07	40													
19	Resource 0 unclassified	02	-40	-30	53	-45	-68	-17	-05	04	-27	17	35	42	31	53	-35	-22	-63												
20	1 Procedure	-05	03	-09	-26	00	04	06	-26	-32	06	-17	30	38	-13	-26	22	28	17	-29											
21	2 Information	-06	-23	-02	30	-33	-42	-54	03	14	-49	04	04	02	-13	09	10	-19	-32	11	-06										
22	3 Irrelevant information	26	40	18	-42	54	56	24	09	-03	42	01	-33	-25	04	-24	05	19	40	-48	-01	-77									
23	4 Acknowledgement +	56	27	12	-29	37	08	17	27	21	-32	34	-07	13	51	-22	21	-21	-16	10	01	08	-02								
24	5 Acknowledgement -	60	42	10	-28	45	16	31	57	51	-30	39	-40	12	47	-26	17	00	00	-04	-05	09	00	74							
25	6 Outcomes	-54	-34	-18	53	-46	-20	-19	-26	-20	05	-23	40	15	-16	17	-12	-02	-02	31	11	06	-62	-32	-31						
26	Referent 0 unclassified/no referent	11	-04	-11	19	-08	-22	03	-17	-22	-09	27	25	41	09	-15	25	-07	-21	37	06	08	-24	19	-10	16					
27	1 Self	-25	02	18	-22	07	35	-08	14	20	19	-23	-35	-35	-24	-03	-05	29	43	-01	05	05	-14	12	12	12	-62				
28	2 Other person excluding speaker	-01	33	29	-19	30	42	13	17	11	58	12	-36	04	-05	-38	06	44	73	32	04	44	-30	08	-12	-19	12	27			
29	3 Others including speaker	11	29	11	-18	23	23	18	05	02	-18	11	19	16	07	-32	22	08	25	-15	01	-41	-06	26	17	19	-04	07	05		
30	4 Third parties	02	-12	-11	02	-09	-10	-05	03	09	-20	-22	04	-29	06	37	-31	-13	-23	-01	-13	07	11	-09	-01	-26	-70	-05	-31	-14	

evidence of the abnormalities and impairments which the literature had led us to anticipate. There was nothing to suggest that the 'asymmetry' of the blind–sighted condition created any special difficulties for either partner, and we could find no differences between the congenital and adventitious groups.

From the second experiment in our series we turn finally to the last. Once again, it was conducted by Kemp (1981a), but this time it was based on questionnaires rather than laboratory observations of behaviour. Because the previous study had been limited to an objective analysis we had been able to discover little if anything about how blind people perceived their difficulties, and it was this that now concerned us.

According to the literature or, more accurately, according to some of it, blind people experience enormous difficulties in social settings – opening and maintaining conversations, forming impressions, conveying information non-verbally and making sense of other people's signals, finding the right distance to stand or sit and, especially, mixing with other people in groups and locating who is speaking and who is being addressed. How far the literature could be trusted, however, we were very unsure; and what was needed, we believed, was a properly controlled study. It would be particularly worthwhile, we thought, to compare congenital with adventitious subjects, because the latter might retain their skills from when they were sighted; and it also would be interesting to ask both of the groups to compare themselves with 'the blind' in general, since it was unclear from the literature quite how they would regard themselves. Congenital subjects would report more difficulties than adventitious subjects, we predicted, and whereas the former would identify themselves with 'the blind' in general, adventitious subjects would regard themselves as distinct.

Six months after the previous study a postal questionnaire was sent to all thirty blind subjects who had taken part – twelve congenital and eighteen adventitious. There were two sections. The first asked subjects to respond to a set of twenty-three items to describe themselves; and the second asked them to complete the same questions, in a different order, to describe 'the blind' in general. The items were derived from the literatures on blind people and visual communication, as well as our own model of cuelessness, and each sought an answer on a five-point scale from 'very often' to 'hardly ever'. Examples included 'When you/blind people first meet someone do you/they have difficulty starting up a conversation?', 'Do you/blind people feel that you/they misunderstand what other people mean?', and 'Do you/blind people nod your/their head when listening?'. The questionnaire was typed, and the covering letter suggested that the subject's usual 'reader' should read out the questions and record the responses on the form. One month after the initial mailing a reminder was sent, and twenty-six of the thirty questionnaires were returned.

To examine the subjects' descriptions of themselves and of 'the blind' in general, the two sets of items were factor-analysed separately, and the factor scores for the congenital and adventitious groups were then compared by analysis of variance. For the first set of comparisons – the subjects' descriptions of themselves – eight factors emerged altogether, but there were no significant differences between the two groups. For the second set of comparisons – the subjects' descriptions of other blind people – there were eight factors again and this time there were two significant effects. The first factor concerned impression formation, and while the congenital group believed that the blind in general can and do form impressions of other people, the adventitious group did not. The other factor concerned interruptions, and while the congenital group believed that blind people in general do not find it hard to make interruptions, the adventitious group believed that they do.

The third and final set of comparisons concerned the extent to which subjects identified with the blind in general. For each of the twenty-three items the difference was calculated between the subject's scores for the 'self' and 'other' versions of the material, and the congenital and adventitious groups were then compared by analysis of variance for each of the questions separately. Only two of the items revealed a significant difference, and both were concerned with the voice. The first asked whether blind people have to raise their voices to make themselves understood, and the second was concerned with whether they find it necessary to make special adjustments, such as speaking clearly and deliberately. In both cases it emerged that the congenital group did identify with 'the blind' in general but the adventitious group did not.

In summary, what our objective analysis had suggested earlier, the subjective reports had now confirmed: despite the assertions of the previous literature there were many blind people who did not experience difficulties in social settings, even though they had obvious and well-researched difficulties in other respects, particularly mobility and locomotion. What is more, the congenital and adventitious groups were very similar in their reports for the most part, and the only differences to emerge concerned their perceptions of others. Adventitious subjects believed that 'the blind' as a group do experience difficulties, and they distanced themselves from them, but congenital subjects did neither. We had begun by expecting that blind people would be seriously hampered in social settings but, in the event, we had been proved wrong.

There were three possible interpretations, we believed, and the first was that we had inferred too much from the literature on blind people. As we have seen already, much of the evidence is difficult to interpret for methodological reasons, and the assertion that blind people are seriously impaired is in any case by no means universal.

The second interpretation concerned sampling, for whereas previous reports had generally been based on institutionalized subjects, Kemp's experiments deliberately chose people who were supporting themselves in the community, living normal, 'sighted' lives. The latter were likely to be more skilled and experienced than the former – and that was precisely what our findings suggested.

The third and final point concerned our own research on visual communication. From laboratory experiments on sighted people we had extrapolated directly to blind people, and we had simply gone too far for, though cuelessness does affect blind people, they learn to cope with it in ways we had not foreseen. The model was right, but our predictions were wrong.

Teleconferencing

The telephone was invented more than a hundred years ago and, by tradition, it has long been regarded as a two-person medium. Recently, however, larger meetings have become possible. Many advances in technology have made their contribution – including group telephone systems, the videotelephone, conference television networks, and computer-mediated systems – and, for some people at least, the 'teleconference' has become almost commonplace. What is uncertain, however, is whether it is effective, given the restrictions in the social cues it makes available, and it is that which provides the focus for the discussion which follows. First, I shall review the numerous systems which have been produced; then I shall consider how they have been used in industry and elsewhere, and whether they have been successful; and, finally, I shall try to draw the discussion to a conclusion by examining some recent research on the role of teleconferencing in teaching.

Developments in technology

Group telephone systems.   The first of the group systems is the 'conference call'. Participants use their own receivers and the public lines, and they are 'bridged' together by the operator. The lines are open, so that everyone can hear and speak directly to everyone else, and typically up to eight people can take part. The main advantage of the system is its flexibility and ease of use, but it is costly and relatively time-consuming to set up, and the acoustic quality is sometimes unsatisfactory. For those reasons, many organizations now choose to install their own 'dedicated' networks away from the public lines and to employ their own operators.

The second system is the loudspeaking telephone, and the best-known prototypes were the British Post Office LST4 and Bell Telephones' Speakerphone. In both examples the handset is connected to a speaker/amplifier unit, participants speak into a built-in microphone, and the signal is then amplified and reproduced through the loudspeaker at the other end of the line. In principle, the systems were intended to accommodate as many as a dozen people around one unit but, because the microphone is unidirectional and requires the speaker to sit no more than 18 inches away, it is seldom possible to cater for more than three or four. Furthermore, only one person can speak at a time, and the automatic voice-switching mechanism which determines which of the two microphones is 'on' often removes the opening and closing syllables – the phenomenon of voice-clipping. Unfortunately, the switch can also be triggered by other loud noises.

In general, the loudspeaking telephone has not been received favourably, but improved versions are now available. British Telecom, for example, has replaced the LST4 with DORIC – and has recently gone on to introduce HARMONY and LST8 – and all three allow speakers to sit up to 10 feet away. There is much less voice-clipping than before, because of a faster switching mechanism, and the transmitter is more sensitive, the volume is greater, and the entire machine is smaller and more manageable. Like their predecessors, the new units can all be bridged in to conference calls.

The third and last of the group telephone systems is the Remote Meeting Table, and the principal user has been the British Civil Service. One of the problems with both the conference call and the loudspeaking telephone is that individual speakers are hard to identify unless they announce themselves each time they contribute, and it was this, in part, which the Remote Meeting Table was designed to overcome. Two tables of up to six people are linked by a telephone line, and every participant has a microphone. Each person at the first table is represented by a loudspeaker at the other and, each time he speaks, his voice is reproduced through his 'own' loudspeaker, and his name appears in letters over the top and a light comes on. Participants and loudspeakers are positioned alternately round the table – so that people have loudspeakers for neighbours and loudspeakers have people – and the physical positions of the 'absent' contributors are thus reproduced.

The videotelephone. The purpose of the videotelephone was to restore, at least in part, the visual information which the traditional telephone denies, and the best known of the prototypes was the Picturephone of American Telegraph and Telephones. The Picturephone was designed as a desk-top unit, and it consisted of a loudspeaking telephone, a camera with zoom lens, a 5 by 5½ inch monochrome monitor, and a built-in microphone. The normal camera position gave a head-and-shoulders image of the speaker, but close-ups were possible too, and material on the desk could also be transmitted, by means of a mirror, though the resolution was insufficient for typescript. Each machine came equipped with a 'privacy' button so that the speaker could switch off the camera but, even so, neither the Picturephone nor its British equivalent, the Post Office Viewphone, were well received. An important factor, apparently, was cost.

Conference television networks. One way to hold a telephone conference with vision is simply to bridge together a number of videotelephones in a conference call but, because the videotelephone has proved unpopular, little progress has been made. The main alternative, at least in this country, has been the British Post Office Confravision. Special studios have been set up in a number of cities, and each can be linked with any of the others, though normally only one at a time. Each has two cameras, one for the group and one for documents, and there are two monitors, one showing the 'home' group, and one showing the other group. The system was piloted in the 1970s, and it is now in full operation.

Similar networks have been developed elsewhere, particularly by Bell Telephones in North America.

Computer-mediated systems. Computer systems are the most recent invention of all, and the very first was set up in 1970 at the Office of Emergency Preparedness of the Executive Office of the President of the USA. Since then there have been many developments but, in essence, the systems are all very similar. Each participant has a computer terminal, into which material can be typed, and all the terminals are linked to a central computer by public or dedicated telephone lines. Every contribution is labelled and stored and is then available for all the participants to retrieve – unless the sender chooses otherwise. Participants need not be 'on line' at the same time – though, if they are not, the network becomes more of a postal system than a conference – and most of the current versions allow members a certain amount of 'private' space which is not accessible to others. Many systems are now established, especially in the USA, and they are particularly common among groups of scientists and branches of government. Useful reviews are to be found in books by Hiltz & Turoff (1978), Johansen, Vallee & Spangler (1979), and Christie (1981).

One other important development, this time from Britain, is CYCLOPS, a computer-based machine devised at the Open University for tutorial teaching by telephone (Read, 1978; McConnell, 1982). Its purpose is to allow visual information, particularly graphics, to be transmitted at the same time as speech, and it is typically used to link two 'study centres' together, each with perhaps three or four people grouped round a monitor and loudspeaking telephone. Pre-recorded graphics can be presented from a cassette player, and material can be added 'live' by means of a light-sensitive pen which is applied direct to the screen or a special 'scribble pad'. All the information appears on both monitors, and both groups of participants can transmit. Preliminary trials are currently in progress.

Uses and effectiveness

With the growth of technology in the last 10 years or so, teleconferencing has developed very rapidly, and many institutions have begun to explore its potential. Industry, commerce, and government are among the principal users, and the main attraction has been the promise of a cost-effective substitute for travel. Distances are especially important in the USA, of course, where most of the early initiatives originated, but even in Britain there have been some limited developments. The Civil Service, for example, has set up a network of Remote Meeting Tables, as described in the previous section, and Short, Williams & Christie (1976) were able to report on a variety of other installations also. Many detailed reviews are to be found, in the work of the New England Rural Society Project, for example, and the Institute for the Future, and there are many manufacturers' reports, by the Long Range Division of British Telecom, in particular, and Bell Telephones.

The other main use for teleconferencing – apart from teaching, which will be discussed in the final section of the chapter – has been scientific conferences. Earlier, I described how computer networks have been applied, and another example is communication satellites, notably 'Symphonie', which was used by UNESCO in 1976. Each year, UNESCO holds a world General Conference, and the venue that year was Nairobi. The organization's headquarters are in Paris, and the satellite made it possible to link the two centres by telephone, video, telex, and facsimile machines for transmitting photocopies. Many benefits were reported – particularly that the administrative staff in Paris could supply last-minute information very quickly and were able to be involved in the proceedings in a way which is usually impossible – and the entire experiment was said to be a great success (Sommerlad, Seeger & Brown, 1978).

As to whether teleconferencing is successful and effective in general, only limited conclusions can be drawn at present, and the reasons are largely methodological. Two main approaches have been taken: laboratory experiments and field studies; but despite a considerable volume of work, relatively little has been achieved because few criteria of effectiveness have been explored. What is more, 'subjective effectiveness' has frequently been confounded with 'objective effectiveness', and it has often been forgotten that success on one dimension may be quite incompatible with success on another. Only in the literature on teaching, as will be shown later, have full-scale investigations been undertaken.

Of the two main approaches to evaluation, the most extensive has been laboratory research, and the most productive contribution has come from the Communications Studies Group at the University of London. Much of the group's work was discussed earlier, in Chapters 4 and 5 of the book, and, as was shown, effectiveness was generally measured in two ways. One was to ask people in advance how appropriate they believed a particular medium would be for a particular task or type of meeting, and the other was to let them experience the medium and then say afterwards how satisfied they felt with it. Both were measures of perceptions or outcome and, unfortunately, there was seldom any attempt to examine process. The approach was, however, rooted firmly in psychological theory, and a medium's 'social presence', it was argued, was the most important determinant of how it was rated. The basis for comparison was face-to-face.

The second approach to evaluation, field studies, has generally been less concerned with psychology and more concerned with economics, and the main criteria for effectiveness have been financial. The over-riding question is how much can be saved on travel by substituting teleconferencing, but there has been concern too about energy costs and pollution. As a rule the studies have been small-scale and atheoretical, and typically they have been based on interviews with experienced users about their frequency and type of usage. What often emerges is that teleconferencing itself is regarded as cheap and effective for all but a minority of occasions, but one of its main effects is to generate a host of supplementary meetings, many of which are held face-to-face. Just as the original transatlantic cable apparently created a new 'need' for communication, so too does teleconferencing, and the *economics* of effectiveness are soon forgotten.

Teaching by telephone

Teaching by telephone began in Iowa, in the 1930s, and today it is very widespread, particularly in North America and Europe. Many systems have been developed, including the conference call and loudspeaking telephone for small group discussions, but perhaps the most elaborate is the Educational Telephone Network (ETN) at the University of Wisconsin, one of the most advanced specialist centres in the world. Wisconsin is the size of England, but with a population of only 5 million, and the ETN was set up in 1965 to provide continuing education for doctors. There are over two hundred study centres, all linked together by dedicated lines, and each has microphones and speakers so that participants can speak to and from anywhere in the system. According to the users, the main advantage over other methods of teaching at a distance – correspondence material, radio, television, computer print – is the opportunity to interact with other people (Moore, 1981).

As well as the ETN itself, the University of Wisconsin has a variety of other telephone services, and one of the most popular is DIAL ACCESS, a library of cassette tapes. Over 100,000 calls a year are received, and subscribers simply ask for particular tapes and listen to them over their own telephones. Like the ETN, the system was set up originally for doctors, and the recordings are intended as an authoritative reference library, particularly for handling emergencies. Another service is SEEN (Statewide Extension Education Network), which operates like a conference call with added graphics and an electronic blackboard, and there is also an automatic conferencing device, called MEET-ME. Before long, it is hoped, there may even be an international network, perhaps making use of satellites.

In Britain there has been much less call for telephone teaching, perhaps because distances are generally short and face-to-face meetings are convenient to arrange, but the one institution which makes extensive use of it is the Open University. The Open University was founded in the late 1960s, for people who wished to study for degrees but had not followed traditional routes into higher education, and it is a 'university of the air'. There is no campus, only a central administration, and most of the teaching is done by television, radio, printed course material, and correspondence with tutors and counsellors who are co-ordinated through the thirteen regional offices. Apart from occasional summer schools, the only face-to-face contact which students have with staff or one another is through tutorials, which typically meet only five or six times a year.

Enrolment at the Open University has always been high – around 74,000 students in 1983 – and initially there were relatively few courses, so that face-to-face tutorials were the most economic way to organize small group teaching. By the mid-1970s, however, the pattern had changed, for the number of courses had increased dramatically, and sometimes a region would find itself with very few students on a particular course, and perhaps no tutor at all. Telephone meetings thus became more attractive, no longer something special for disadvantaged students who were disabled, or housebound, or geographically isolated, but something to be exploited more generally.

In 1979 the Open University began to consider setting up a national network like Wisconsin's ETN but, as yet, the only group systems in common use are the conference call and the loudspeaking telephone – together with the new CYCLOPS. Both the conference call and the loudspeaking telephone were introduced in the early 1970s, and the former is now much the more widespread. Each region is able to set aside its own budget, and there are surprisingly marked differences across the country. In 1981, for example, the Welsh region programmed 140 hours for conference calls, Scotland planned for 120, the East Midlands region 125 (mostly by CYCLOPS), and East Anglia 96. The remainder were well behind, and some regions had no plans at all (Robinson, 1981). To some extent the differences could be explained by geography – a third of students in Scotland have no possibility of face-to-face meetings, for example – but local opinions and attitudes were often the real reason.

Given the significance of telephone teaching, the important question now, of course, is how effective it is. In the USA, as seen already, the telephone has been used in a variety of ways, and evaluative research has been in progress for some years. Becker (1978), for example, reviewed over 200 reports and though her main conclusion was that all but a few of the studies had been conducted very poorly, the telephone was generally regarded as satisfactory. Technical problems sometimes interfered, however (Pinches, 1975), but, provided the tutor managed to 'humanize' the meetings, ensured that students participated fully, adopted an appropriate style of presentation, and made proper use of feedback, the telephone could be just as effective as face-to-face (Monson, 1978). Indeed, objective comparisons between students who had been taught by telephone only, and equivalent students who had covered the identical material face-to-face, sometimes showed that the telephone even held an advantage (Perinchief & Hugdahl, 1982). The most interesting point about that particular study was that the discipline in question was music.

In Britain, where telephone teaching is restricted in the main to small group work in what might be called tutorials or seminars, a rather different approach has been taken to evaluation. In general, the emphasis has been on the processes of teaching and learning, as well as outcome and satisfaction, and one of the issues has been what are the functions of tutorials, whether telephone or face-to-face. In one detailed study, for example, Murgatroyd (1980) examined the content of thirty face-to-face tutorials recorded in Wales, and four main categories emerged: clarification by the tutor, development by the tutor, critical comments about the course, and attempts to encourage students to participate. The proportion of time spent on each was 38%, 17%, 8%, and

32% respectively and while tutors spoke more than 60% of the time, the average time per student was 8 minutes each 2-hour session. There was little evidence that tutors were following what is sometimes called the 'facilitation model'. Instead, they devoted most of their time to explication and remedial help. Whatever tutors may hope and believe, concluded Murgatroyd, students appeared to want 'chalk and talk', and they were reluctant to discuss their own academic ideas and problems. Similar conclusions were drawn by L'Henry-Evans (1982).

Apart from Murgatroyd's work there have been only two attempts to examine Open University teaching in any systematic way. One is our own, which will be examined at the end of the chapter, and the other was by Hammond, Young & Cook (1978) who, some years before, had been members of the Communications Studies Group at the University of London. Holloway & Hammond (1975) had already published a small pilot study on tutors' and students' reactions to tutorials by conference call and LST4, and now they embarked on an extensive investigation in which measures of content and style were collected also. The overall aim was to evaluate the effectiveness of the telephone and to decide upon practical recommendations.

The study was based on the London and East Anglian regions of the Open University, which were the heaviest users of the telephone at the time, and four main issues were explored. How far can telephone tutorials be an effective substitute for face-to-face – that is, fulfil the same functions and satisfy the participants? Are certain ways of organizing and conducting telephone tutorials more successful than others, and do they differ from successful face-to-face methods? Does experience lead to adaptation and, if so, might training accelerate the process? What are the relative costs, financially, to the Open University, to the student, and to the tutor?

According to the Open University, the main purpose of a tutorial is remedial, and a 'successful' session should therefore be one which dwells on the students' academic problems and is 'student centred'. In fact, as we have seen from Murgatroyd (1980), a remedial tutorial is not what students appear to want, and a satisfactory meeting for them would be one which met quite different criteria. What Hammond, Young & Cook chose to do, therefore, was to abandon any objective criterion of outcome – such as how much students learned or remembered, and how much support they received from the tutor – and instead to define success as satisfaction, leaving the research team to identify the components of success and the processes which led up to it.

The experimental design was as follows. A series of tutorials was tape-recorded, some face-to-face and some over a conference call, and question-naire responses were collected from the participants at the end of each session. A variety of disciplines was represented, including mathematics and music, and each tutorial was part of the planned programme for the region, so that every session was built into the annual schedule as a normal provision, and telephone tutorials were substitutes for face-to-face and not supplements. Each student was allocated to either face-to-face or telephone for the whole course, but tutors often taught over both media. For each tutorial group an attempt was made to record one session early in the year and another later, and the eventual outcome was thirty-two face-to-face and thirty-three telephone recordings, 287 questionnaires, and a number of additional interviews and questionnaires from a sample of participants approached one final time at the end of the academic year.

To analyse the content of the tutorials from the tape-recordings, the research team first tried to apply the schemes of Flanders and Bales, but what emerged eventually was a tailor-made adaptation they devised themselves to examine both the 'functions' of the tutorial and its 'socio-emotional' aspects. There were sixteen categories in all, together with twenty-one stylistic indices which examined the way the content was structured, and the whole analysis was conducted direct from the tapes without transcripts. The brief questionnaires collected after each session consisted of two sides of items about how the participants perceived the processes and functions of the tutorials, and how they evaluated them, and the interviews and longer questionnaires administered at the end of the year covered much the same ground. For the latter, fifty-two subjects were interviewed and fifty-five replied by post, but the data were not analysed statistically because they were largely qualitative in nature.

The main analysis of the data concentrated on the functions of the tutorials and how well they were fulfilled, and the first thing to emerge was that students expected telephone tutorials to meet exactly the same criteria as face-to-face. The most important requirement was that the tutor should provide guidance on the significant academic areas, the second was that he should summarize the Open University's own printed course material for them, and the third was that he should provide remedial help for their academic problems. For both the first and third functions the telephone was regarded as more successful than face-to-face according to the students' questionnaires, while for the second there was no difference. Face-to-face, the function which was seen to be fulfilled the most successfully was moral support through contact with the tutor.

For the tutors the pattern was rather different. First of all, the most important function for them was to help the students with their academic problems, and guidance on the important areas came only second, and students' discussion of their own ideas was third – a pattern which provided good support for Murgatroyd's (1980) concern that there may be a 'mismatch' between students and tutors. The other main finding was that, unlike the students, the tutors saw no difference between face-to-face and telephone in the extent to which the functions were fulfilled. Indeed, in general, tutors were much less satisfied than students, but the difference held for telephone and face-to-face alike.

As to the objective analysis of the content and structure of the tutorials, there were only two significant differences between face-to-face and telephone for the students, and both were concerned with discussion of their own ideas: most of the students spent proportionately more time talking over the telephone than face-to-face; and their utterances were shorter than face-to-face.

Thus, just as their questionnaires had suggested, if one of the objectives of a tutorial is to give students the chance to talk about their own ideas, the telephone may well be *more* successful than face-to-face rather than less. Face-to-face tutorials are easily dominated by a verbose minority but, over the telephone, tutors are more able to encourage an equitable distribution. Questions to particular individuals by the tutor were more numerous over the telephone than face-to-face, as were agreements by the tutor, but questions to the group as a whole were less so. There was little if any evidence that participants adapted to the constraints of the telephone as time went on.

For most of the remaining analyses the investigators concentrated on the participants' ratings of the tutorials. Students found the material discussed in telephone tutorials 'more interesting' than the face-to-face material, but there was no difference between conditions in either their overall satisfaction or how much they believed they had understood. The main advantage of the telephone, they said, was the efficient use of time. but the lack of a writing-board was a problem, and almost half believed face-to-face meetings would have been more successful. Interestingly enough, though, there were no complaints about the social limitations of the telephone sessions, and the authors were led to suggest that 'satisfaction' meant different things to the students depending upon the experimental condition. Face-to-face, their overall satisfaction correlated positively with an absence of silences and an absence of interruptions by the tutor, while over the telephone the significant measures were the proportion of time each student spoke, the number of laughs, and the level of audibility. There were no differences between the various academic disciplines, and no effects either for tutor's teaching style. Tutors who were successful over the telephone were also, according to the students, successful face-to-face.

Like the students, the tutors reported no difference between conditions in their overall satisfaction, though 61% believed their face-to-face sessions were the more successful. In fact, as shown already, tutors were altogether less satisfied than students and, curiously enough, the two sets of ratings correlated negatively, so that the more satisfied the student, the less satisfied the tutor. No obvious explanation could be detected but, once again, the findings confirmed the mismatch to which Murgatroyd (1980) was to draw attention. Most of the objective measures revealed no significant correlation with tutors' satisfaction, but the two which did were the proportion of time devoted to problems raised by students and the proportion of time devoted to their progress. The shorter the time, the happier the tutor – even though it was precisely those areas which tutors, unlike students, regarded as the most important.

At the end of what had been an impressive piece of work, Hammond, Young & Cook (1978) were able to conclude with a series of practical recommendations to the Open University, and it was practical issues which had provided the focus throughout the investigation. The one thing missing had been any serious attempt to link the project to theory, and it was to that that we turned ourselves. Naturally, we too hoped to say something of practical value, but our principal aims were theoretical: to test how well our model of cuelessness would stand up outside the laboratory; and to exploit the new setting as a source of further hypotheses.

The first of our experiments took place in the East Midlands Region of the Open University, in 1976. At the time, very little of the region's teaching was conducted by telephone, and we were unable to make use of pre-arranged telephone sessions in the way that Hammond, Young & Cook (1978) had done. Instead, we invited a number of groups at the start of the academic year to substitute two telephone meetings for two of the face-to-face sessions which had already been planned for them, and all six who were approached agreed. All were from Course E201, 'Personality and Learning', and each of the groups consisted of one tutor and three to six students. Each met face-to-face for the first meeting of the year, and the experiment was based on the next four sessions. Three groups met twice face-to-face and then twice over the telephone, and three did the reverse, giving a cross-over design which provided a useful control for participants' familiarity with one another and with the course material. All the sessions were tape-recorded, but one of the groups was lost, unfortunately, because the technical quality was poor. Our design was therefore reduced to five (Figure 6.1).

	Face-to-face tutorials	Telephone tutorials
Groups		
1	2,3	4,5
2	2,3	4,5
3	2,3	4,5
4	4,5	2,3
5	4,5	2,3

Figure 6.1   Rutter & Robinson (1981): experimental design. (Reproduced by permission of John Wiley & Sons Ltd.)

Each tutorial lasted just over an hour, and two sessions from each group were selected for analysis, the first of the experimental face-to-face sessions, so far as possible, and the first of the telephone sessions. Verbatim transcripts were made of the whole recording, and the second 20-minute period was analysed for content, and the whole session for style. The content analysis was based on a modified version of CPA (Figure 6.2), in which the original Referents were amended and a number of Resources were added, and style was examined by means of our normal system. In addition, participants were asked to keep a tape-recorded diary of their impressions of each tutorial, to give us a measure of outcome. Some of the impressions were responses to a printed check-list, while others were the participants' free comments, and the diary was designed to be recorded immediately the session ended.

Mode	0	unclassifiable
	1	offer
	2	accept
	3	reject
	4	seek
Resource	0	unclassifiable
	1	procedure
	2	procedure for topic (academic)
	3	procedure for course (OU)
	4	evaluation (academic)
	5	evaluation of course (OU)
	6	information (academic)
	7	information about course (OU)
	8	information (relevant)
	9	information (irrelevant)
	10	praise
	11	blame
Referent	0	unclassifiable/no referent
	1	self
	2	student (or students as individuals)
	3	students as a group
	4	tutor
	5	tutor + student (or students as individuals)
	6	tutor + students (as a group)
	7	third party (academic)

Figure 6.2   Rutter & Robinson (1981): CPA categories. (Reproduced by permission of John Wiley & Sons Ltd.)

The first of our analyses examined content, and we predicted from our model that telephone tutorials would be more task-oriented than face-to-face, and probably depersonalized. In the event, however, not one of the comparisons revealed a significant effect, either for tutors or for students. Irrespective of medium, all five groups maintained a very high level of task-orientation throughout the experiment – Resources 4–8 (academic substance) accounting for almost 80% of tutors' units and almost 90% of students' units – and there was very little interpersonal content of any sort.

What did distinguish between the conditions, however, was the way in which the task was approached. Over the telephone, tutors sought contributions from the students much more than face-to-face ($t = 6 \cdot 6$; d.f. 4; $P < 0 \cdot 01$), and students responded with correspondingly more offers ($t = 4 \cdot 4$; d.f. 4; $P < 0 \cdot 05$), while seeking by the students ($t = 2 \cdot 9$; d.f. 4; $P < 0 \cdot 05$) and offering by the tutors ($t = 4 \cdot 3$; d.f. 4; $P < 0 \cdot 05$) showed the opposite pattern. Tutors were more likely over the telephone than face-to-face to call on particular individuals ($t = 5 \cdot 8$; d.f. 4; $P < 0 \cdot 01$) and, in their replies, students were more likely to refer to themselves ($t = 3 \cdot 6$; d.f. 4; $P < 0 \cdot 05$).

The second of our analyses was concerned with style, and our prediction was that the telephone condition would be less spontaneous than face-to-face, with fewer interruptions. The results are given in Table 6.4, and the prediction was confirmed. Students interrupted almost twice as frequently face-to-face as over the telephone, and tutors responded similarly, though less strongly. It was also noticeable that both types of participant used many more filled pauses over the telephone, presumably because they were trying harder to plan what to say. Students gave more acknowledgement signals in the face-to-face condition than over the telephone, and they also asked more questions of their own, whilst devoting fewer of their utterances to answering questions from the tutor. Tutors meanwhile said much more over the telephone than face-to-face, and the pattern overall was one of greater spontaneity face-to-face, but greater structuring over the telephone.

The other main feature of the analysis concerned a suggestion made by Stephenson, Ayling & Rutter (1976). As shown in Chapter 4, Stephenson, Ayling & Rutter argued that one of the consequences of removing social cues was to magnify the effects of role. In that particular experiment, 'union' and 'management' representatives held a discussion about industrial relations, and it proved to be much easier to identify who was who from the telephone transcripts than the face-to-face transcripts. The behavioural differences between the subjects were more less marked. In the present experiment a very

Table 6·4 Rutter & Robinson (1981): style. (Reproduced by permission of John Wiley & Sons Ltd.)

	Face-to-Face		Telephone		d.f.	t
	Mean	SD	Mean	SD		
Tutor						
No. utterances	157·2	33·4	148·0	30·5	4	0·7
No. words	748·0	1071·5	4942·2	755·5	4	5·4**
Word length of utterances	50·0	18·4	33·5	8·0	4	2·0
No. interruptions	17·8	11·1	12·0	7·1	4	1·2
No. questions	48·6	12·4	69·0	19·8	4	2·0
No. acknowledgement signals	86·6	46·1	100·6	52·3	4	0·5
Filled pause ratio (% words)	2·5	1·4	4·9	2·8	4	3·3*
Students						
No. utterances	186·4	47·4	173·4	38·9	4	0·5
No. words	3990·0	678·0	4706·0	857·0	4	2·7
Word length of utterances	23·1	9·9	28·5	9·1	4	1·7
No. interruptions	33·4	20·0	17·6	10·2	4	2·9*
No. questions	36·4	12·4	20·0	8·0	4	5·0**
Percentage utterances which = response to tutor question	23·2	4·9	36·4	10·0	4	2·8*
No. acknowledgement signals	68·0	29·5	41·0	17·3	4	3·2*
Filled pause ratio (% words)	1·9	0·6	3·4	0·6	4	14·0**

* $P < 0·05$ (two-tailed); ** $P < 0·01$ (two-tailed).

similar pattern was revealed for content, but for style there was a tendency in the opposite direction: both the length of utterances and the number of words spoken produced a significantly smaller difference between tutors and students in the telephone condition than face-to-face ($t = 4\cdot4$; d.f. 4; $P < 0\cdot05$, and $t = 7\cdot5$; d.f. 4; $P < 0\cdot01$, respectively).

The third and last of our analyses examined outcome. Because many of the subjects failed to complete their diaries, no attempt was made at a proper, statistical analysis. Instead, we simply counted the most frequent comments, and what emerged was that the telephone was seen as the more 'business-like', 'structured', 'formal', and efficient at covering the material. Tutors and students alike reported that they spent longer preparing for the telephone sessions – the students because they felt more exposed to the tutor's questions, perhaps – and both groups regarded the tutor as more 'chairman-like' in the telephone condition, and necessarily so. Almost all the respondents reported greater anxiety over the telephone, and face-to-face was generally much preferred, even though it was regarded as the less effective medium academically.

In summary, then, content, style, and outcome all showed marked differences between face-to-face and telephone. While the tutorials were highly task-oriented and impersonal in both conditions, there were noticeable differences in the way the task was approached, tutors seeking more contributions over the telephone than face-to-face, and students making more responses. Stylistically, telephone tutorials were the less spontaneous and the more deliberately structured, and both content and style were reflected accurately in the participants' impressions.

The purpose and design of our first experiment had been very straightforward, but now, perhaps for precisely that reason, we were faced with a variety of new and unresolved issues, and two in particular caused us some concern. The first was whether the findings would generalize beyond the Open University – whose students come from a wide range of backgrounds and ages, and whose organization and teaching methods are very different from those of other institutions. The second was whether the results were attributable to physical separation, the lack of visual information, or both, since the comparison between face-to-face and telephone confounds the variables. What was needed was a follow-up study, using a traditional university and manipulating cuelessness properly, and accordingly we designed our second experiment. Conducted by Janet Taylor, the experiment was based at Nottingham, and it was first reported in Rutter & Robinson (1981). Content, style, and structuring were all examined together, but outcome was excluded.

The experiment took place in the Department of Psychology at the University of Nottingham, and six tutorial groups took part. Four consisted of three students and their tutor, and two consisted of four students and their tutor. All the participants were well acquainted because the experiment took place towards the middle of the academic year when the groups had already been meeting regularly for some weeks. Normally, tutorials in the department were held face-to-face in an ordinary room but, for the purposes of the experiment, each group met for two of its timetabled sessions in the laboratory, once face-to-face and once behind screens. Face-to-face, the participants sat on easy chairs in a circle and, in the other condition, cloth screens were placed between them, measuring 2 metres by 1 metre, so that they remained in physical proximity but visual communication was denied. Seating position was the same in both conditions, and the screens were the same as those used by Rutter et al. (1984). Three groups held their face-to-face tutorial first and the screen tutorial second, while the remainder did the reverse, and all twelve of the sessions were tape-recorded in stereo. Verbatim transcripts were prepared in our usual way and, once the opening and closing remarks had been excluded, the first, middle, and last 5-minute segments were examined. The sessions generally lasted 45 or 50 minutes and, just as in our first experiment, the topic varied from group to group. All six of the groups came from the same introductory course, however, and the discussions were intended to cover similar ground.

The first of our analyses examined content, and coding was based on the modified form of CPA we had introduced in the previous experiment. Once again, it was found that task orientation was very high throughout the experiment, though this time there was no evidence that the task was approached differently under the two media. Around 80% of the units were concerned with the task in both conditions, for tutors and students alike, and this time there was evidence of greater concern with procedures in the screen condition than face-to-face ($t = 2 \cdot 9$; d.f. 5; $P < 0 \cdot 05$ for tutors, and $t = 4 \cdot 0$; d.f. 5; $P < 0 \cdot 05$ for students). There was no evidence of depersonalization.

For structuring and style the results were similarly mixed. For tutors there were no differences between the two conditions, but students were more likely to talk to one another face-to-face than in the screen condition – where the norm was tutor–student–tutor – and a greater proportion of their utterances came as responses to the tutor. When tutor and students were taken together, it was found that pauses at switches of speaker lasted longer face-to-face than in the screen condition ($t = 2 \cdot 7$; d.f. 5; $P < 0 \cdot 05$), and there was a trend towards more frequent interruptions, though the effect was not significant statistically.

In summary, then, several of the findings from the first experiment were confirmed – suggesting that the results went beyond the Open University – while others were not. The effects were often smaller than before and, although the differences in design and procedures meant that interpretation was not easy, the pattern was exactly what our model of cuelessness would predict, since the screen allows proximity but denies visual information, while the telephone denies them both. The differences between screen and face-to-face should be less marked than between telephone and face-to-face and, in general, that was exactly what we had found.

The laboratory experiment had provided us with some useful findings and hypotheses, and now we were ready to return to the Open University, for what was to be the most important and extensive study in the series. There were three main issues that interested us, and the first concerned our dependent measures. Throughout our research on cuelessness we had tried to explore a wide variety of measures of content, style, and outcome, but in our work on teaching, neither the content measures nor the outcome measures had been as sensitive as we might have hoped. A new approach was needed, and the first objective of the study was to develop and test some alternatives, and then to re-examine very carefully how content, style, and outcome fitted together. In particular, we were concerned to measure the tutor's strategy and the discourse structure of the two types of meeting, and to gauge objectively how much the students had benefited – something which Hammond, Young & Cook (1978) had rejected as impossible.

The second issue concerned generalization. In our first experiment we had examined only one faculty and only one course within that faculty, and now it was important to know how well the findings would stand up elsewhere. In the new study, therefore, two faculties were incorporated rather than one – Social Sciences as well as Education – and each was represented by five different courses.

The third and final issue concerned adaptation and the effects of time. So far, and in common with most other writers, we had restricted ourselves to cross-sectional designs and relatively brief periods of observation, with the result that we knew very little about whether people may adapt to cuelessness as they grow accustomed to its constraints. An ideal solution would have been to examine tutorial groups who only ever met over the telephone, and to follow them longitudinally through the year and compare them with groups who always met face-to-face. Unfortunately, however, that proved impossible, and we therefore did the next best thing. Each of our ten groups met in both conditions, and all were observed through the whole year, with the result that changes from medium to medium and changes over time were both able to be traced. The only substantial difference from a full longitudinal study was the reduced number of sessions per medium per group.

The experiment took place in the South-East Region of the Open University, and five Education and five Social Science groups took part, all of them from full-year post-foundation courses. The experiment began at the start of the 1980 academic year, and every group which was scheduled to meet in Canterbury, Maidstone, or Chatham was approached – with the exception of two whose tutors were already involved with the project and knew the predictions we were testing. There were two refusals, and we were left with five groups from Education and two from the Social Sciences. To complete the design the following year, every Social Science group which was due to meet in Canterbury was approached, provided there were to be at least five sessions in the year and the tutor had not already refused in 1980, and five accepted. One had to be excluded because the tutor was already teaching a group in the experiment – and another was eventually discarded because a telephone tutorial was cancelled at the last moment – and the full design was therefore five Education groups from 1980, and two Social Science groups from 1980 and three from 1981.

Almost all of the South-East Region's teaching is done face-to-face, and there were no scheduled telephone sessions for any of our ten groups. Each of them was therefore invited to hold two supplementary meetings at the project's expense, and both were to take place towards the middle of the year over a conference call link. No more than eight students were to take part each time, and it was left to the group to decide who they would be. The only constant was thus the tutor, but often the students were those who attended the face-to-face meetings the most regularly, and sometimes the same individuals took part in both the telephone sessions. Most of the tutors, like the students, were inexperienced at telephone teaching – though one or two had used it occasionally on previous courses – but all had had at least a little training from the Open University.

The main purpose of our experiment was to examine the content, style, and outcome of the tutorials, and the procedures we adopted were as follows. Each of the groups held from four to nine face-to-face meetings, and the two telephone sessions were inserted towards the middle, in such a way that at least one face-to-face meeting fell between them. Tape-recordings were made of both the telephone sessions and, in general, four of the face-to-face sessions, and our eventual analyses were based on four recordings altogether – the two telephone sessions, and the face-to-face sessions which immediately preceded and followed them, giving face-to-face, telephone, telephone, face-to-face for each group. The design is given in Figure 6.3, and the recorded sessions are underlined, while those selected for analysis appear in italics. Almost all the recordings were made by the research assistant who worked on the project, or by myself, and the final number was twenty telephone sessions and thirty-seven face-to-face, excluding one telephone session and four face-to-face sessions from the group which was eventually discarded.

The first stage of our analysis, as usual, was to prepare verbatim transcripts. The face-to-face tutorials generally lasted around 90 minutes, the telephone tutorials 45, and the middle ½-hour was selected in each case. Typescripts were

Education	1	F	F	*F*	T*	F	*T*	F	*T*	*F*	F	F	F
	2	F	*F*	T*	F	*T*	F	*T*	*F*	F			
	3	F	F	*F*	*T*	F	F	*T*	*F*	F	F		
	4	F	F	*F*	*T*	F	*T*	F	*F*	F	F		
	5	F	*F*	*T*	F	F	*T*	*F*	F				
Social science	6	F	*F*	*T*	F	F	*T*	*F*	F				
	7	F	*F*	*T*	F	*T*	F	*F*					
	8	F	*F*	F	*T*	F	*T*	*F*	F				
	9	F	*F*	*T*	F	*T*	*F*						
	10	F	*F*	*T*	F	*T*	F	*F*	F				

Figure 6.3 Open University experiment: experimental sessions. * Recording abandoned because of technical problems. Underlining means recorded; italics with underlining means recorded and analysed

prepared, and analyses of content, style, and structuring were conducted. To examine outcome we relied on questionnaires – no longer the tape-recorded diaries we had introduced in the first experiment – and a postal system was used. For each of the forty-one recorded face-to-face sessions the assistant distributed the questionnaire at the end of the tutorial, and the participants were asked to complete it as soon as possible and return it to us in the stamped, addressed envelope we supplied. For the twenty-one telephone sessions the questionnaires were posted to the participants individually before the tutorial, and again a stamped, addressed envelope was enclosed. Thirty-seven of the forty (93%) face-to-face questionnaires distributed to tutors were completed and returned to us safely, and the other figures were 228/315 (72%) for face-to-face students, 17/21 (81%) for telephone tutors, and 86/112 (77%) for telephone students.

For all our data there were wide discrepancies between sessions in the number of students present, and it was hard to know how to treat the scores. For the face-to-face recordings the range was two to thirteen with a median of 8, and for the telephone recordings it was three to eight with a median of 5, and eventually we decided to examine the data in the way we had chosen for the first experiment. For content, the scores for the students were totalled for each recording, and for style, structuring, and outcome they were averaged, giving one value for the combined students and one for the tutor. The data were then analysed by analysis of variance (Figure 6.4), with Faculty (Education/Social Sciences) a between-subjects factor, and Medium (face-to-face/telephone), Occasion (first/second), and Participant (tutor/student) within-subjects factors (Winer, 1971, p. 571). Where analysis of variance was inappropriate – the qualitative items from the outcome questionnaire – non-parametric analyses were used instead, and the totals and means for students were replaced by frequencies.

The first of our analyses examined content, and our prediction was that, in comparison with face-to-face tutorials, telephone tutorials would be noticeably task-oriented and depersonalized. The analysis was based on a newly amended form of CPA and, while the Modes from the original version were retained, the Resources were extended and modified, and the Referents were abandoned altogether. It was now also possible to code a number of Resources without Modes (Figure 6.5). Each utterance was divided into units of two lines of typescript (or less if the utterance was shorter), and each unit was coded once. In the event, many of the possible codes were used very seldom, and we chose eventually to base our statistical analyses on just twenty-three categories (Figure 6.6). To be included, the category had either to account for an average of 1% or more of the units or to be an index of personal content – a criterion which was essential for our theoretical purposes since personal contributions were comparatively uncommon and would have been almost excluded by the 1% rule. Together, the twenty-three categories accounted for 93·8% of the units.

The results of the analysis are given in Table 6.5. All twenty-three measures

	Face-to-face				Telephone			
	Occasion 1		Occasion 2		Occasion 1		Occasion 2	
	Tutor	Student	Tutor	Student	Tutor	Student	Tutor	Student
Education groups 1								
2								
3								
4								
5								
Social science groups 6								
7								
8								
9								
10								

Figure 6.4   Open University experiment: experimental design

200

MODES AND RESOURCES

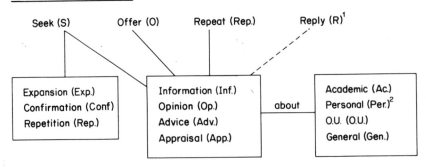

¹ Reply may be coded alone or with a resource.

² Personal is divided into Personal-procedure (Per. Proc.), Personal-example (Per. Eg.), and Personal-irrelevant (Per. Irrel.).

Resources coded without modes

Agreement (Ag.)	Exclamation (!)
Disagreement (D)	Apology (Ap.)
Procedure (Proc.)	Praise (Pr.)
Academic procedure (Ac. Proc.)	Laugh (L)
Acknowledgement (Ack.)	Uncodable (U.C.)

Figure 6.5   Open University experiment: CPA categories

are included and, whenever a significant *F* was revealed by the analysis of variance, the level of significance is reproduced and the direction of the effect is noted. What emerged in particular was two principal findings. The first was that only four of the measures produced a significant main effect of Medium. Furthermore, in every one of the four cases, the effect was against our prediction – more offering of academic information face-to-face, less responding with

Seek	Offer	Reply	No mode
Exp.	Inf. Ac.	Inf. Ac.	Ag.
Conf.	Inf. Per. Proc.	Inf. Per. Proc.	Proc.
Inf. Ac.	Inf. Per. Eg.	Inf. Per. Eg.	Ac. Proc.
Inf. Per. Proc.	Inf. O.U.	Op. Ac.	Ack.
Inf. Per. Eg.	Op. Ac.	Reply (no resource)	
Op. Ac.	Op. O.U.		
	Adv. O.U.		
	App. Ac.		

Figure 6.6   Open University experiment: principal CPA categories

Table 6·5   Open University experiment: content

		%	Faculty	Medium	Occasion	Participant	Two-way	Three-way	Four-way
1	S.Expansion	1·7				T > S*	MP**		
2	S.Confirmation	1·3				T > S*			
3	S.Inf.Ac.	2·8				T > S**	PF**		
4	S.Inf.Per.Proc.	0·8				T > S***	MP*		
5	S.Inf.Per.Eg.	0·5					MP*		
6	S.Op.Ac.	4·1				T > S**	MP*	MOF*	MOPF*
7	O.Inf.Ac.	19·9		FF > Tel*	1 > 2*	T > S**			
8	O.Inf.Per.Proc.	2·4				T > S*		OPF**	
9	O.Inf.Per.Eg.	3·3							
10	O.Inf.O.U.	3·1			1 < 2*				
11	O.Op.Ac.	14·9							
12	O.Op.O.U.	1·5							
13	O.Adv.O.U.	1·6							
14	O.App.Ac.	2·5				T > S**			
15	R.Inf.Ac.	3·6				T < S***			
16	R.Inf.Per.Proc.	1·0		FF < Tel*	1 < 2*	T < S**	MP*		
17	R.Inf.Per.Eg.	0·6		FF < Tel*		T < S**	MP *		
18	R.Op.Ac.	4·7				T < S**		MOP*	
19	Reply	5·7				T < S***			
20	Agree	3·1					MO*		
21	Proc.	4·9			1 > 2*	T > S**	MO*	OPF*	
22	Ac.Proc.	4·1				T > S***	MP*		
23	Ack.	5·7		FF < Tel*		T > S*	MP**		

* $P < 0·05$; ** $P < 0·01$; *** $P < 0·001$

202

personal examples and personal information about procedures, and less acknowledgement.

The second finding concerned the interaction between Medium and Participant (Table 6.6). As might be expected, there were many overall differences between tutor and student. However, and this was the most important result, eight of the measures produced a strong interaction between Medium and Participant – and in every single case the effect of cuelessness was to increase the difference between tutor and students (Figure 6.7). Thus, even though the main effects of Medium were not what we had expected, cuelessness nevertheless had a significant impact, namely – just as we had found in Stephenson, Ayling & Rutter (1976) and Rutter & Robinson (1981) – to strengthen the way in which the participants fulfilled their roles and executed what they perceived to be their tasks. There were no main effects for Faculty, it should be added, and there were few effects of time, and few subsidiary interactions.

The second of our analyses examined style and structuring, and there were two predictions: the first that telephone tutorials would be less spontaneous

Table 6·6 Open University experiment: content means for medium and participant

		Face-to-face		Telephone	
		Tutor	Student	Tutor	Student
1	S.Expansion	3·0	1·4	5·2	0·7
2	S.Confirmation	2·5	1·3	3·8	0·7
3	S.Inf.Ac.	5·6	2·2	7·6	1·8
4	S.Inf.Per. Proc.	1·4	0·5	3·0	0·2
5	S.Inf.Per. Eg.	0·2	0·4	2·6	0·1
6	S.Op.Ac.	6·5	2·4	15·0	1·5
7	O.Inf.Ac.	55·9	15·8	38·9	12·8
8	O.Inf.Per. Proc.	3·5	4·2	2·4	4·8
9	O.Inf.Per. Eg.	4·2	7·9	2·0	6·5
10	O.Inf.O.U.	9·4	3·9	4·1	1·8
11	O.Op.Ac.	23·9	28·4	20·4	19·5
12	O.Op.O.U.	3·5	3·3	1·9	0·9
13	O.Adv.O.U.	5·5	0·1	4·7	0·0
14	O.App.Ac.	4·9	1·2	9·2	0·4
15	R.Inf.Ac.	2·5	7·8	1·8	10·3
16	R.Inf.Per. Proc.	0·3	1·3	0·3	4·1
17	R.Inf.Per. Eg.	0·0	0·9	0·0	3·1
18	R.Op.Ac.	1·1	8·4	1·3	18·2
19	Reply	2·8	11·9	2·9	17·9
20	Agree	3·5	6·4	5·2	4·0
21	Proc.	6·2	5·1	13·2	5·6
22	Ac.Proc.	10·4	1·4	12·3	1·2
23	Ack.	6·8	6·6	17·1	4·7

$N = 20$ throughout.

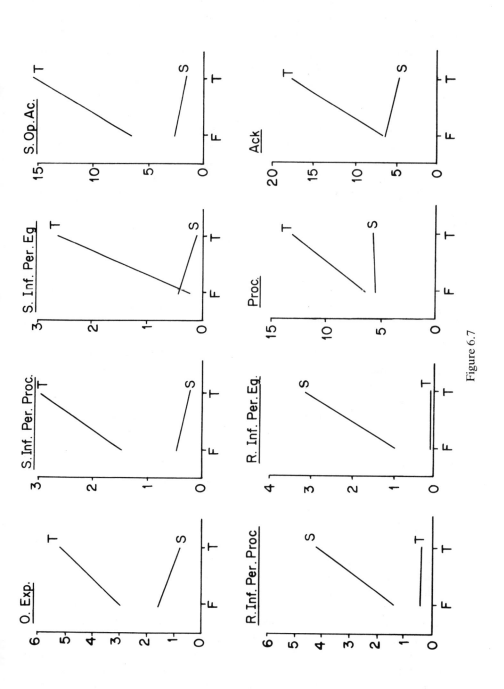

Figure 6.7

than face-to-face tutorials, the second that they would be more deliberately structured by the tutor. The results are given in Tables 6.7 and 6.8, and both predictions received good support.

To measure spontaneity, our first approach as usual was to consider interruptions and, for all four indices, the pattern was as predicted, though significantly so only for interruptions which did not lead to a change of speaker. Students, in general, interrupted rather more than tutors and for two of the measures there was a significant interaction such that the greatest frequency of all was for students face-to-face, especially students interrupting other students. Apart from interruptions, the other measures to produce significant effects were laughter, acknowledgement signals and filled pauses. Laughter was significantly more common among students than tutors, especially face-to-face; acknowledgment signals showed exactly the same pattern; and filled pausing, which often indicates a concern with planning what to say, was much more frequent over the telephone than face-to-face, especially for students.

To measure structuring by tutors we examined a variety of measures, and the first was the types of question they asked. For both direct questions (those aimed at named individuals) and general questions (those for the group at large), the values were much greater for tutors than students, as would be expected; but, more importantly, in both cases the difference was especially marked over the telephone. For question tags, in contrast (expressions like 'isn't it?' and 'don't they?' which turn statements into questions), there was no main effect. Again, however, there was an interaction, but this time the greatest frequency was for students face-to-face, perhaps indicating a degree of hesitancy at the end of what would otherwise have been statements and assertions.

Apart from questions, the other principal measure to produce a significant effect was the links between utterances and, just as in the laboratory study, there was a pronounced and rigid pattern over the telephone – tutor–student–tutor – with very little student–student interaction. Face-to-face, in contrast, there were just as many switches from student to student as from tutor to student and student to tutor. The only other important effects concerned the amount said, and tutors, it emerged, spoke more words overall than students, in longer but less frequent utterances, and this time the differences were most noticeable face-to-face. Otherwise, the remaining results for style and structuring revealed just one significant main effect for Faculty, another for Occasion, and a handful of two-way and three-way interactions.

The third of our analyses examined outcome, and there were two sets of measures, both based on the questionnaire administered at the end of each session. The first was concerned with a variety of open-ended questions about what had happened during the tutorial – how many issues had been raised, had anything unexpected been discussed or anything expected omitted, were there any additional comments the subject wished to make to us, and so on. The second was based on a checklist of twenty-four five-point adjective scales intended to tap task-orientation, depersonalization, spontaneity, and the

Table 6·7 Open University experiment: style and structuring

	Mean	Faculty	Medium	Occasion	Participant	Two-way	Three-way	Four-way
No. words	2439·0							
No. utterances	85·6				T > S*	MP*	OPF*	
Length utterances	43·0				T < S*	MP*	OPF*	
Acknowledgement signals	32·0			1 < 2*	T > S*	MP**		
Filled pause ratio	2·8		FF < Tel***			MP**		
Laughs	10·0				T < S**	MP**		
Successful interruptions	13·6				T < S*		MOP*	
Unsuccessful interruptions	8·5				T < S*			
Other interruptions	6·8		FF > Tel*			MP*		
Direct questions	10·1	Ed < SS*	FF < Tel*		T > S*	MP**		
General questions	6·7				T > S***	PF* MP*	MPF*	
Question tags	6·7					MP*	OPF*	
Interruptions (excl. sim. speech)	3·9					MP*		

*$P < 0·05$; **$P < 0·01$; ***$P < 0·001$.

206

Table 6·8   Open University experiment: means for style and structure for medium and participant

	Face-to-face		Telephone	
	Tutor	Student	Tutor	Student
No. words	3217·5	1716·3	3005·0	1817·2
No. utterances	56·7	121·9	74·6	89·2
Length utterances	83·5	15·3	51·9	21·4
Acknowledgement signals	21·7	54·6	30·1	21·8
Filled pause ratio	2·2	1·6	3·1	4·3
Laughs	2·3	22·7	5·4	9·8
Successful interruptions	11·4	22·8	8·3	11·9
Unsuccessful interruptions	5·4	17·1	4·3	7·2
Other interruptions	3·7	16·3	4·1	3·4
Direct questions	5·9	5·7	24·0	4·7
General questions	8·4	3·5	13·2	1·9
Question tags	5·7	9·4	7·0	4·9
Interruptions (excl. sim. speech)	2·3	7·1	3·4	3·0

$N = 20$ throughout

subject's overall evaluation. In the event most participants made very few responses to the open-ended questions, except to list the topics which had been raised, and our analysis was therefore restricted to just that one item from the open-ended section and the twenty-four items from the other section. Two-hundred-and-thirty-four questionnaires were examined altogether – 17 telephone tutor, 82 telephone student, 19 face-to-face tutor, and 116 face-to-face student – and there were no formal predictions, except that there would be differences between the two types of session.

The results are given in Figure 6.8, and the first comment to make is that there were very few significant effects, noticeably fewer than for either content or style. There were three main effects for Medium – with telephone tutorials perceived as more 'formal' and 'tiring' than face-to-face, and less 'humorous' – but, beyond that, all that emerged was one main effect for Faculty, one for Occasion, two for Participant, and a handful of interactions, several of them involving Faculty for the first time in any of our analyses. In general, the tutorials were evaluated very favourably and, for tutors and students alike, there was little to choose between them on any of our dimensions.

The fourth and last of our analyses concerned the relationships between the three sets of dependent measures, content, style, and outcome. According to our model the only direct effect of cuelessness is upon content, and style and outcome are influenced only *indirectly*, through the *mediation* of content. The way we had explored the relationships before was simply to examine the correlations, but now we went on to use multiple regression. If the model was

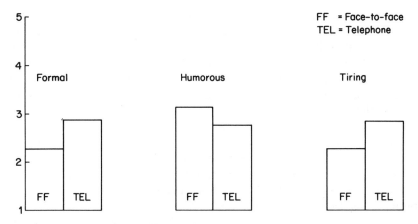

Figure 6.8   Open University experiment: outcome

correct, content would *predict* style and outcome, not merely *correlate* with them, and it was that which multiple regression allowed us to test.

The first stage of the analysis was to reduce the measures to a manageable number and, for that, we used factor-analysis, the Maximum Likelihood method, with Varimax rotation. All forty sessions were incorporated, irrespective of experimental condition, and seven factors emerged for content, three for style, and six for the perceptual measures of outcome (Figure 6.9). The variables which loaded significantly (calculated by the Burt–Banks formula)

	VP
Content	
1. Tutor seeking and commenting	3·5
2. Offering and replying with academic information	2·3
3. Open university	2·2
4. Offering and replying with personal information	1·9
5. Agreeing/offering opinions	1·6
6. Seeking/offering academic information and confirmation	1·6
7. Replying with opinions and personal examples	1·3
Style and structuring	
1. Spontaneity	5·8
2. Speech quantity	1·8
3. Questioning	1·1
Outcome	
1. Evaluation	3·4
2. Anxiety	3·0
3. Interaction/democracy	2·8
4. Structure	2·1
5. Personal evaluation	1·7
6. Academic relevance	1·4

Figure 6.9   Open University experiment: content factors

were then inspected and, for each of the sixteen factors, the one which loaded the most strongly was selected, and both style and outcome were regressed on content, each of the nine measures one at a time. All seven content variables were used as predictors in the equations, and two types of analysis were conducted, the first simple multiple linear regression to estimate the total variance explained, the second stepwise regression to determine the rank-order of the predictors.

The first of the analyses examined style (Table 6.9), and all three of the measures were predicted very strongly by content, the variance explained being 69% for the first, 63% for the second, and 56% for the third. More important still, however, the relationship was exactly what our model predicted – the more personal and the less task-oriented the content, the more spontaneous the style (Factor 1). Speech quality too was predicted strongly (Factor 2), and so was questioning (Factor 3), and altogether the evidence for our model was among the most persuasive we had found.

The second of the analyses examined outcome (Table 6.10), and this time there was rather less support for our predictions. The more task-oriented the tutorial – that is, the more it followed the typical pattern of question and answer – the less favourable the overall evaluation (Factor 1) and the greater the reported anxiety (Factor 2), but beyond that there were no significant relationships.

The third and last of our analyses again examined outcome, but this time using style rather than content as the predictor. Outcome and style would be independent, we predicted, and that is exactly what emerged (Table 6.11), for there was no single significant effect, and the average variance explained was less than 5%. Style and outcome were independent, but both were predicted by content – and that is precisely what our model contends.

The experiment had begun with three principal objectives, and all three had now been met. The first was to refine and extend our measures and to examine the relationships between them. Tutor's strategy, discourse structure, and the relationships between content, style, and outcome had all been examined successfully, and the findings had offered good support for our model. The second objective was to examine how far our previous findings would generalize, especially across faculties and across courses within faculties, and what had emerged was a pattern of findings very similar to before, but stronger, with little evidence of differences between faculties or courses. Much more important than those sources of variance was the medium of communication, and especially its effects upon role performance, for the more cueless the setting, the more the participants retreated into traditional forms of behaviour, tutors becoming even more 'like' tutors, and students even more 'like' students. The third and last of our objectives was to examine whether people might adapt to cuelessness as time went on, and the short answer, confirming the previous literature, was that they did not. There were few effects of Occasion and no interactions at all with Medium.

So we come to the final study in our series – or, at least, the final study so far

Table 6·9 Open University experiment: relationships between content and style

	Cumulative MR	Cumulative MR²	Simple r	Standardized Beta	F
Factor 1: spontaneity (V55)	MR 0·83	MR² 0·69			21·6***
Step 1 Factor 5 – Agreeing and offering opinions (V36)	0·67	0·45	0·67	0·77	96·2***
Step 2 Factor 6 – Seeking and offering ac. info. and confirmation (V14)	0·75	0·57	−0·08	−0·34	18·6***
Step 3 Factor 4 – Offering and replying with personal info. (V5)	0·81	0·66	0·39	0·33	22·3***
Factor 2: speech quantity (V49)	MR 0·79	MR² 0·63			16·2***
Step 1 Factor 2 – Offering and replying with ac. info. (V40)	0·53	0·28	0·53	0·43	24·2***
Step 2 Factor 4 – Offering and replying with personal info. (V5)	0·66	0·43	0·40	0·41	29·1***
Step 3 Factor 6 – Seeking and offering ac. info. and confirmation (V14)	0·72	0·52	0·40	0·24	7·7**
Step 4 Factor 3 – Open University (V2)	0·76	0·57	0·30	0·29	12·0***
Step 5 Factor 1 – Tutor seeking and commenting (V19)	0·77	0·60	0·26	0·20	5·0*
Step 6 Factor 7 – Replying with opinions and personal eg's (V32)	0·79	0·62	−0·17	0·15	2·9
Factor 3: questioning (V44)	MR 0·75	MR² 0·56			12·3***
Step 1 Factor 1 – Tutor seeking and commenting (V19)	0·73	0·54	0·73	0·79	68·2***

*P < 0·05; **P < 0·01; ***P < 0·001.

Table 6·10 Open University experiment: relationships between content and outcome

	Cumulative MR	Cumulative MR²	Simple r	Standardized Beta	F
Factor 1: evaluation (V61)	MR 0·35	MR² 0·12			1·4
Step 1 Factor 2 – Offering and replying with ac. info. (V40)	0·27	0·07	−0·27	−0·22	2·8
Factor 2: anxiety (V81)	MR 0·43	MR² 0·18			2·2*
Step 1 Factor 2 – Offering and replying with ac. info. (V40)	0·35	0·13	0·35	0·38	8·7**
Factor 3: interaction (V68) No steps	MR 0·26	MR² 0·07			1·1
Factor 4: structure (V59) No steps	MR 0·29	MR² 0·08			<1
Factor 5: personal evaluation (V66) No steps	MR 0·31	MR² 0·10			<1
Factor 6: academic relevance (V58) No steps	MR 0·26	MR² 0·07			<1
Var. 82: points noted No steps	MR 0·22	MR² 0·05			<1

$*P < 0.05; **P < 0.01.$

Table 6·11   Open University experiment: relationships between style and outcome

		MR	MR^2	F
Factor 1:	Evaluation (V61)	0·20	0·04	1·0
Factor 2:	Anxiety (V81)	0·12	0·02	<1
Factor 3:	Interaction (V68)	0·27	0·07	1·9
Factor 4:	Structure (V59)	0·13	0·02	<1
Factor 5:	Personal evaluation (V66)	0·13	0·02	<1
Factor 6:	Academic relevance (V58)	0·10	0·01	<1
Var. 82	Points noted	0·21	0·05	1·1

Note: No steps for any of the seven analyses

completed, since another is still in progress, an examination of CYCLOPS. This time our objective was very simple. Because of the constraints of the design in the previous experiment, where only forty of the sixty-two sessions we attended were incorporated into the analysis, we were left with a large number of outcome questionnaires we had had to exclude. The purpose of the final study was to examine the entire collection. From the previous experiment there were 234, and to those we were able to add the 9 telephone and 111 face-to-face questionnaires from the sessions we had excluded, and a further 35 telephone

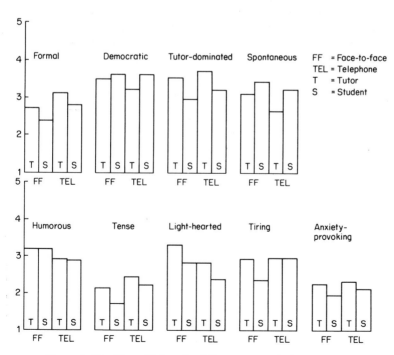

Figure 6.10   Open University follow-up experiment: outcome

and 23 face-to-face questionnaires from supplementary tutorials gathered elsewhere. The combined total was thus 410, and the breakdown was 141 telephone (24 tutor and 117 student), and 269 face-to-face (37 tutor and 232 student). This time there was sufficient material to incorporate the free responses as well as the five-point scales, and both were examined in two-by-two analyses (Medium and Participant), using independent factors and ignoring the possible relatedness between respondents. Chi-square, corrected for continuity, was used for the non-parametric data, and analysis of variance for the remainder.

For the non-parametric data – topics which participants felt had been omitted, others which had been discussed unexpectedly, positive comments about the proceedings, negative comments, and absence of comments – a total of nineteen analyses was conducted, but only one produced a significant effect, almost precisely the number expected by chance. For the parametric data, however, the pattern was quite different (Figure 6.10), and there were significant effects both for Medium and Participant and the interaction between them. Thus, more discussion points were recalled face-to-face than over the telephone, and face-to-face was regarded as more 'spontaneous', 'humorous', and 'light-hearted' but less 'formal' and 'tense'; and tutors saw the proceedings as more 'formal' than students, and more 'tutor-dominated', 'tense', 'light-hearted', 'tiring', and 'anxiety-provoking', but less 'democratic' and 'spontaneous'. For 'tiring', the only measure to produce an interaction, the lowest rating of all was for students face-to-face.

In conclusion, then, the results both confirmed and extended what we had found before: perceptions reflected both content and style, and tutors and students were frequently different. In general, the ratings were strong and positive, and students especially were particularly pleased. Both the media were regarded with satisfaction.

CONCLUSION

Research on visual communication began in the 1960s, and the purpose of this book has been to integrate the literature theoretically and empirically. The book started with research on looking, and examined the normal pattern (Chapter 1). People look more when they listen than when they speak, it was discovered, looks are more frequent at certain points in utterances than others, and eye-contact, or mutual looking, is generally very brief. Moreover, while a particular individual may behave consistently from encounter to encounter, there are noticeable differences between individuals, and sex, personality, and psychopathology are all important sources of variance.

By Chapter 2, the late 1960s had been reached, and structure had given way to function. The purpose of gaze, it appeared, was threefold: to express emotions and attitudes, to regulate the flow of conversation, and to monitor the other's behaviour for feedback. Expression was the most popular function to explore, and the central concept was emotion, while the leading model was intimacy. But gradually, a new approach took shape, for though gaze was salient, arousing, and involving, it had no intrinsic meaning. Not intimacy but attribution theory was the real key to expression.

Chapter 3 moved on to regulation and monitoring, and now a major turning-point was reached. Eye-contact had been exposed as a chance event, and information had replaced emotion as the central concept, but what emerged from regulation and monitoring was that looking, in fact, played little part in either. The information which mattered came from facial expression, gestures, and posture – but looking was gaze at the eyes. Visual access to the whole person was what people really sought – and the concept of seeing was born.

So, by the late 1970s, looking was overtaken by seeing, and a whole new literature was under way (Chapter 4); but even now there were problems, for the most common approach to seeing was to compare face-to-face with audio – and so to confound visual presence with physical presence. Disentangle them, we discovered, and the result was striking, for what mattered above all was the interaction, the aggregate of social cues from whatever source. The more cueless the encounter, the greater the feeling that one was psychologically distant from one's partner – and so the more depersonalized and task-oriented the content of the discussion and, in turn, the less spontaneous the style and the less likely an eventual compromise (Chapter 5). Content is influenced directly, we believe, and style and outcome are secondary.

In cuelessness, at last we had found a theoretical framework, and the questions which concerned us in the final chapter of the book were how well the model would stand up outside the laboratory, and how valuable it would be in everyday applications (Chapter 6). Blindness and telecommunications were the areas we explored, and the conclusions we drew were positive. The pattern of findings was just as before – or sometimes even stronger – and the practical value of our work was confirmed.

With that, I hope, the main objectives of the book have been achieved – a review of the major developments and a theoretical integration of the findings. Practical implications have emerged as well, of course – especially for training, perhaps, and organizational development – but since theory has been my major concern, it is with theory that I should like to conclude.

There are three main points that I wish to make, and the first concerns the overall significance of visual signalling. When research on nonverbal communication began, gaze was assumed to be central, and looking and eye-contact were pre-eminent. But first looking gave way to seeing, and then seeing gave way to cuelessness, and gradually it emerged that vision was much less significant than it had seemed at first. People communicated perfectly well without it – as everyday experience ought already to have told us – and their behaviour was changed remarkably little. Visual cues might be important, but seldom were they essential.

The second point leads on from the first, and concerns the relationship between gaze and the other signals. Two opposing trends have always been present in the literature on nonverbal communication – to examine each cue in isolation, and to explore the full range together. The former has been much the most common, but the more gaze is controlled and manipulated, the more its relationships with its context are over-looked. With the move towards cuelessness the balance was redressed, and it is in that direction, I hope, that research will now turn – particularly to functional analyses (Patterson, 1982; Edinger & Patterson, 1983).

The final point concerns language. Just as the literature on nonverbal communication concentrated on isolated signals, so the links with language were all but ignored. Seeing, we knew, had important effects, and cuelessness made them explicit. Language and nonverbal communication do more than work in parallel – they are integrated together – and we must not forget. Words matter too.

REFERENCES

Abele, A. (1981) Acquaintance and visual behaviour between two interactants. Their communicative function for the impression formation of an observer. *European Journal of Social Psychology*, **11**, 409–25.

Aiello, J. R. (1972) A test of equilibrium theory: visual interaction in relation to orientation, distance and sex of interactants. *Psychonomic Science*, **27**, 335–6.

Aiello, J. R. (1977a) A further look at equilibrium theory: visual interaction as a function of interpersonal distance. *Environmental Psychology and Nonverbal Behaviour*, **1**, 122–40.

Aiello, J. R. (1977b) Visual interaction at extended distances. *Personality and Social Psychology Bulletin*, **3**, 83–6.

Allen, D. E. & Guy, R. F. (1977) Ocular breaks and verbal output. *Sociometry*, **40**, 90–6.

Anderson, D. (1976) Eye contact, topic intimacy, and equilibrium theory. *Journal of Social Psychology*, **100**, 313–14.

Archer, D. & Akert, R. M. (1977) Words and everything else: verbal and nonverbal cues in social interpretation. *Journal of Personality and Social Psychology*, **35**, 443–9.

Argyle, M. (1967) *The Psychology of Interpersonal Behaviour* (first edition). Harmondsworth: Penguin.

Argyle, M. (1969) *Social Interaction*. London: Methuen.

Argyle, M. (1970) Eye-contact and distance: a reply to Stephenson and Rutter. *British Journal of Psychology*, **61**, 395–6.

Argyle, M. (1978) *The Psychology of Interpersonal Behaviour* (third edition). Harmondsworth: Penguin.

Argyle, M., Alkema, F. & Gilmour, R. (1971) The communication of friendly and hostile attitudes by verbal and non-verbal signals. *European Journal of Social Psychology*, **1**, 385–402.

Argyle, M. & Cook, M. (1976) *Gaze and Mutual Gaze*. London: Cambridge University Press.

Argyle, M. & Dean, J. (1965) Eye-contact, distance and affiliation. *Sociometry*, **28**, 289–304.

Argyle, M. & Graham, J. A. (1976) The central European experiment: looking at persons and looking at objects. *Environmental Psychology and Nonverbal Behaviour*, **1**, 6–16.

Argyle, M. & Ingham, R. (1972) Gaze, mutual gaze and proximity. *Semiotica*, **6**, 32–49.

Argyle, M., Ingham, R., Alkema, F. & McCallin, M. (1973) The different functions of gaze. *Semiotica*, **7**, 19–32.

Argyle, M. & Kendon, A. (1967) The experimental analysis of social performance. In L. Berkowitz (ed.), *Advances in Experimental Social Psychology*, **3**, 55–98. New York: Academic Press.

Argyle, M., Lalljee, M. & Cook, M. (1968) The effects of visibility on interaction in a dyad. *Human Relations*, **21**, 3–17.

Argyle, M., Lefebvre, L. & Cook, M. (1974) The meaning of five patterns of gaze. *European Journal of Social Psychology*, **4**, 125–36.

Argyle, M. & McHenry, R. (1971) Do spectacles really affect judgements of intelligence? *British Journal of Social and Clinical Psychology*, **10**, 27–9.

Argyle, M., Salter, V., Nicholson, H., Williams, M. & Burgess, P. (1970) The communication of inferior and superior attitudes by verbal and nonverbal signals. *British Journal of Social and Clinical Psychology*, **9**, 222–31.

Argyle, M. & Williams, M. (1969) Observer or observed? A reversible perspective in person perception. *Sociometry*, **32**, 396–412.

Asch, S. E. (1956) Studies of independence and conformity. A minority of one against a unanimous majority. *Psychological Monographs*, **70**, No. 416.

Ashcroft, S. C. (1963) Blind and partially sighted children. In L. M. Dunn (ed.). *Exceptional Children in the Schools*. New York: Holt, Rinehart & Winston.

Baker, E. & Shaw, M. E. (1980) Reactions to interpersonal distance and topic intimacy: a comparison of strangers and friends. *Journal of Nonverbal Behaviour*, **5**, 80–91.

Bakken, D. (1978) Behavioural adjustment in nonverbal immediacy: a methodological note. *Personality and Social Psychology Bulletin*, **4**, 300–3.

Bales, R. F. (1950) *Interaction Process Analysis*. Cambridge, Mass.: Addison-Wesley.

Bales, R. F. (1970) *Personality and Interpersonal Behaviour*. New York: Holt, Rinehart & Winston.

Beattie, G. W. (1977) The dynamics of interruption and the filled pause. *British Journal of Social and Clinical Psychology*, **16**, 283–284.

Beattie, G. W. (1978) Floor apportionment and gaze in conversational dyads. *British Journal of Social and Clinical Psychology*, **17**, 7–15.

Beattie, G. W. (1981) A further investigation of the cognitive interference hypothesis of gaze patterns during conversation. *British Journal of Social Psychology*, **20**, 243–8.

Beattie, G. W. (1982) Turn-taking and interruption in political interviews: Margaret Thatcher and Jim Callaghan compared and contrasted. *Semiotica*, **39**, 93–114.

Beattie, G. W. & Barnard, P. J. (1979) The temporal structure of natural telephone conversations (Directory Enquiry Calls). *Linguistics*, **17**, 213–229.

Beattie, G. W. & Bogle, G. (1982) The reliability and validity of different video-recording techniques used for analysing gaze in dyadic interaction. *British Journal of Social Psychology*, **21**, 31–4.

Becker, A. de V. (1978) Teleconferencing: a survey and evaluation. *Journal of Communication*, **28** (3), 120–4.

Beebe, S. A. (1974) Eye-contact: a nonverbal determinant of speaker credibility. *The Speech Teacher*, **23**, 21–5.

Bem, D. J. (1967) Self-perception: an alternative explanation of cognitive dissonance phenomena. *Psychological Review*, **74**, 183–200.

Bem, D. J. (1972) Self-perception theory. In L. Berkowitz (ed.) *Advances in Experimental Social Psychology*, **6**, 1–62.

Bem, D. J. & Allen, A. (1974) On predicting some of the people some of the time. *Psychological Review*, **81**, 506–20.

Bendig, A. W. (1962) The Pittsburgh scales of social extraversion-introversion and emotionality. *Journal of Psychology*, **53**, 199–209.

Berman, H. J., Shulman, A. D. & Marwit, S. J. (1976) Comparison of multidimensional decoding of affect for audio, video and audio video recordings. *Sociometry*, **39**, 83–9.

Bowers, K. S. (1973) Situation in psychology: an analysis and a critique. *Psychological Review*, **80**, 307–36.

Brand, C. R. (1969) Two types of dominance. Annual Conference of the Social Psychology Section of the British Psychological Society. September, 1969. Loughborough.

Breed, G. (1972) The effect of intimacy: reciprocity or retreat. *British Journal of Social and Clinical Psychology*, **11**, 135–42.

217

Breed, G. R. & Porter, M. (1972) Eye contact, attitudes, and attitude change among males. *Journal of Genetic Psychology,* **120**, 211–17.

Brieland, D. M. (1950) A comparative study of the speech of blind and sighted children. *Speech Monographs,* **17**, 99–103.

Broadbent, D. E. (1958) *Perception and Communication.* Oxford: Pergamon Press.

Buchanan, D. R., Goldmann, M. & Juhnke, R. (1977) Eye contact, sex, and the violation of personal space. *Journal of Social Psychology,* **103**, 19–25.

Bugental, D., Kaswan, J. & Love, L. (1970) Perception of contradictory meanings conveyed by verbal and nonverbal channels. *Journal of Personality and Social Psychology,* **16**, 647–55.

Bull, R. & Gibson-Robinson, E. (1982) The influences of eye-gaze, style of dress, and locality on the amounts of money donated to a charity. *Human Relations,* **34**, 895–905.

Burns, K. L. & Beier, E. G. (1973) Significance of vocal and visual channels in the decoding of emotional meaning. *Journal of Communication,* **23**, 118–30.

Burroughs, W., Schultz, W. & Aubrey, S. (1973) Quality of argument, leadership roles and eye contact in three person leaderless groups. *Journal of Social Psychology,* **90**, 89–93.

Butterworth, B., Hine, R. R. & Brady, K. D. (1977) Speech and interaction in sound-only communication channels. *Semiotica,* **20**, 81–99.

Byrne, D. & Clore, G. L. (1966) Predicting interpersonal attraction toward strangers presented in three different stimulus modes. *Psychonomic Science,* **4**, 239–40.

Campbell, D. E. & Lancioni, G. E. (1979) The effects of staring and pew invasion in church settings. *Journal of Social Psychology,* **108**, 19–24.

Carlsmith, J. M., Ellsworth, P. C. & Aronson, E. (1976) *Methods of Research in Social Psychology.* Reading, Mass.: Addison-Wesley.

Carr, S. J. & Dabbs, J. M. (1974) The effects of lighting, distance and intimacy of topic on verbal and visual behaviour. *Sociometry,* **37**, 592–600.

Carroll, T. J. (1961) *Blindness.* Boston: Little, Brown & Co.

Cary, M. S. (1978) The role of gaze in the initiation of conversation. *Social Psychology,* **41**, 269–271.

Castell, R. (1970) Physical distance and visual attention as measures of social interaction between child and adult. In S. J. Hutt & C. Hutt (eds), *Behaviour Studies in Psychiatry.* Oxford: Pergamon Press, pp. 91–102.

Cegala, D. J., Alexander, A. F., and Sokuvitz, S. (1979) An investigation of eye gaze and its relation to selected verbal behaviour. *Human Communications Research,* **5**, 99–108.

Champness, B. G. (1972a) Attitudes towards person-person media. Communications Studies Group paper (mimeo) No. E/72011/CH.

Champness, B. G. (1972b) The perceived adequacy of four communication systems for a variety of tasks. Communications Studies Group paper (mimeo) No. E/72245/CH.

Champness, B. G. (1972c) Feelings Towards Media in Group Situations. Communications Studies Group paper No. E/72160/CH.

Champness, B. G. (1973) *The Assessment of User Reactions to Confravision: II. Analysis and Conclusions.* Unpublished Communications Studies Group paper No. E/73250/CH.

Champness, B. G. & Davies, M. F. (1971) *The Maier pilot experiment.* Unpublished Communications Studies Group paper No. E/71030/CH.

Champness, B. G. & Reid, A. A. L. (1970). *The Efficiency of Information Transmission: A Preliminary Comparison Between Face-to-Face Meetings and the Telephone.* Unpublished Communications Studies Group paper No. P/70240/CH.

Chance, M. R. A. (1962) The interpretation of some agonistic postures: the role of 'cut-off' acts and postures. *Symposium of the Zoological Society of London,* **8**, 71–89.

Chapanis, A. (1971) Prelude to 2001: Explorations in human communication. *American Psychologist*, **26**, 949–61.

Chapanis, A., Ochsman, R. B., Parrish, R. N. & Weeks, G. D. (1972) Studies in interactive communication. I. The effects of four communication modes on the behaviour of teams during cooperative problem-solving. *Human Factors*, **14**, 487–510.

Chapman, A. J. (1975) Eye contact, physical proximity and laughter: a re-examination of the equilibrium model of social intimacy. *Social Behaviour and Personality*, **3**, 143–155.

Christie, B. (1972) *Report on series I experiments.* Unpublished paper from New Rural Society project, Fairfield University, Connecticut.

Christie, B. (1973) Appendix M. In P. C. Goldmark *et al.*, *The 1972/73 New Rural Society Project.* Research report available from Fairfield University, Connecticut.

Christie, B. (1974) *Semantic Differential Judgements of Communications Media and other Concepts: I. Differences between the media.* Unpublished Communications Studies Group paper No. E/74120/CR.

Christie, B. (1981) *Face to File Communication: a psychological approach to information systems.* Chichester: Wiley.

Clark, N. K. & Rutter, D. R. (1983) Visual information, social categorization and impression formation. Unpublished. University of Kent at Canterbury.

Cline, V. B., Atzet, J. & Holmes, E. (1972) Assessing the validity of verbal and nonverbal cues in accurately judging others. In D. C. Speer (ed.), *Nonverbal Communication*. Beverley Hills: Sage.

Collis, G. M. & Bryant, C. A. (1981) Interactions between blind parents and their young children. *Child: Care, Health and Development*, **7**, 41–50.

Cook, M. (1969) Anxiety, speech disturbances and speech rate. *British Journal of Social and Clinical Psychology*, **8**, 13–21.

Cook, M. (1970) Experiments on orientation and proxemics. *Human Relations*, **23**, 61–76.

Cook, M. (1979) *Perceiving Others*. London: Methuen.

Cook, M. & Lalljee, M. G. (1972) Verbal substitutes for visual signals. *Semiotica*, **3**, 212–21.

Cook, M. & Smith, J. M. C. (1975) The role of gaze in impression formation. *British Journal of Social and Clinical Psychology*, **14**, 19–25.

Coulthard, R. M. (1973) The analysis of classroom discourse. In AILA/BAAL seminar: *The Communicative Teaching of English*.

Coutts, L. M. & Ledden, M. (1977) Nonverbal compensatory reactions to changes in interpersonal proximity. *Journal of Social Psychology*, **102**, 283–90.

Coutts, L. M. & Schneider, F. W. (1975) Visual behaviour in an unfocused interaction as a function of sex and distance. *Journal of Experimental Psychology*, **11**, 64–77.

Coutts, L. M. & Schneider, F. W. (1976) Affiliative conflict theory: an investigation of the intimacy equilibrium and compensation hypothesis. *Journal of Personality and Social Psychology*, **34**, 1135–1142.

Cranach, M. von (1971) The role of orienting behaviour in human interaction. In A. H. Esser (ed.), *Environmental Space and Behaviour*. New York: Plenum Press.

Cranach, M. von & Ellgring, J. H. (1973) The perception of looking behaviour. In M. von Cranach & I. Vine (eds), *Social Communication and Movement*. London: Academic Press.

Cranach, M. V., Frenz, H. G. & Frey, S. (1968) Die 'Angenehmste Entfernung zur Betrachtung Sozialer Objecte'. *Psychologische Forschung*, **32**, 89–103.

Cranach, M. von & Vine, I. (eds) (1973) *Social Communication and Movement*. London: Academic Press.

Creak, M. (1961) Schizophrenic syndrome in children. *Cerebral Palsy Bulletin*, **3**, 501–4.

Creak, M. (1964) Schizophrenic syndrome in childhood: further progress report of a working party. *Developmental Medicine and Child Neurology*, **6**, 530–5.

Crowne, D. P. & Marlowe, D. A. (1960) A new scale of social desirability independent of psychopathology. *Journal of Consulting Psychology*, **24**, 349–54.

Cullinan, T. R. (1977) The epidemiology of visual disability: studies of visually disabled people in the community. HSRU Report No. 28. University of Kent at Canterbury.

Cutsforth, T. D. (1951) *The Blind in School and Society*. New York: American Foundation for the Blind.

Dabbs, J. M., Evans, M. S., Hopper, C. H. & Purvis, J. A. (1980) Self-monitors in conversation: what do they monitor? *Journal of Personality and Social Psychology*, **39**, 278–84.

Davey, A. G. & Taylor, L. J. (1968) The role of eye-contact in inducing conformity. *British Journal of Social and Clinical Psychology*, **7**, 307–8.

Davies, M. (1971a) Cooperative problem solving. A follow-up study. Communications Studies Group paper (mimeo) No. E/71252/DV.

Davies, M. (1971b) Cooperative problem solving. Communications Studies Group paper (mimeo) No. E/71159/DV.

De Alberdi, M. (1982) More opinion change over audio: process or pseudoprocess? *Annual Conference of the Social Psychology Section of the British Psychological Society*, Edinburgh, September 1982.

De Paulo, B. M., Rosenthal, R., Eisenstat, R. A., Rogers, P. L. & Finkelstein, S. (1978) Decoding discrepant nonverbal cues. *Journal of Personality and Social Psychology*, **36**, 313–23.

Dilley, J., Lee, J. L. & Verrill, E. L. (1971) Is empathy ear-to-ear or face-to-face? *Personnel and Guidance Journal*, **50**, 188–91.

Domangue, B. (1978) Decoding effects of cognitive complexity, intolerance of ambiguity, and verbal–nonverbal inconsistency. *Journal of Personality*, **46**, 519–35.

Douglas, A. (1957) The peaceful settlement of industrial and intergroup disputes. *Journal of Conflict Resolution*, **1**, 69–81.

Douglas, A. (1962) *Industrial Peacemaking*. New York: Columbia University Press.

Dovidio, J. F. & Ellyson, S. L. (1982) Decoding visual dominance: attributions of power based on relative percentages of looking while speaking and looking while listening. *Social Psychology Quarterly*, **45**, 106–13.

Duncan, S. (1972) Some signals and rules for taking speaking turns in conversations. *Journal of Personality and Social Psychology*, **23**, 283–92.

Duncan, S. D. Jr. (1974) On the structure of speaker-auditor interaction during speaking turns. *Language in Society*, **2**, 161–80.

Duncan, S. (1975) Interaction units during speaking turns in dyadic face-to-face conversations. In A. Kendon & R. M. Harris (eds), *The Organisation of Behaviour in Face-to-Face Interaction*. The Hague: Mouton.

Duncan, S., Brunner, L. J. & Fiske, D. W. (1979) Strategy signals in face-to-face interaction. *Journal of Personality and Social Psychology*, **37**, 301–13.

Duncan, S. & Fiske, D. W. (1977) *Face-to-face Interaction: Research, Methods and Theory*. New Jersey: Erlbaum.

Duncan, S. D. Jr. & Niederehe, G. (1974) On signalling that it's your turn to speak. *Journal of Experimental Social Psychology*, **10**, 234–47.

Edinger, J. A. & Patterson, M. L. (1983) Nonverbal involvement and social control. *Psychological Bulletin*, **93**, 30–56.

Efran, J. S. (1968) Looking for approval: effect on visual behavior of approbation from persons differing in importance. *Journal of Personality and Social Psychology*, **10**, 21–5.

Efran, J. S. & Broughton, A. (1966) Effect of expectancies for social approval on visual behavior. *Journal of Personality and Social Psychology*, **4**, 103–7.

Efran, M. G. & Cheyne, J A. (1974) Affective concomitants of the invasion of shared space: Behavioral, physiological, and verbal indicators. *Journal of Personality and Social Psychology*, **29**, 219–226.

Eibl-Eibesfeldt, I. (1970) The expressive behaviour of the deaf and blind born. In M. von Cranach & I. Vine (eds), *Nonverbal Behaviour and Expressive Movements*. London: Academic Press.

Eibl-Eibesfeldt, I. (1972) Similarities and differences between cultures in expressive movements. In R. Hinde (ed.), *Non-Verbal Communication*. Cambridge: Cambridge University Press.

Ekman, P. & Friesen, W. V. (1969) Nonverbal leakage and clues to deception. *Psychiatry*, **32**, 88–105.

Ekman, P. & Oster, H. (1979) Facial expressions of emotion. *Annual Review of Psychology*, **30**, 527–54.

Ellsworth, P. C. (1975) Direct gaze as a social stimulus: The example of aggression. In P. Pliner, L. Krames & T. Alloway (eds), *Nonverbal communication of aggression*. New York: Plenum Press, pp. 53–76.

Ellsworth, P. C. (1978) The meaningful look. (Review of Argyle & Cook, 1976). *Semiotica*, **24**, 341–51.

Ellsworth, P. C. & Carlsmith, J. M. (1968) Effects of eye contact and verbal content on affective response to a dyadic interaction. *Journal of Personality and Social Psychology*, **10**, 15–20.

Ellsworth, P. & Carlsmith, J. M. (1973) Eye contact and gaze aversion in an aggressive encounter. *Journal of Personality and Social Psychology*, **28**, 280–92.

Ellsworth, P. C., Carlsmith, J. M. & Henson, A. (1972) The stare as a stimulus to flight in human subjects: a series of field experiments. *Journal of Personality and Social Psychology*, **21**, 302–11.

Ellsworth, P. C. & Langer, E. J. (1976) Staring and approach: An interpretation of the stare as a nonspecific activator. *Journal of Personality and Social Psychology*, **33**, 117–22.

Ellsworth, P. C. & Ludwig, L. M. (1972) Visual behaviour in social interaction. *Journal of Communication*, **22**, 375–403.

Ellsworth, P. C. & Ross, L. D. (1975) Intimacy in response to direct gaze. *Journal of Experimental Social Psychology*, **11**, 592–613.

Ellyson, S. L., Dovido, J. F. & Corson, R. L. (1981) Visual behaviour differences in females as a function of self-perceived expertise. *Journal of Nonverbal Behaviour*, **5**, 164–71.

Ellyson, S. L., Dovidio, J. F., Corson, R. L. & Vinicur, D. L. (1980) Visual dominance behaviour in female dyads: situational and personality factors. *Social Psychology Quarterly*, **43**, 328–36.

Elman, D., Schulte, D. C. & Bukoff, A. (1977) Effects of facial expression and stare duration on walking speed: two field experiments. *Environmental Psychology and Nonverbal Behavior*, **2**, 93–9.

Elwell, C., Brown, R. J. & Rutter, D. R. (1983) Effects of speech style and visual cues on impression formation. Unpublished. University of Kent at Canterbury.

English, R. W. & Jelenevsky, S. (1971) Counsellor behaviour as judged under audio, visual, and audiovisual communication conditions. *Journal of Counselling Psychology*, **18**, 509–13.

Erlichman, H. (1981) From gaze aversion to eye-movement suppression: an investigation of the cognitive interference explanation of gaze patterns during conversation. *British Journal of Social Psychology*, **20**, 233–41.

Exline, R. V. (1963) Explorations in the process of person perception: visual interaction in relation to competition, sex and need for affiliation. *Journal of Personality*, **31**, 1–20.

Exline, R. V. (1971) Visual interaction: the glances of power and preference. *Nebraska Symposium on Motivation*, pp. 163–206.

Exline, R. V. & Eldridge, G. (1967) Effects of two patterns of a speaker's visual behavior upon the authenticity of his verbal message. Paper presented to the Eastern Psychological Association, Boston. Unpublished. University of Delaware.

Exline, R. V., Ellyson, S. L. & Long, B. (1975) Visual behaviour as an aspect of power role relationships. In P. Pliner, L. Krames & T. Alloway (eds), *Nonverbal Communication of Aggression*. New York: Plenum.

Exline, R. V. & Fehr, B. J. (1982) The assessment of gaze and mutual gaze. In K. R. Scherer & P. Ekman (eds), *Handbook of Methods in Nonverbal Behaviour Research*. Cambridge: Cambridge University Press.

Exline, R. V., Gray, D. & Schuette, D. (1965) Visual behavior in a dyad as affected by interview content and sex of respondent. *Journal of Personality and Social Psychology*, **1**, 201–9.

Exline, R. V. & Messick, D. (1967) The effects of dependency and social reinforcement upon visual behaviour during an interview. *British Journal of Social and Clinical Psychology*, **6**, 256–66.

Exline, R. V. & Winters, L. C. (1965a) Effects of cognitive difficulty and cognitive style on eye to eye contact in interviews. *Paper to Eastern Psychological Association*, Atlantic City, April, Mimeo.

Exline, R. V. & Winters, L. C. (1965b) Affective relations and mutual glances in dyads. In S. Tomkins and C. Izard (eds), *Affect, Cognition and Personality*. New York: Springer.

Exline, R. V. & Yellin, A. (1969) Eye contact as a sign between man and monkey. Symposium on Non-Verbal Communication, 19th International Congress of Psychology, London. Unpublished. University of Delware.

Exline, R. V., Thibaut, J., Brannon, C., & Gumpert, P. (1961) Visual interaction in relation to Machiavellianism and an unethical act. *American Psychologist*, **16**, 396.

Exline, R. V., Gottheil, I., Paredes, A. & Winklemayer, R. (1968) Gaze direction as a factor in judgement of non-verbal expressions of affect. *Proceedings, 76th Annual Convention of the A.P.A.*, **3**, 415–16.

Exline, R. V., Thibaut, J., Hickey, C. B. & Gumpert, P. (1970) Visual interaction in relation to Machiavellianism and an unethical act. In R. Christie and F. L. Geis (eds), *Studies in Machiavellianism*. New York: Academic Press.

Exline, R. V., Paredes, A., Gottheil, E. & Winkelmayer, R. (1979) Gaze patterns of normals and schizophrenics retelling happy, sad, and angry experiences. In C. E. Izard (ed.), *Emotions in Personality and Psychopathology*. New York: Plenum.

Fairbanks, L. A., McGuire, M. T. & Harris, C. J. (1982) Nonverbal interaction of patients and therapists during psychiatric interviews. *Journal of Abnormal Psychology*, **91**, 109–19.

Feldstein, S., Brenner, M. S. & Jaffé, J. (1963) The effect of subject sex, verbal interaction, and topical focus on speech disruption. *Language and Speech*, **6**, 229–39.

Felipe, N. J. & Sommer, R. (1966) Invasions of personal space. *Social Problems*, **14**, 206–14.

Foddy, M. (1978) Patterns of gaze in cooperative and competitive negotiations. *Human Relations*, **31**, 925–38.

Foulds, G. A. & Hope, K. (1968) *Manual of the Symptom-Sign Inventory (SSI)* London: University of London Press.

Freedman, J. L. (1969) Role playing: psychology by consensus. *Journal of Personality and Social Psychology*, **13**, 107–14.

French, E. G. (1955) Development of a measure of complex motivation. Unpublished. Lackland Air Force Base, Texas.

Friedman, H. S. (1978) The relative strength of verbal versus nonverbal cues. *Personality and Social Psychology Bulletin*, **4**, 147–50.

Fromme, D. K. & Schmidt, C. K. (1972) Affective role enactment and expressive behaviour. *Journal of Personality and Social Psychology*, **24**, 413–19.

Fugita, S. S. (1974) Effects of anxiety and approval on visual interaction. *Journal of Personality and Social Psychology*, **29**, 586–92.

Furnham, A., Trevethan, R. & Gaskell, G. (1981) The relative contribution of verbal, vocal and visual channels to person perception: experiment and critique. *Semiotica*, **37**, 39–57.

Gale, A., Lucas, B., Nissim, R. & Harpham, B. (1972) Some EEG correlates of face-to-face contact. *British Journal of Social and Clinical Psychology*, **11**, 326–32.

Gardin, H., Kaplin, K. J., Firestone, I. J. & Cowan, G. A. (1973) Proxemic effects on cooperation, attitude and approach avoidance in a prisoner's dilemma game. *Journal of Personality and Social Psychology*, **27**, 13–18.

Ghodsian, M. (1977) Children's behaviour and the BSAG: some theoretical and statistical considerations. *British Journal of Social and Clinical Psychology*, **16**, 23–8.

Giedt, F. H. (1955) Comparison of visual content and auditory cues in interviewing. *Journal of Consulting Psychology*, **19**, 407–19.

Goffman, E. (1963) *Behavior in public places*. Glencoe: The Free Press.

Goldberg, G. N., Kiesler, C. A. & Collins, B. E. (1969) Visual behavior and face-to-face distance during interaction. *Sociometry*, **32**, 43–53.

Goldberg, G. N. & Mettee, D. R. (1969) Liking and perceived communication potential as determinants of looking at another. *Psychonomic Science*, **16**, 277–8.

Goldberg, M. L. & Wellens, A. R. (1979) A comparison of nonverbal compensatory behaviours within direct face-to-face and television-mediated interviews. *Journal of Applied Social Psychology*, **9**, 250–60.

Goldman, M. (1980) Effect of eye contact and distance on the verbal reinforcement of attitude. *Journal of Social Psychology*, **111**, 73–78.

Goodwin, C. (1981) *Conversational Organization*. New York: Academic Press.

Gottheil, E., Paredes, A., Exline, R. V. & Winkelmayer, R. (1970) Communication of affect in schizophrenia. *Archives of General Psychiatry*, **22**, 439–444.

Grant, E. C. (1965) An ethological description of some schizophrenic patterns of behaviour. *Proceedings of the Leeds Symposium on Behaviour Disorders*. Dagenham: May & Baker.

Grant, E. C. (1970) An ethological description of non-verbal behaviour during interviews. In S. J. Hutt & C. Hutt (eds), *Behaviour Studies in Psychiatry*. Oxford: Pergamon.

Grant, E. C. (1972) Non-verbal communication in the mentally ill. In R. A. Hinde (ed.) *Non-verbal Communication*. Cambridge: Cambridge University Press.

Griffitt, W., May, J., & Veitch, R. (1974) Sexual stimulation and interpersonal behavior: Heterosexual evaluative responses, visual behavior, and physical proximity. *Journal of Personality and Social Psychology*, **30**, 367–77.

Guild, P. D. (1976) Distance, gaze, and the intimacy equilibrium in video-mediated dyads. Unpublished. University of Oxford.

Haase, R. F. & Tepper, D. T. Jr. (1972) Nonverbal components of empathic communication. *Journal of Counseling Psychology*, **19**, 417–24.

Hagiwara, S. (1975) Visual versus verbal information in impression formation. *Journal of Personality and Social Psychology*, **32**, 692–8.

Hall, E. T. (1955) The anthropology of manners. *Scientific American*, **192**, 85–9.

Hall, E. T. (1966) *The Hidden Dimension*. Garden City, New York: Doubleday.

Hammond, S., Young, I. & Cook, A. (1978) Teaching by telephone. *Final Report to S.S.R.C.* HR 4487.

Hargreaves, C. P. & Fuller, M. F. (in press) Some analyses of data from eye contact studies. *British Journal of Social Philosophy*.

Harper, R. G., Wiens, A. N. & Matarazzo, J. D. (1978) *Nonverbal Communication: the state of the art*. Chichester: Wiley.

Harris, S. E. (1968) Schizophrenic mutual glance patterns. Doctoral dissertation, Columbia University. *Dissertation Abstracts*, **29**, 2202B.

Hayduk, L. A. (1978) Personal space: an evaluative and orienting overview. *Psychological Bulletin*, **85**, 117–34.

Hedge, B. J., Everitt, B. S. & Frith, C. D. (1978) The role of gaze in dialogue. *Acta Psychologica*, **42**, 453–75.

Heron, A. (1956) A two-part personality measure for use as a research criterion. *British Journal of Psychology*, **47**, 243–52.

Hiltz, S. R. & Turoff, M. (1978) *The Network Nation: human communication via computer*. Reading, Mass.: Addison-Wesley.

Hinchliffe, M., Lancashire, M. & Roberts, F. J. (1970) Eye contact and depression: a preliminary report *British Journal of Psychiatry*, **117**, 571–2.

Hinchliffe, M. K., Lancashire, M. & Roberts, F. J. (1971) A study of eye-contact changes in depressed and recovered psychiatric patients. *British Journal of Psychiatry*, **119**, 213–15.

Hobson, G. N., Strongman, K. T., Bull, D. & Craig, G. (1973) Anxiety and gaze aversion in dyadic encounters. *British Journal of Social and Clinical Psychology*, **12**, 122–9.

Holloway, S. & Hammond, S. (1975) *Tutoring by Telephone: A Case Study in the Open University*. Communications Studies Group paper No. P/75025/HL.

Holstein, C. M., Goldstein, J. M. & Bem, D. J. (1971) The importance of expressive behaviors, involvement, sex, and need-approval in induced liking. *Journal of Experimental Social Psychology*, **7**, 534–544.

Hutt, S. J. & Hutt, C. (1970) *Behaviour Studies in Psychiatry*. Oxford: Pergamon.

Hutt, C. & Ounsted, C. (1966) The biological significance of gaze aversion: with special reference to childhood autism. *Behavioural Science*, **11**, 346–56.

Hutt, C. & Ounsted, C. (1970) Gaze aversion and its significance in childhood autism. In S. J. Hutt & C. Hutt (eds), *Behaviour Studies in Psychiatry*. Oxford: Pergamon.

Jackson, D. N. (1964) *Personality Research Form*. London: Canada.

Jaffé, J. & Feldstein, S. (1970) *Rhythms of Dialogue*. New York: Academic Press.

Johansen, R., Vallee, J. & Spangler, K. (1979) *Electronic Meetings: Technical Alternatives and Social Choices*. New York: Addison-Wesley.

Jones, I. H. & Pansa, M. (1979) Some nonverbal aspects of depression and schizophrenia occurring during the interview. *Journal of Nervous and Mental Disorders*, **167**, 402–9.

Jourard, S. M. & Friedman, R. (1970) Experimenter-subject and self-disclosure. *Journal of Personality and Social Psychology*, **15**, 278–282.

Kagan, J. & Lewis, M. (1965) Studies of attention in the human infant. *Merrill-Palmer Quarterly*, **2**, 95–122.

Kasl, S. V. & Mahl, G. F. (1965) The relationship of disturbances and hesitations in spontaneous speech to anxiety. *Journal of Personality and Social Psychology*, **1**, 425–33.

Kemp, N. J. (1981a) An experimental analysis of visual communication and social interaction. Unpublished Ph.D. thesis. University of Kent at Canterbury.

Kemp, N. J. (1981b) Social psychological aspects of blindness: a review. *Current Psychological Reviews*, **1**, 69–89.

Kemp, N. J. & Rutter, D. R. (1982) Cuelessness and the content and style of conversation. *British Journal of Social Psychology*, **21**, 43–9.

Kemp, N. J., Rutter, D. R., Dewey, M. E., Harding, A. G. & Stephenson, G. M. (in press) Visual communication and impression formation. *British Journal of Social Psychology*.

Kendon, A. (1967) Some functions of gaze direction in social interaction. *Acta Psychologica*, **26**, 1–47.

224

Kendon, A. (1968) The gaze-direction of the interviewer as a factor regulating temporal aspects of the interviewer's utterance patterns. Unpublished. Canberra University.

Kendon, A. (1978) Looking in conversation and the regulation of turns at talk: a comment on the papers of G. Beattie and D. R. Rutter *et al.*, *British Journal of Social and Clinical Psychology*, **17**, 23–4.

Kendon, A. (1982) The organisation of behaviour in face-to-face interaction: observations on the development of a methodology. In K. R. Scherer & P. Ekman (eds), *Handbook of Methods in Nonverbal Behaviour Research*. Cambridge: Cambridge University Press.

Kendon, A. & Cook, M. (1969) The consistency of gaze patterns in social interaction. *British Journal of Psychology*, **69**, 481–94.

Kendon, A. & Ferber, A. (1973) A description of some human greetings. In R. P. Michael and J. H. Crook (eds), *Comparative Ecology and Behavior of Primates*. London: Academic Press.

Kendon, A., Harris, R. M. & Key, M. R. (eds) (1975) *Organization of Behavior in Face-to-Face Interaction*. The Hague: Mouton.

Kleck, R. (1968) Physical stigma and nonverbal cues emitted in face-to-face interaction. *Human Relations*, **21**, 19–28.

Kleck, R. E. & Nuessle, W. (1968) Congruence between the indicative and communicative functions of eye-contact in interpersonal relations. *British Journal of Social and Clinical Psychology*, **7**, 241–6.

Kleck, R. E. & Rubinstein, S. (1975) Physical attractiveness, perceived attitude similarity, and interpersonal attraction in an opposite-sex encounter. *Journal of Personality and Social Psychology*, **31**, 107–14.

Kleck, R., Buck, P. L., Goller, W. L., London, R. S., Pfeiffer, J. R. & Vukcevic, D. P. (1968) The effect of stigmatizing conditions on the use of personal space. *Psychological Reports*, **23**, 111–18.

Kleinke, C. L. (1977) Compliance to requests made by gazing and touching experimenters in field settings. *Journal of Experimental Social Psychology*, **13**, 218–23.

Kleinke, C. L. (1980) Interaction between gaze and legitimacy of request on compliance in a field setting. *Journal of Nonverbal Behaviour*, **5**, 3–12.

Kleinke, C. L., Meeker, F. B. & Fong, C. L. (1974) Effects of gaze, touch, and use of name on evaluation of 'engaged' couples. *Journal of Research in Personality*, **7**, 368–73.

Kleinke, C. L. & Pohlen, P. D. (1971) Affective and emotional responses as a function of other person's gaze and cooperativeness in a two-person game. *Journal of Personality and Social Psychology*, **17**, 308–13.

Kleinke, C. L., Staneski, R. A. & Berger, D. E. (1975) Evaluation of an interviewer as a function of interviewer gaze, reinforcement of subject gaze, and interviewer attractiveness. *Journal of Personality and Social Psychology*, **31**, 115–22.

Kleinke, C. L., Bustos, A. A., Meeker, F. B. & Staneski, R. A. (1973) Effects of self-attributed and other-attributed gaze in interpersonal evaluations between males and females. *Journal of Experimental Social Psychology*, **9**, 154–63.

Klemmer, E. T. & Stocker, L. P. (1971) *Picturephone Versus Speakerphone for Conversation Between Strangers*. Unpublished company data.

Knapp, M. L., Hart, R. P. & Dennis, H. S. (1974) The rhetoric of duplicity: An exploration of deception as a communication construct. *Human Communications Research*, **1**, 15–29.

Knapp, M. L., Hart, R. P., Fredrich, G. W. & Shulman, G. M. (1973) The rhetoric of good-bye: Verbal and nonverbal correlates of human leave taking. *Speech Monographs*, **40**, 182–98.

Knight, D. J., Langmeyer, D. L. & Lundgren, D. C. (1973) Eye-contact, distance and affiliation: the role of observer bias. *Sociometry*, **36**, 390–401.

225

Kogan, N. & Wallach, M. A. (1964) *Risk-taking: a study in cognition and personality.* New York: Holt, Rinehart & Winston.

Krasner, L. (1958) Studies on the conditioning of verbal behaviour. *Psychological Bulletin*, **55**, 148–70.

LaCrosse, M. B. (1975) Nonverbal behavior and perceived counselor attractiveness and persuasiveness. *Journal of Counseling Psychology*, **22**, 563–6.

Laing, R. D. (1960) *The Divided Self.* London: Tavistock.

Laing, R. D. (1961) *The Self and Others.* London: Tavistock.

Lalljee, M. & Cook, M. (1973) Uncertainty in first encounters. *Journal of Personality and Social Psychology*, **26**, 137–41.

Lamb, T. (1981) Nonverbal and paraverbal control in dyads and triads: sex or power differences? *Social Psychology Quarterly*, **44**, 49–53.

Laplante, D. (1971) *Communication, Friendliness, Trust and the Prisoners Dilemma.* M.A. thesis, University of Windsor.

Lazzerini, A. J. & Stephenson, G. M. (1975) Visual interaction and affiliative-conflict theory. Unpublished. University of Nottingham.

Lazzerini, A. J., Stephenson, G. M. & Neave, H. (1978) Eye-contact in dyads: a test of the independence hypothesis. *British Journal of Social and Clinical Psychology*, **17**, 227–9.

LeCompte, W. F. & Rosenfeld, H. M. (1971) Effects of minimal eye contact in the instruction period on impressions of the experimenter. *Journal of Experimental Social Psychology*, **7**, 211–20.

Lefcourt, H. M., Rotenberg, F., Buckspan, R. & Steffy, R. A. (1967) Visual interaction and performance of process and reactive schizophrenics as a function of examiner's sex. *Journal of Personality*, **35**, 535–46.

Lefebvre, L. (1975) Encoding and decoding of ingratiation in modes of smiling and gaze. *British Journal of Social and Clinical Psychology*, **14**, 33–42.

Lesko, W. A. (1977) Psychological distance, mutual gaze, and the affiliative-conflict theory. *Journal of Social Psychology*, **103**, 311–12.

Levine, J. M. & Ranelli, C. J. (1977) Observer visibility and comfort in a surveillance situation. *Sociometry*, **40**, 343–50.

Levine, M. H. & Sutton-Smith, B. (1973) Effects of age, sex, and task on visual behavior during dyadic interaction. *Developmental Psychology*, **9**, 400–5.

Levitt, E. A. (1964) The relationship between abilities to express emotional meanings vocally and facially. In J. R. Davitz (ed.), *The Communication of Emotional Meaning.* New York: McGraw-Hill.

L'Henry-Evans, O. (1982) Anatomy of a tutorial (or when is a tutorial not a tutorial?) *Teaching at a Distance*, **21**, 71–5.

Libby, W. L. (1970) Eye contact and direction of looking as stable individual differences. *Journal of Experimental Research in Personality*, **4**, 303–12.

Libby, W. L. & Yaklevich, D. (1973) Personality determinants of eye contact and direction of gaze aversion. *Journal of Personality and Social Psychology*, **27**, 197–206.

Lochman, J. E. & Allen, G. (1981) Nonverbal communication of couples in conflict. *Journal of Research in Personality*, **15**, 253–69.

Lorenz, K. (1966) *On Aggression.* New York: Harcourt Brace Jovanovich.

Lowenfield, B. (1971) Psychological problems of children with impaired vision. In W. M. Cruickshank (ed.), *Psychology of Exceptional Children and Youth (Third edition).* New York: Prentice-Hall.

Machotka, P. (1965) Body movement as communication. In *Dialogue: Behavioral Science Research.* Boulder, Colorado: Western Interstate Commission for Higher Education.

Maclay, H. & Osgood, C. E. (1959) Hesitation phenomena in spontaneous English speech. *Word*, **15**, 19–44.

Magnusson, D. & Endler, N. S. (1977) *Personality at the Crossroads*. Hillsdale, New Jersey: Erlbaum.
Mahl, G. F. (1956) Disturbances and silences in the patients' speech in psychotherapy. *Journal of Abnormal and Social Psychology*, **53**, 1–15.
Mahoney, E. R. (1974) Compensatory reactions to spatial immediacy. *Sociometry*, **37**, 423–31.
Maier, N. R. F. & Thurber, J. A. (1968) Accuracy of judgements of deception when an interview is watched, heard and read. *Personnel Psychology*, **21**, 23–30.
Martin, W. W. & Rovira, M. L. (1981) An experimental analysis of discriminability and bias in eye-gaze judgement. *Journal of Nonverbal Behaviour*, **5**, 115–63.
McBride, G., King, M. G. & James, J. W. (1965) Social proximity effects on galvanic skin responsiveness in adult humans. *Journal of Psychology*, **61**, 153–7.
McConnell, D. (1982) CYCLOPS telewriting tutorials. *Teaching at a Distance*, **22**, 20–5.
Mehrabian, A. (1968a) Inference of attitudes from the posture, orientation and distance of a communicator. *Journal of Consulting and Clinical Psychology*, **32**, 296–308.
Mehrabian, A. (1968b) Relationship of attitudes to seated posture orientation and distance. *Journal of Personality and Social Psychology*, **10**, 26–32.
Mehrabian, A. (1969) Significance of posture and position in the communication of attitude and status relationships. *Psychological Bulletin*, **71**, 359–72.
Mehrabian, A. (1971) Nonverbal communication. *Nebraska Symposium on Motivation, 1971*, 107–161.
Mehrabian, A. (1972) *Nonverbal Communication*. New York: Aldine-Atherton.
Mehrabian, A. & Ferris, S. R. (1967) Inference of attitudes from non-verbal communication in two channels. *Journal of Consulting Psychology*, **31**, 248–52.
Mehrabian, A. & Friar, J. F. (1969) Encoding of attitude by a seated communicator via posture and position cues. *Journal of Consulting and Clinical Psychology*, **33**, 330–6.
Mehrabian, A. & Ksionzky, S. (1972) Categories of social behavior. *Comparative Group Studies*, **3**, 425–36.
Mehrabian, A. & Wiener, M. (1967) Decoding of inconsistent information. *Journal of Personality and Social Psychology*, **6**, 109–14.
Mehrabian, A. & Williams, M. (1969) Nonverbal concomitants of perceived and intended persuasiveness. *Journal of Personality and Social Psychology*, **13**, 37–58.
Milgram, S. (1965) Some conditions of obedience to authority. *Human Relations*, **18**, 57–75.
Milgram, S. (1974) *Obedience to Authority*. London: Tavistock.
Miller, N. E. (1944) Experimental studies of conflict. In J. McV. Hunt (ed.), *Personality and the Behavior Disorders*. New York: Ronald.
Mischel, W. (1968) *Personality and Assessment*. New York: Wiley.
Mischel, W. (1979) On the interface of cognition and personality: beyond the person-situation debate. *American Psychologist*, **34**, 740–754.
Mobbs, N. A. (1968) Eye-contact in relation to social introversion-extraversion. *British Journal of Social and Clinical Psychology*, **7**, 305–6.
Modigliani, A. (1971) Embarrassment, facework and eye-contact: testing a theory of embarrassment. *Journal of Personality and Social Psychology*, **17**, 15–24.
Monson, N. K. (1978) Teleconferencing: designing for the participants. *Journal of Communication*, **28**, 132–6.
Moore, M. (1981) Educational telephone networks. *Teaching at a Distance*, **19**, 24–31.
Morley, I. E. & Stephenson, G. M. (1969) Interpersonal and inter-party exchange: a laboratory simulation of an industrial negotiation at the plant level. *British Journal of Psychology*, **60**, 543–45.
Morley, I. E. & Stephenson, G. M. (1970a) Formality in experimental negotiations: a validation study. *British Journal of Psychology*, **61**, 383–4.
Morley, I. E. & Stephenson, G. M. (1970b) Strength of case, communication systems

and outcomes of simulated negotiations: some social psychological aspects of bargaining. *Industrial Relations Journal*, **1**, 19–29.

Morley, I. E. & Stephenson, G. M. (1977) *The Social Psychology of Bargaining*. London: Allen & Unwin.

Moscovici, S. (1967) Communication processes and the properties of language. In L. Berkowitz (ed.) *Advances in Experimental Social Psychology*, **3**, 225–70.

Moscovici, S. & Plon, M. (1966) Les situations-colloques: observations théoriques et experimentales. *Bulletin de Psychologie*, **247**, 702–22.

Muirhead, R. D. & Goldman, M. (1979) Mutual eye contact as affected by seating position, sex and age. *Journal of Social Psychology*, **109**, 201–6.

Murgatroyd, S. (1980) What actually happens in tutorials? *Teaching at a Distance*, **18**, 44–53.

Nevill, D. (1974) Experimental manipulation of dependency motivation and its effects on eye contact and measures of field dependency. *Journal of Personality and Social Psychology*, **29**, 72–9.

Nichols, K. A. & Champness, B. G. (1971) Eye gaze and the GSR. *Journal of Experimental Social Psychology*, **7**, 623–6.

Nielsen, G. (1962) *Studies in Self Confrontation*. Copenhagen: Monksgaard.

Nolter, P. (1980). Gaze in married couples. *Journal of Nonverbal Behaviour*, **5**, 115–29.

Norman, E. (1955) Affect and withdrawal in schizophrenic children. *British Journal of Medical Psychology*, **28**, 1–18.

O'Connor, N. & Hermelin, B. (1967) The selective visual attention of psychotic children. *Journal of Child Psychology and Psychiatry*, **8**, 167–79.

Patterson, M. L. (1973a) Compensation in non-verbal immediacy behaviors: a review. *Sociometry*, **36**, 237–52.

Patterson, M. L. (1973b) Stability of non-verbal immediacy behaviors. *Journal of Experimental Social Psychology*, **9**, 97–109.

Patterson, M. L. (1975) Eye contact and distance: a re-examination of measurement problems. *Personality and Social Psychology Bulletin*, **1**, 600–4.

Patterson, M. L. (1976) An Arousal Model of Interpersonal Intimacy. *Psychological Review*, **83**, 235–45.

Patterson, M. L. (1977) Interpersonal distance, affect, and equilibrium theory. *Journal of Social Psychology*, **101**, 205–14.

Patterson, M. L. (1978) Arousal change and cognitive labelling: pursuing the mediators of intimacy exchange. *Environmental Psychology, and Nonverbal Behaviour*, **3**, 17–22.

Patterson, M. L. (1982) A sequential functional model of nonverbal exchange. *Psychological Review*, **89**, 231–49.

Patterson, M. L., Mullens, S. & Romano, J. (1971) Compensatory reactions to spatial intrusion. *Sociometry*, **34**, 114–21.

Patterson, M. L., Jordan, A., Hogan, M. B. & Frerker, D. (1981) Effects of nonverbal intimacy on arousal and behavioural adjustment. *Journal of Nonverbal Behavior*, **5**, 184–98.

Pellegrini, R. J., Hicks, R. A. & Gordon, L. (1970) The effect of an approval seeking conduct on eye contact in dyads. *British Journal of Social and Clinical Psychology*, **9**, 373–4.

Pennington, D. C. & Rutter, D. R. (1981) Information or affiliation? Effects of intimacy on visual interaction. *Semiotica*, **35**, 29–39.

Perinchief, R. & Hugdahl, E. O. (1982) Teaching music by telephone. *Teaching at a Distance*, **22**, 33–5.

Pinches, C. (1975) Some technical aspects of teaching by telephone. *Teaching at a Distance*, **3**, 39–43.

Pruitt, D. G. & Lewis, S. A. (1976) The dynamics of integrative bargaining. Paper to XXI International Congress of Psychology. Paris.

228

Read, G. A. (1978) *CYCLOPS – an audio-visual system.* Walton Hall, Milton Keynes. Open University Press.

Reid, A. A. L. (1970) Electronic person-person communications. *Communications Studies Group* paper No. P/70244/RD.

Riemer, M. D. (1949) The averted gaze. *Psychiatric Quarterly*, **23**, 108–15.

Riemer, M. D. (1955) Abnormalities of the gaze: a classification. *Psychiatric Quarterly*, **29**, 659–72.

Rimé, B. (1982) The elimination of visible behaviour from social interactions: effects on verbal, nonverbal and interpersonal variables. *European Journal of Social Psychology*, **12**, 113–29.

Rimé, B. & McCusker, L. (1976) Visual behaviour in social interaction; the validity of eye-contact assessments under different conditions of observation. *British Journal of Psychology*, **67**, 507–14.

Robinson, B. (1981) Telephone tutoring in the Open University: a review. *Teaching at a Distance*, **20**, 57–65.

Rochester, S. R. (1973) The significance of pauses in spontaneous speech. *Journal of Psycholinguistic Research*, **2**, 51–81.

Rosa, E. & Mazur, A. (1979) Incipient status in small groups. *Social Forces*, **58**, 18–37.

Ross, M. *et al.* (1973) Affect, facial regard, and reactions to crowdings. *Journal of Personality and Social Psychology*, **28**, 69–76.

Rubin, A. (1970) Measurement of romantic love. *Journal of Personality and Social Psychology*, **16**, 265–73.

Russo, N. F. (1975) Eye contact, interpersonal distance, and the equilibrium theory. *Journal of Personality and Social Psychology*, **31**, 497–502.

Rutter, D. R. (1973) Visual interaction in psychiatric patients: a review. *British Journal of Psychiatry*, **123**, 193–202.

Rutter, D. R. (1976) Visual interaction in recently admitted and chronic long-stay schizophrenic patients. *British Journal of Social and Clinical Psychology*, **15**, 295–303.

Rutter, D. R. (1977a) Speech patterning in recently admitted and chronic long-stay schizophrenic patients. *British Journal of Social and Clinical Psychology*, **16**, 47–55.

Rutter, D. R. (1977b) Visual interaction and speech patterning in remitted and acute schizophrenic patients. *British Journal of Social and Clinical Psychology*, **16**, 357–61.

Rutter, D. R. (1978) Visual interaction in schizophrenic patients: the timing of Looks. *British Journal of Social and Clinical psychology*, **17**, 281–2.

Rutter, D. R., Morley, I. E. & Graham, J. C. (1972) Visual interaction in a group of introverts and extraverts. *European Journal of Social Psychology*, **2**, 371–84.

Rutter, D. R. & O'Brien, P. (1980) Social interaction in withdrawn and aggressive maladjusted girls: a study of gaze. *Journal of Child Psychology and Psychiatry*, **21**, 59–66.

Rutter, D. R. & Robinson, B. (1981) An experimental analysis of teaching by telephone: theoretical and practical implications for social psychology. *Progress in Applied Social Psychology, Vol. 1*, 345–374. Chichester: Wiley.

Rutter, D. R. & Stephenson, G. M. (1972a) Visual interaction in a group of schizophrenic and depressive patients. *British Journal of Social and Clinical Psychology*, **11**, 57–65.

Rutter, D. R. & Stephenson, G. M. (1972b) Visual interaction in a group of schizophrenic and depressive patients: a follow-up study. *British Journal of Social and Clinical Psychology*, **11**, 410–11.

Rutter, D. R. & Stephenson, G. M. (1977) The role of visual communication in synchronising conversation. *European Journal of Social Psychology*, **7**, 29–37.

Rutter, D. R., & Stephenson, G. M. (1979a) The role of visual communication in social interaction. *Current Anthropology*, **20**, 124–5.

Rutter, D. R. & Stephenson, G. M. (1979b) The functions of Looking: effects of friendship on gaze. *British Journal of Social and Clinical Psychology*, **18**, 203–5.

Rutter, D. R., Stephenson, G. M. & Dewey, M. E. (1981) Visual communication and the content and style of conversation. *British Journal of Social Psychology*, **20**, 41–52.

Rutter, D. R., Stephenson, G. M., Lazzerini, A. J., Ayling, K. & White, P. A. (1977) Eye-contact: a chance product of individual Looking? *British Journal of Social and Clinical Psychology*, **16**, 191–2.

Rutter, D. R., Stephenson, G. M., Ayling, K. & White, P. A. (1978) The timing of looks in dyadic conversation. *British Journal of Social and Clinical Psychology*, **17**, 17–21.

Rutter, D. R., Dewey, M. E., Harding, A. & Stephenson, G. M. (1984). Medium of communication and group size: effects of cuelessness on the content, style, and outcome of discussions. Unpublished. University of Kent at Canterbury.

Rutter, M. (1968) Concepts of autism. In P. J. Mittler (ed.), *Aspects of Autism*. London: British Psychological Society.

Rutter, M. & Lockyer, L. (1967) A five to fifteen year follow-up study of infantile psychosis. I. Description of sample. *British Journal of Psychiatry*, **113**, 1169–82.

Sacks, H., Schegloff, E. A., & Jefferson, G. A. (1974) A simplest systematics for the organization of turn-taking for conversation. *Language*, **50**, 697–735.

Sartre, J. P. (1943) *L'Etre et le Néant*. (Translated by H. Barnes, *Being and Nothingness*). London: Rider.

Scherer, K. R. & Ekman, P. (eds.) (1982) *Handbook of Methods in Non-verbal Behavior Research*. Cambridge: Cambridge University Press.

Scherer, S. E. & Schiff, M. R. (1973) Perceived intimacy, physical distance, and eye contact. *Perceptual and Motor Skills*, **36**, 835–41.

Scherwitz, L. & Helmreich, R. (1973) Interactive effects of eye contact and verbal content on interpersonal attraction in dyads. *Journal of Personality and Social Psychology*, **25**, 6–14.

Schulz, R. & Barefoot, J. (1974) Non-verbal responses and affiliative conflict theory. *British Journal of Social and Clinical Psychology*, **13**, 237–43.

Schutz, W. C. (1958) *FIRO: A Three-dimensional Theory of Interpersonal Behavior*. New York: Holt, Rinehart, & Winston.

Scott, R. (1969) *The Making of Blind Men*. New York: Russell Sage Foundation.

Short, J. A. (1971a) Bargaining and negotiation: an exploratory study. Unpublished Communications Studies Group paper No. E/71065/SH.

Short, J. (1971b) Conflicts of interest and conflicts of opinion in an experimental bargaining game conducted over three media. Communications Studies Group paper (mimeo) No. E/71245/SH.

Short, J. (1972a) Medium of communication, opinion change, and the solution of a problem of priorities. Communications Studies Group paper (mimeo) No. E/72245/SH.

Short, J. (1972b) Conflicts of opinion and medium of communication. Communications Studies Group paper (mimeo) No. E/72001/SE.

Short, J. (1972c) Medium of communication and consensus. Communications Studies Group paper (mimeo) No. E/72210/SH.

Short, J. A. (1973) The Effects of Medium of Communication on Persuasion, Bargaining and Perceptions of the Other. Unpublished Communications Studies Group paper No. E/73100/SH.

Short, J. A. (1974) Effect of medium of communication on experimental negotiation. *Human Relations*, **27**, 225–34.

Short, J., Williams, E. & Christie, B. (1976) *The Social Psychology of Telecommunications*. Chichester: Wiley.

Siegman, A. W. & Pope, B. (eds) (1972) *Studies in Dyadic Communication*. New York: Pergamon Press.

Sissons, M. (1971) The psychology of social class. In *Money, Wealth and Class*, pp. 115–31. The Open University Press.

Smith, D. H. (1969) Communication and negotiation outcome. *Journal of Communication*, **19**, 248–56.

Smith, B. J., Sanford, F. & Goldman, M. (1977) Norm violations, sex and the 'blank stare'. *Journal of Social Psychology*, **103**, 49–55.

Snyder, M., Grether, J. & Keller, C. (1974) Staring and compliance: a field experiment on hitchhiking. *Journal of Applied Social Psychology*, **4**, 165–70.

Sommer, R. (1969) *Personal Space*. Englewood Cliffs, NJ: Prentice-Hall.

Sommerlad, E. L., Seeger, W. & Brown, M. (1978) A UNESCO experiment. *Journal of Communication*, **28**, (Summer), 149–156.

Sorsby, A. (1972) The incidence and causes of blindness in England and Wales, 1963–68. DHSS Reports on Health and Medical Subjects, No. 128. London: DHSS.

Steer, A. B., Charles, C. R. & Lake, J. A. (1973) Some characteristics of transition points occurring in social and task activity. *Bulletin of the British Psychological Society*, **26**, 168.

Stephenson, G. M. (in press) Intergroup and interpersonal dimensions of bargaining and negotiation: In J. Jaspars and C. Fraser (eds) *Social Dimensions, Volume 1*. Cambridge: Cambridge University Press.

Stephenson, G. M., Ayling, K. & Rutter, D. R. (1976) The role of visual communication in social exchange. *British Journal of Social and Clinical Psychology*, **15**, 113–20.

Stephenson, G. M. & Kniveton, B. H. (1978) Interpersonal and interparty exchange: an experimental study of the effect of seating position on the outcome of negotiations between teams representing parties in dispute. *Human Relations*, **31**, 555–65.

Stephenson, G. M., Kniveton, B. H. & Morley, I. E. (1977) Interaction analysis of an industrial wage negotiation. *Journal of Occupational Psychology*, **50**, 231–41.

Stephenson, G. M. & Rutter, D. R. (1970) Eye-contact, distance, and affiliation: a re-evaluation. *British Journal of Psychology*, **61**, 385–93.

Stephenson, G. M., Rutter, D. R. & Dore, S. R. (1973) Visual interaction and distance. British Journal of Psychology, **64**, 251–7.

Strahan, C. & Zytowski, D. G. (1976) Impact of visual, vocal, and lexical cues on judgements of counselor qualities. *Journal of Counseling Psychology*, **23**, 387–93.

Strickland, L. H., Guild, P. D., Barefoot, J. C. & Patterson, S. A. (1978) Teleconferencing and leadership emergence. *Human Relations*, **31**, 583–96.

Strongman, K. T. & Champness, B. G. (1968) Dominance hierarchies and conflict in eye contact. *Acta Psychologica*, **28**, 376–86.

Sumby, W. H. & Pollack, I. (1954) Visual contribution to speech intelligibility in noise. *Journal of the Acoustics Society of America*, **26**, 212–15.

Summerfield, A. B. & Lake, J. A. (1977) Non-verbal and verbal behaviours associated with parting. *British Journal of Psychology*, **68**, 133–6.

Sundstrom, E. (1978) A test of equilibrium theory: effects of topic intimacy and proximity on verbal and nonverbal behaviour in pairs of friends and strangers. *Environmental Psychology and Nonverbal Behaviour*, **3**, 3–16.

Swain, J., Stephenson, G. M. & Dewey, M. E. (1982) Seeing a stranger: Does eye-contact reflect intimacy? *Semiotica*, **42**, 107–118.

Thayer, S. (1969) The effect of interpersonal looking duration on dominance judgements. *Journal of Social Psychology*, **79**, 285–6.

Thayer, S. & Schiff, W. (1974) Observer judgement of social interaction. *Journal of Personality and Social Psychology*, **30**, 110–14.

Thayer, S. & Schiff, W. (1977) Gazing patterns and attribution of sexual involvement. *Journal of Social Psychology*, **101**, 235–46.

Tinbergen, N. (1960) Comparative study of the behaviour of gulls: a progress report. *Behaviour*, **15**, 1–70.

Tysoe, M. (in press) Social cues and the negotiation process. *British Journal of Social Psychology*.

Valentine, M. E. (1980) The attenuating influence of gaze upon the bystander intervention effect. *Journal of Social Psychology*, **111**, 197–203.

Valentine, M. E. & Erlichman, H. (1979) Interpersonal gaze and helping behaviour. *Journal of Social Psychology*, **107**, 193–8.

Van Hooff, J. A. R. A. M. (1967) The facial displays of the Catarrhine monkey and apes. In D. Morris (ed.), *Primate Ethology*. Chicago: Aldine.

Vine, I. (1971) Judgement of direction of gaze – an interpretation of discrepant results. *British Journal of Social and Clinical Psychology*, **10**, 320–31.

Vitz, P. C. & Kite, W. R. (1970) Factors affecting conflict and negotiation within an alliance. *Journal of Experimental Social Psychology*, **6**, 233–47.

Wagner, H., Clarke, A. H. & Ellgring, J. H. (1983) Eye-contact and individual looking: the role of chance. *British Journal of Social Psychology*, **22**, 61–2.

Walker, M. B. (1977) The relative importance of verbal and nonverbal cues in the expression of confidence. *Australian Journal of Psychology*, **29**, 45–57.

Walsh, N. A., Meister, L. A. & Kleinke, C. L. (1977) Interpersonal attraction and visual behaviour as a function of perceived arousal and evaluation by an opposite sex person. *Journal of Social Psychology*, **103**, 65–74.

Warren, D. H. (1977) *Blindness and Early Childhood Development*. New York: American Foundation for the Blind.

Watson, O. M. (1970) *Proxemic Behavior: a cross-cultural study*. The Hague: Mouton.

Waxer, P. (1979) Therapist training in nonverbal behavior: towards a curriculum. In A. Wolfgang (ed.), *Nonverbal Behavior: applications and cultural implications*. New York: Academic Press.

Weitz, S. (ed.) (1979) *Nonverbal Communication: readings with commentary* (second edition). New York: Oxford University Press.

Welford, A. T. (1960) The measurement of sensory-motor performance: survey and reappraisal of twelve years' progress. *Ergonomics*, **3**, 189–230.

Weston, J. R. & Kristen, C. (1973) *Teleconferencing: A Comparison of Attitudes, Uncertainty and Interpersonal Atmospheres in Mediated and Face-to-face Group Interaction*. Department of Communications, Canada.

White, J. H. Hegarty, J. R. & Beasley, N. A. (1970) Eye contact and observer bias: a research note. *British Journal of Psychology*, **61**, 271–3.

Wichman, H. (1970) Effects of isolation and communication on co-operation in a two-person game. *Journal of Personality and Social Psychology*, **16**, 114–20.

Wiener, M., Devoe, S., Rubinow, S. & Geller, J. (1972) Nonverbal behavior and nonverbal communication. *Psychological Review*, **79**, 185–214.

Wiener, M. & Mehrabian, A. (1968) *Language within language: Immediacy, a channel in verbal communication*. New York: Appleton-Century-Crofts.

Williams, E. (1972) Factors Influencing the Effect of Medium of Communication upon Preferences for Media, Conversations and Person. Unpublished Communications Studies Group paper No. E/72227/WL.

Williams, E. (1973) Coalition Formation in Three-person Groups Communication via Telecommunications Media. Unpublished Communications Studies Group paper No. E/73037/WL.

Williams, E. (1975a) Medium or message: Communications medium as a determinant of interpersonal evaluation. *Sociometry*, **38**, 119–30.

Williams, E. (1975b) Speech patterns during mediated communication within small groups. Unpublished Communications Studies Group paper No. E/75275/WL.

Williams, E. (1975c) Coalition formation over telecommunications media. *European Journal of Social Psychology*, **5**, 503–507.

Williams, E. (1977) Experimental comparisons of face-to-face and mediated communication: a review. *Psychological Bulletin*, **84**, 963–976.

Williams, E. (1978) Visual interaction and speech patterns: an extension of previous results. *British Journal of Social and Clinical Psychology*, **17**, 101–2.

Williams, F. & Sundene, B. (1965) Dimensions of recognition: visual vs. vocal expression of emotion. *Audio Visual Communication Review*, **18**, 44–52.

Wilson, C. (1974) Interpretation of media effects. Unpublished Communications Studies Group paper No. P/74157/CW.

Wilson, C. & Williams, E. (1977) Watergate words: a naturalistic study of media and communication. *Communication Research*, **4**, 169–78.

Winer, B. J. (1971) *Statistical Principles in Experimental Design*. (Second edition). New York: McGraw-Hill.

Wish, M. (1977) Measuring the dimensions of interpersonal communication. *Report to Bell Laboratories*.

Wolff, S. & Chess, S. (1964) A behavioural study of schizophrenic children. *Acta Psychiatrica Scandinavica*, **40**, 438–66.

Woodside, C. M., Cavers, J. K. & Buck, L. (1971) Evatec: evaluation of a video addition to the telephone for engineering conversation. Unpublished. Bell Northern Research Laboratories.

Young, I. (1974a) Telecommunicated Interviews: An Exploratory Study. Unpublished Communications Studies Group paper No. E/74165/YN.

Young, I. (1974b) Understanding the Other Person in Mediated Interactions. Unpublished Communications Studies Group paper No. E/74266/YN.

Young, I. (1975) A Three Party Mixed-Media Business Game: A Progress Report on Results to Date. Unpublished Communications Studies Group paper No. E/75189/YN.

Zimbardo, P. G. (1969) The human choice: individuation, reason, and order versus deindividuation, impulse, and chaos. In W. J. Arnold & D. Levine (eds), *Nebraska Symposium on Motivation, 1969*, 237–306.

AUTHOR INDEX

SUBJECT INDEX

240

242